RULES

1. Books may be kept two weeks and may be renewed once for the same period.

2. A fine of five cents a day will be charged on each book which is not returned according to the above rule. No book will be issued to any person incurring a fine until that fine has been paid.

3. All injuries to books beyond reasonable wear and all losses shall be made good to the satisfaction of the Librarian.

4. Each borrower is held responsible for all books drawn on his number and for all fines on the same.

Friedrich Schiller.

Heath's Modern Language Series

Schillers

Maria Stuart

EDITED WITH INTRODUCTION AND NOTES

BY

LEWIS A. RHOADES, Ph. D.

Late Professor of Germanic Languages and Literatures in the Ohio State University

D. C. HEATH & CO., PUBLISHERS

BOSTON NEW YORK CHICAGO

Maria Stuart is published both with and without a vocabulary. In ordering please specify which edition is desired.

I D 5

PREFACE.

ONE of Schiller's dramas is usually chosen as an introduction to the study of the German classics, and to serve this end the present edition of Maria Stuart has been prepared. In writing the grammatical and lexical notes I have, accordingly, intended to give aid whenever the pupil, who knows the ordinary facts of German grammar, would be puzzled in making a correct and felicitous translation. On the other hand I have aimed to avoid giving an amount of assistance that will lead him to rely upon the notes, rather than upon a careful and intelligent use of one of the ordinary dictionaries. Often a grammatical reference has been given and the pupil has been left the valuable exercise of working out the translation for himself. As far as practicable, the grammars by Brandt, Joynes-Meissner and Whitney have been cited in each instance. The biographical and historical notes have been made somewhat full, in order that the student may see, not how far Schiller has followed the facts of history, but, what is of vastly more importance, how he has employed or transformed the facts to suit his artistic purpose.

In the Introduction I have attempted to put the pupil in possession of the material necessary for the appreciation of the drama as a work of literary art, and have particularly sought to show that it fulfills the essential requirements of tragedy. No biographical sketch of the author however has been undertaken, for anything within the scope of this volume is supplied equally well by any one of several encyclopedias.

The text is a reprint of Boxberger's, as contained in Volume 122 of Kürschner's Deutsche National-Litteratur. In the Introduction and Notes I have intended to acknowledge each instance of particular indebtedness. The commentaries of Düntzer, Bellermann and Fielitz, as well as the editions by Boxberger and Heskamp, have been frequently consulted, and have often been suggestive when it has not been possible to trace my specific indebtedness.

For constant encouragement and helpful advice in the preparation of the volume, I desire to thank Professors Calvin Thomas, George Hench, F. N. Scott and Alexander Ziwet of the University of Michigan. The notes were read in part by Miss May Carpenter and others. My special thanks are also due to Professor R. W. Deering of Western Reserve University, and to Dr. H. P. Jones of Cornell University, who have kindly read the proof sheets, and offered valuable suggestions.

LEWIS A. RHOADES.

ITHACA, January, 1894.

INTRODUCTION.

I.

Composition of the Drama.

Schiller had no sooner completed Wallenstein than he began to feel the need of some new dramatic project. March 19, 1799, he writes[1] to Goethe, that without the incentive of a definite purpose, he is incapable of any work, and adds: "I shall not be contented till my thoughts are again fixed with hope and enthusiasm upon some definite subject." The historical material however had been such a source of difficulty, that he inclined toward a subject of his own invention, and desired Goethe's advice, that he might not make a mistake in his choice.

What plans Schiller had in mind is not certain, but it is probable that he was thinking of the subject of his later tragedy, Die Braut von Messina, as well as of Maria Stuart, and it is in part, at least, due to Goethe's influence that, in spite of the difficulties of the subject, he determined to make the Queen of Scots the heroine of his next work. The idea of treating her career dramatically was no new one, for at Bauerbach, in December, 1782, he had thought of it, but after some preparatory reading he had given it up for Don Carlos. Just when he decided to resume the old subject is not known, but it was doubtless during his stay at Weimar, for April 26, the day after his return to Jena, he wrote[2] to Goethe: "I have begun to study the trial of Mary Stuart. Several tragic *motifs* have at once suggested

[1] Briefwechsel zwischen Schiller und Goethe. 4te Auflage. Stuttgart, 1881. 585.
[2] Briefwechsel, 591.

themselves to me, and have given me great faith in this subject, which undeniably has very many satisfactory aspects." The general plan of the work was forming in his mind, but though Goethe spent the greater part of the month of May with him, other matters occupied their attention and no progress was made.

After Goethe's departure, Schiller worked earnestly at his new subject, and June 4 he writes[1]: "Since the plan for the first acts of the Mary was complete and in the last acts only a single point was still undetermined, I could not refrain, in order not to lose time, from proceeding at once to the composition. Before beginning the second act everything in the last acts must be clear to me. Accordingly to-day, June 4, I have begun this *opus* with delight and pleasure, and during this month I hope to put behind me a considerable portion of the exposition." The work progressed, however, somewhat slowly, for it was necessary to lay the foundation for the whole and to guard, at the beginning, against making any mistake. But Schiller worked industriously and gained confidence in the tragic quality of his subject. July 12 he wrote[2]: "Aside from the fact that I am not familiar with such matters, the necessary exposition of the trial and of the legal form has a tendency to dullness, which I hope that I have overcome. In doing so, however, I have lost a good deal of time, but the exposition was not to be avoided." A few days later he again wrote[3]: "This act has taken a long time and will take another week, because I had to encounter in it the poetic struggle with the historical material, and took pains to allow my imagination a certain freedom with the history, while at the same time I sought to appropriate everything useful that it afforded." Before the end of the month, however, the second act was begun, and August 9 he wrote[4] to Körner: "A third

---

[1] Briefwechsel, 601. [2] Briefwechsel, 621.
[3] Briefwechsel, 625.
[4] Briefwechsel mit Körner, Th. II. S. 329. Hsg. Goedeke. Leipzig, 1878.

of the new tragedy, and the most difficult part of the whole, I have already behind me." A week later he had finished the first draft of the act, which he completed August 26, and began the third act the following day. Sept. 3 he had reached the famous quarrel scene, but here the work which he was obliged to do on the Musenalmanach compelled him to pause.

Beside other lyrics Schiller was occupied with Das Lied von der Glocke till the end of the month. He was then able to devote a few days to his drama, and made such progress that he began to think of new plans[1] for the following year. His wife's serious illness interrupted him, however, till the beginning of December, so that he had to give up all thought of bringing out the play in January. December 23 he wrote[2] to Goethe: "I intended to visit you yesterday evening, but got deeply engaged in my work, and the time passed. As I wish to read the first three acts to Mellish to-morrow, there was and still is much to do, which keeps me at home. There is nothing, as you know by experience, that takes more time than filling in the little gaps that one has left in his work."

The last day of December he was busy with the scene of Mortimer's death, and a few days later he wrote[3] to Körner that he would perhaps finish the work by the end of February. His adaptation of Macbeth and the revision of Wallenstein hindered him, and in February he was prostrated by a severe illness, so that the first four acts were not finally completed till May 5, 1800. A few days later he wrote[4] to Goethe that he had neither been able nor desired to begin the fifth act, because for it he needed a peculiar mood. Accordingly, May 15, he withdrew to the ducal castle of Ettersburg, where, in profound solitude, he wrote the concluding act. The drama was completed

---

[1] Düntzer, Erläuterungen, 18.
[2] Briefwechsel, 685.
[3] Briefwechsel mit Körner, II. 337.
[4] Briefwechsel, 739.

June 9, but three days later, at the command of the duke, Goethe wrote[1] to him, desiring that the representation of the communion might be omitted. "I can now confess to you," he wrote, "that I was not pleased with the idea myself, and since it has been protested against in advance, it is doubly unadvisable. Perhaps you might like to let me see the fifth act, and to visit me this morning after ten o'clock, so that we might talk over the matter." This was of course equivalent to a direct command from the duke, and Schiller accordingly so altered[2] the stage version that no offense was given. June 14 the tragedy was played for the first time, and was received with great approval. Schiller was himself satisfied[3] with its success, and Goethe wrote[4] to him: "There is every reason to be thoroughly satisfied with the presentation, and the piece has pleased me extraordinarily."

II.

SCHILLER'S SOURCES.

In a letter to Goethe, Jan. 5, 1798, Schiller defined his general attitude toward historical subjects. "I will not deny," he wrote[5], "that I ought to choose only historical subjects; freely invented ones would be dangerous for me. Idealizing the real is quite another task from realizing the ideal, and the latter is essentially the case in pure fiction. It is possible for me to animate a given subject, that is defined and limited, to impart warmth to it, and, as it were, to make it spring up; at the same time the objective definiteness of such a subject curbs my imagination and limits my choice." From this standpoint the history of Mary Stuart afforded the poet a suitable subject. The

---

1 Briefwechsel, 741.
2 For changes cf. l. 3625, *note*.
3 Briefwechsel mit Körner, II. 345.
4 Briefwechsel, 743.
5 Briefwechsel, 398.

essential facts and the tragic climax were supplied; it remained for him to transmute them into an organic and dramatic whole.

Of the use that he made of the historical material, he wrote[1]: "Since the subject, historically considered, affords abundant material, I have treated it somewhat more fully in this respect, and have made use of *motifs* that can give pleasure to the thoughtful and educated reader, but which, in the representation, when the object is moreover visibly present, are not necessary and, on account of the historical ignorance of the masses, are also uninteresting." A careful study of the drama shows that this is true. It must of course be remembered that Schiller's purpose was to write poetry and not history. In so doing he groups historical facts to suit himself and when dramatic necessity requires, either alters the facts to suit his purpose or introduces characters and events that are purely fictitious. Of the subject-matter, however, he made a thorough and careful study in the course of which he consulted all available sources. Düntzer mentions the following list of authorities which he is known to have had in hand:

Archenholz, Geschichte der Königin Elisabeth von England.

Brantôme, Sammlung historischer Memoires. Hsg. von Schiller. Bd. 10.

Buchanan, Rerum Scotiarum Historia.

Camden, Annales rerum Anglicarum et Hibernicarum regnante Elizabetha.

Du Chesne. Histoire d'Écosse avec l'histoire d'Angleterre.

Genz, Aufsatz über Maria Stuart in Viewegs Taschenbuch für 1799.

Hume, History of England.

De Rapin Thoyras, Histoire d'Angleterre.

Robertson, History of Scotland.

---

[1] Briefwechsel, 640.

Beside these he consulted various general works of reference for biographical details, local customs and the like. He also used a volume of theological miscellanies in preparing for the last act.

Of this list it seems desirable to mention particularly only those works whose influence seems to have been specially marked in determining Schiller's conception of his characters. Among these the most important is the essay by Archenholz, with whose view of Mary's character Schiller in many points agrees. It is to this work that Düntzer refers the letter of April 26, already cited, in which the poet spoke of taking up a history of the reign of Queen Elizabeth and beginning the study of Mary Stuart's trial.

Archenholz based his sketch of the Scottish queen upon Robertson and in conclusion remarks: "Philanthropy inclines us to draw a veil over her past and to attribute her actions more to her situation than to her disposition. Both in degree and duration her sufferings surpass those tragic misfortunes which the imagination invents in order to arouse pity upon the stage. If we reflect upon these sufferings with all their circumstances, we are disposed to forget the faults of the unhappy queen, and to give our tears free course." Düntzer quotes at length those portions of Archenholz that are of special interest to the student of Schiller's drama. Elizabeth's jealousy of Mary's superior charms and her hypocrisy in everything pertaining to the fate of her rival are *motifs* that he found more sharply presented here than in any of the other works that he consulted.

In keeping the English locality and character vividly before his imagination, Schiller found de Rapin Thoyras[1] particularly useful. In matters of detail throughout the drama he seems to have followed this authority closely. Especially is this true of

---

[1] Cf. Briefwechsel, 621.

Mary's trial and of legal affairs in general, and in several instances he has freely adapted such portions of Rapin's text as he found available.

In the fifth act one of Schiller's chief authorities was Brantôme. His account of Mary's execution purports to be copied from the verbal account of two of her ladies, who were present. This was probably the most detailed account with which Schiller was familiar, though he had also read Robertson and Hume. It contains much that is exaggerated or untrue, but is written in a style so naïve and sympathetic, that it was especially suited to his purpose. He availed himself of many of its details, though in some points he follows other authors. The use of Brantôme has been especially pointed out by Boxberger, and in his introduction to the drama he reprints the greater part of the article. In his foot-notes he also gives the passages from Rapin that seem to have been especially suggestive to the poet.

III.

CRITICAL DISCUSSION OF THE TRAGEDY.

A just appreciation of Maria Stuart must of necessity first concern itself with the question of Schiller's intention in writing the drama. From what standpoint did he regard the subject? In determining this question the information that can be gathered from his correspondence with Goethe is particularly valuable.

It will be remembered that after finishing Wallenstein, Schiller's first idea for a new tragedy was a subject[1] dealing with some question of human passion and of his own invention rather than historical. But as above remarked, his sober judgment dictated an historical subject as better suited to the bent of his

---

[1] Briefwechsel, 586.

peculiar genius, and this feeling seems to have determined his choice. It was, however, only natural that he was disposed to select a subject in which it was still possible to realize, in part at least, his original wish. This opportunity Maria Stuart afforded him, and it seems to have been this form of the subject that first presented itself to his mind, for no sooner had he begun work upon it, than he wrote[1] to Goethe: "I see a possibility of setting aside the whole judicial process, together with all political affairs, and of beginning the tragedy with the condemnation."

But apart from the fact that the difficulties encountered in his great trilogy inclined him to select a subject dealing with human passion, such a method of treating historical material was in accord with the development of his own and Goethe's views upon the use of history in dramatic composition. It was while at work upon Maria Stuart that he wrote,[2] apropos of another historical subject, "I think on the whole it would be well always to take only the general situation, the time and the persons from history, and to invent every thing else with poetic freedom." To this Goethe replied[3]: "There is no question that if history supply the simple fact, the bare object, and the poet the subject-matter and treatment, it is better and more convenient than if we make a more detailed and circumstantial use of history; for when one is always compelled to accept the peculiarity of the situation, he turns away from the purely human element, and poetry is involved in difficulties."

Had Schiller written his drama sixteen years before, when the subject first occurred to him, it is probable that he would have represented[4] the catholic princess as opposed to the irresistible progress of English protestantism, and falling a sacrifice to the

---

[1] Briefwechsel, 591. [2] Briefwechsel, 642.
[3] Briefwechsel, 643.
[4] Cf. Scherer, Geschichte der deutschen Literatur, 598.

religious and political interests of a great nation. The judicial and political elements would have then formed the chief part of the work, and its character would have been essentially polemic. But now, not only from inclination but also in harmony with clearly defined principles, Schiller undertook simply to represent upon an historical background a tragedy of human passion. Various critics, and notably Hettner, have censured him for not making the plot of his drama turn upon the conflict of historic forces. Such criticism, however, is either manifestly unjust, or is based upon a misconception of the poet's purpose. As well might one find fault with a landscape, because the artist had not preferred to paint a portrait.

In certain tragic requirements the subject seemed especially suited for a drama of passion. By a skillful exposition of Mary's situation and sufferings, it was easy to arouse the pity that Aristotle characterizes as essential to tragedy. The element of tragic fear also occasioned no great difficulty. In beginning with the condemnation, the catastrophe is at once foreseen and the feature of surprise is thus sacrificed. But the poet distinguished clearly between surprise and suspense. The latter alone is essential, and the absence of the former he even regarded as an advantage, for he wrote[1] to Goethe that the plot, while seeming to turn away from the catastrophe, constantly approached it, and thus aroused the Aristotelian fear.

The chief difficulty that confronted the poet was to invent a plot in which the heroine should appear as acting, and not simply as suffering. Dramatic art required that the inevitable climax should be the necessary result of Mary's own action, as exhibited in the drama. To this end Schiller invented the character of Mortimer, Mary's relation to Leicester and her meeting with Elizabeth. In this way he aimed at arousing hope

[1] Briefwechsel, 607.

for the condemned queen, and showing her ultimate destruction as the immediate result of her own tragic guilt. How far he succeeded in this attempt, it is the purpose of the following analysis of the drama to show.

In a discussion of the drama for this purpose, it is of the utmost importance to comprehend clearly Mary's mental attitude when the play begins. She feels keenly the wrong that she is suffering at Elizabeth's hands, but long imprisonment, separation from her servants, suspense regarding her fate and the refusal of religious consolation have brought her to the verge of despair. In her wretchedness she is further tortured with remorse at the murder of Darnley. Penance can not atone for that crime nor absolution free her from the overwhelming sense of her guilt. His implacable ghost will never be at peace with her till the measure of her misfortunes is full. Her old spirit is broken. Paulet's outrage provokes no burst of passion, but with patient dignity she ignores his insults and urges him to deliver to Elizabeth the letter that he has seized. The very fact that she makes an appeal to her shows how far she has given up hope. She does not indeed think that Elizabeth will order her execution, but she looks forward to life-long imprisonment and, in constant fear of assassination, regards herself as one dying. Her course is thus parallel to that of Elizabeth and, as long as she continues in it, a tragic collision is impossible.

Under these circumstances Mortimer reveals himself to Mary as a convert to her faith and the devoted adherent of her cause. She had believed herself abandoned by the world. His story vividly recalls to her the old life and its bright associations. Friends are still faithful to her and regard her imprisonment as a martyrdom. Sympathy and the promise of aid arouse her from her melancholy and work an entire change in her mental condition, so that she utterly refuses to believe in the possibility of her execution and attempts to dissuade Mortimer from his plan of rescuing her by force. She looks for rescue at Leicester's hands and had despaired because every way to him was barred. But now she accepts the unexpected opportunity and sends him a letter. Thus she ceases to be simply passive and acts in her own behalf.

Aroused by the thought of life and freedom, she hears from Burleigh the formal announcement of her sentence. With queenly majesty she declines to recognize the jurisdiction of the court and presents, in the strongest light, the injustice and illegality of her trial. She may fall a sacrifice to Elizabeth's safety, but tyranny, not justice, seals her doom. She leaves the stage, and Burleigh's hint of her assassination shows that, though determined to compass her destruction, he feels himself in the wrong.

The act is a masterpiece of exposition, and arouses the keenest interest in Mary's fate. She is not faultless, but both remorse for her guilt and innocence of the wrong for which she suffers excite pity in her behalf. Fear is aroused by the doom that hangs over her, and her own action is made a factor that must either avert or hasten it. In a word, all the elements of genuine tragedy are present.

The scene of the second act is laid at Elizabeth's court. From the conversation between Davison and Kent it appears that, according to general opinion, Mary's execution is imminent. The queen's determination to be rid of her rival is shown in her reply to the French ambassador's plea in her behalf, and still more clearly is this the case in her replies to Shrewsbury and the sharp reproof with which she finally silences his eloquent appeal in the Council. But she dreads the blame of the deed and is ready to resort to any means to escape it. Upon receiving Mary's letter she realizes as clearly as Burleigh and her remaining councillors, that an interview, as an act looking toward reconciliation, would be incompatible with a death sentence, but she sheds tears over the letter and, in dismissing her Council, promises to find means of reconciling mercy and necessity. She at once recalls Mortimer, however, and attempts to win him to undertake Mary's murder. In order to prevent her intrusting the deed to another hand he agrees, and Elizabeth, relying upon his promise, is not disinclined to gain the appearance of mercy by granting the interview.

In the following scene Leicester receives from Mortimer Mary's letter. His jealous disappointment at failing to win Elizabeth's hand had suggested to him the chance of rescuing and marrying Mary, and the letter contains her assent to his proposals. Mortimer's plot, however, alarms him. He does not dare to take a decided step in her behalf, but on learning of Elizabeth's request for her assassination, he sees the possibility of bringing about an interview between the two queens, and thus hindering the execution of Mary's sentence. By his adroit flattery of Elizabeth's beauty he gains her consent, and plans an interview that shall seem to have occurred accidentally.

Thus the act entangles the threads of Mary's destiny. Leicester has formed no definite plan for her rescue, but her letter leads him to bring about the interview. Mortimer's devotion protects her from assassination, and thus it seems that Elizabeth, in spite of her implacable hatred, will find her hands fettered for proceeding against her rival.

The park at Fotheringhay is the scene of the third act. Mary exults in her unwonted liberty, and regards it as the harbinger of final and complete freedom that Leicester will gain for her. Her mental condition is the very opposite of that in which she had appealed to Elizabeth for an interview. At this moment anything like a reconciliation is as far from her thoughts as it is from Elizabeth's real purpose. The sudden announcement of her rival's approach fills her mind with a burning sense of the wrongs she has suffered, and every other thought gives place to hatred. She controls herself, however, when she hears that Elizabeth is accompanied by Leicester and, in spite of the dissimulation and scornful treatment with which she is met, she approaches humbly and touchingly pleads her cause. She ignores the proud contempt with which she is repulsed and with gentle dignity deprecates Elizabeth's harsh threats. She appeals to her generosity to grant life and freedom as a gift, and is met with bitter insult. But the attempt to make her shameful in Leicester's eyes is unendurable. Justly incensed she answers taunt with taunt. The world knows the worst of her, and she is better than her name, but Elizabeth covers unchastity with the garb of honor, and as a bastard defiles the English throne. Silenced and defeated the queen withdraws and Mary exults that, with Leicester as her witness and strengthened by his presence, she has humiliated her rival and oppressor.

Her triumph however is of short duration. In the following scene she learns that Leicester will risk nothing in her behalf, and it is evident that her own conduct has destroyed every chance of mercy. Her only hope rests in Mortimer's plan, and here complete humiliation awaits her. He will attempt her rescue only to possess her as the object of his passionate love. Neither her sorrow nor her royal person is sacred in his eyes. The act closes with the attempt upon Elizabeth's life and the discovery of the conspiracy. Mary has sealed her own doom and what her friends have undertaken in her behalf has only served to hasten and ensure her destruction.

The scene of the fourth act is laid at court. Command has been given to prepare the death-warrant, and Burleigh intimates to Leicester that his relations with Mary are known. This is confirmed by Mortimer, who warns him that another letter, which Mary had begun to him, has been seized. He urges him to take desperate measures for his own and her rescue, to invent excuses and to avert the worst. But with cowardly selfishness

Leicester thinks only of concealing his own treason. He orders Mortimer's arrest as a traitor, and the youth stabs himself and dies, while Leicester rushes into Elizabeth's presence. Burleigh confronts him with Mary's letter, in which she had urged him to keep his promise. He replies that, presuming upon his position as the queen's favorite, he had begun a secret correspondence with Mary for the purpose of ensnaring her and compassing her destruction. In this manner he had discovered and frustrated Mortimer's conspiracy, which had escaped Burleigh's vigilance. He crowns his base conduct by now urging Mary's immediate execution, and with Burleigh is ordered to see the sentence fulfilled.

The death-warrant, which has been prepared, is now laid before Elizabeth and while Burleigh urges its signature, Shrewsbury pleads for delay. The question is argued simply as one of expediency, the former urging the advantage of the State, the latter its effect upon Elizabeth's popularity. In the following soliloquy the queen decides the question. Her autocratic nature despises public opinion and she rebels at the necessity which has hitherto dictated justice as her policy and thus fettered her hands for an arbitrary act. But the force of circumstances, not her own choice, has dictated this policy. She recognizes that her throne rests upon the good-will of her people, and on that account has always striven to cover her doubtful title by the exercise of lofty virtue. In this attempt, however, Mary Stuart has constantly stood like a threatening spectre before her. Still it is not so much this thought as that of personal jealousy that rankles in her bosom. Mary has come between her and every hope and pleasure of her life. She has robbed her of her favorite Leicester and has been the cause of every misfortune that has befallen her. At the recollection of her contemptuous taunts, she seizes the pen and, recalling the epithet "bastard," she signs the warrant with a quick, firm stroke. After a moment she rings and, when Davison enters, she leaves the warrant with him, but without definite commands. From him Burleigh receives it and puts it into immediate execution.

In this act, then, Mary's fate, which was practically decided at its beginning, is formally determined and, as the poet has clearly shown, not only is the quarrel scene the controlling factor in the determination, but by undertaking a second appeal to Leicester, Mary has still further hastened the inevitable catastrophe.

The fifth act accordingly represents the tragic ending of Mary's career. As dramatic necessity dictated, the poet has represented her death as a martyrdom, for, while the sentence is precipitated by her own fault, she is perfectly innocent of the crime for which she suffers. In harmony with this idea, the conversation of her servants describes the composure and resignation with which she received the order to prepare for death. In the same manner the falseness of the testimony against her and the awful preparations for her execution are reported. When Mary appears it is rather to comfort her grief-stricken servants than to be ministered to and comforted by them. After the humiliation she had experienced at Mortimer's hands, death seems her only release, and exalted in its presence, she regards it as a triumph. After confiding to Melvil the last messages for her friends, she tells her servants that she has recommended them to the protection of the king of France and, receiving from them a promise to leave England, she divides among them her personal possessions and bids each one farewell.

Thus the last earthly duty is performed and it remains for her to make her peace with God. She had earnestly desired a priest of her own faith, from whom she might receive absolution and the holy sacrament, and this happiness is unexpectedly permitted her. Melvil has taken orders that he might hear her last confession. Kneeling before him she acknowledges her envious hatred of Elizabeth and her sinful love of Leicester. The crime of her youth, too, she again confesses, and, protesting her innocence of any plot against Elizabeth, she goes calmly to her fate. At the sight of Leicester, however, she pauses and falls half-fainting, so that he supports her. In another sense than she had expected, it is his arm that leads her from her prison. But Mary has risen above all the hopes and desires of human love, and, though something of reproach is mingled with her words, she forgives him and bids him farewell. Too overcome to follow her, he remains behind and his broken soliloquy traces the progress of the tragedy enacted below, till at the fatal stroke he falls unconscious upon the stage.

But the drama does not end here. As Shakespeare has indicated Iago's punishment, so Schiller's poetic and dramatic insight forbade his permitting Elizabeth to triumph over the victim of her jealousy and hypocrisy. Her deed avenges itself upon her. Shrewsbury leaves the queen, whose nobler nature he could not save, her favorite Leicester abandons her and, tortured by her own guilty conscience, she is left in complete and tragic isolation.

The analysis of the drama thus makes it evident that Schiller carefully kept in mind the requirements of tragic art. A common criticism of the piece is that, while it is pathetic and contains scenes of great dramatic power, Mary is only passive and that the whole thus fails to make the impression of tragedy. But this criticism is not well founded, for there is no question that Schiller has clearly shown the tragic guilt of his heroine. Her sufferings are indeed out of all proportion to her fault, but the same is true of Cordelia and Desdemona, yet it is never questioned that King Lear and Othello belong to genuine tragedy.

IV.

CHARACTERIZATION, LANGUAGE AND METER.

In the delineation of his characters Schiller seems to have kept in mind the principles formulated in Lessing's Hamburgische Dramaturgie, — namely, that in an historical drama, while the poet may treat the details of time, place and the like as freely as he wishes, the characters must remain sacred to him. "To strengthen them,"[1] says Lessing, "to present them in the best light, is all that he may add to them on his own account. The smallest essential change would do away with the reason why they bear these instead of other names." As the notes of this edition point out in detail, the poet has included a large element of fiction in his plot, but even in the case of Mary's admission[2] of her complicity in Darnley's murder, this element serves to define more clearly and dramatically the characters as they were presented in the poet's sources. The view of Mary's career and of Elizabeth's conduct toward her, which they afforded, does not agree with that held by various recent historians. But with this fact the student of the tragedy is not concerned, for it is his task to study the characters simply as they are presented in the drama.

As the heroine of the play, Mary's character first demands attention, and Goedeke is undoubtedly right, that it is her conduct in the quarrel scene that furnishes the key for understanding its consistent development. This seems at first impossible, for in that scene her conduct appears to be a direct contradiction of her character as shown in the first and fifth acts. But a more careful consideration of the question shows that the feeling with which she exults in her triumph over Elizabeth formed the baser

---

[1] Hamburgische Dramaturgie, Nr. 23.

[2] Cf. l. 272, *note*.

element of her nature, from which it is the purpose[1] of the drama to show her purification.

The first act throws much light upon Mary's past life. Endowed with a deeply passionate nature, her education and environment had contributed to make her thoughtless. The sense of her power as a sovereign tempted her and, influenced by her infatuation for Bothwell, she consented to the murder of Darnley, whose base ingratitude and rude treatment had changed her love for him into bitter hatred. In consequence of her crime she was deposed from her throne and driven from her kingdom. At the beginning of the play, however, her better nature has reasserted itself and, as Kennedy testifies, her life in England has been blameless. But though the guilt, in which her sinful love and her hatred have involved her, deserves death, she regards this merited retribution as vengeance, from which she still hopes to escape. She has not surrendered her claim to the pleasures of life, and upon Leicester's promise to set her free, she is ready to throw herself into his arms. Yet in discouraging Mortimer's plot she stands upon higher moral ground than before, though she is attracted to Leicester in the same manner that she had been to Bothwell and for a similar reason. In the quarrel scene also, she shows her moral development, for the self-control that she exercises would have been impossible in her earlier years. When however she does give way to her scornful hatred, she is for the moment capable of herself striking a blow at Elizabeth's life. But when betrayed by Leicester and face to face with death, it is her nobler nature that prevails. She resolutely renounces earthly hope, and death, which she had dreaded as vengeance, appears as a mercy, graciously vouchsafed, by which she is deemed worthy to expiate her crime. Her sinful love and her hatred are thus sacrificed to God, the

[1] Cf. Fielitz, Studien zu Schillers Dramen, S. 59.

moral law is satisfied, and as a spirit, already radiant and redeemed, Mary triumphs completely over the lower and baser elements of her nature.

The best characterization of Elizabeth is found in one of Schiller's letters,[1] in which he refers to her as his "royal hypocrite." This phase of her character he found emphasized in his sources and it was especially suited to his purpose, for the more he exalted Mary, the more detestable it was necessary to represent her rival. Only by such a contrast could he win and retain sympathy for a heroine who was confessedly guilty of her husband's murder. He has succeeded, however, in making her character comprehensible. He represents her as possessed of a cold, intellectual nature, whose natural bent had been still further developed by the harsh fortunes of her early life. Vanity and jealousy are her most conspicuous traits. Her doubtful legitimacy causes her bitter hatred for Mary, but at the same time forbids the tyrannical exercise of her power against her, for she is forced to court the favor of her people. Deceit thus becomes her policy, and her only care is to preserve the appearance of virtue.

The other characters of the drama hardly require special mention. Leicester's rôle is in accord with his historical character, a selfish, ambitious and cowardly courtier. Mortimer, an impulsive, passionate enthusiast, ready to dare anything and regardless of consequences, is contrasted with him. Burleigh is the type of a cool and calculating statesmen, who knows no scruple in seeking the welfare of the State. Except in the case of Mary, the poet has made no attempt to show any development of character.

In point of language and style the drama is classical, and there is little attempt to suit the diction to the speaker. Schil-

[1] Briefwechsel, 630.

ler's tendency to declamation is less marked than in some of his other works. The dialogue is generally well managed, and the interest sustained.

In point of verse the drama shows less irregularity than might be expected, for Schiller especially mentions [1] the fact that he allowed himself greater freedom or rather variety in this respect than had before been his custom. It is probable however that he referred especially to the lyric passages at the beginning of the third act, for elsewhere, as Zarncke remarks,[2] the general character of the work does not differ especially from Wallenstein, except perhaps that the iambics are somewhat smoother. The same author gives a careful analysis of the drama from the metrical standpoint and cites each line that varies from the regular iambic pentameter. Rhyme occurs frequently at the close of scenes and in the lyrics, both alternate and in couplets. Its irregular use serves to add color to the passages in which it is used, and heightens the dramatic effect.

The tragedy was at once successful upon the German stage and still remains a popular favorite. It has been repeatedly translated, and is frequently presented both in England and America.

---

[1] Briefwechsel, 651.

[2] Über den fünffüßigen Jambus, u. s. w. 71.

Maria Stuart.

Ein Trauerspiel.

[1800.]

Personen.

Elisabeth, Königin von England.
Maria Stuart, Königin von Schottland, Gefangene in England.
Robert Dudley, Graf von Leicester.
Georg Talbot, Graf von Shrewsbury.
Wilhelm Cecil, Baron von Burleigh, Großschatzmeister.
Graf von Kent.
Wilhelm Davison, Staatssekretär.
Amias Paulet, Ritter, Hüter der Maria.
Mortimer, sein Neffe.
Graf Aubespine, französischer Gesandter.
Graf Bellievre, außerordentlicher Botschafter von Frankreich.
Okelly, Mortimers Freund.
Drugeon Drury, zweiter Hüter der Maria.
Melvil, ihr Haushofmeister.
Burgoyn, ihr Arzt.
Hanna Kennedy, ihre Amme.
Margareta Kurl, ihre Kammerfrau.
Sherif der Grafschaft.
Offizier der Leibwache.
Französische und englische Herren.
Trabanten.
Hofdiener der Königin von England.
Diener und Dienerinnen der Königin von Schottland.

Erster Aufzug.

Im Schloß zu Fotheringhay. Ein Zimmer.

Erster Auftritt.

Hanna Kennedy, Amme der Königin von Schottland, in heftigem Streit mit Paulet, der im Begriff ist, einen Schrank zu öffnen. Drugeon Drury, sein Gehilfe, mit Brecheisen.

Kennedy.

Was macht Ihr, Sir? Welch neue Dreistigkeit!
Zurück von diesem Schrank!

Paulet.

Wo kam der Schmuck her?
Vom obern Stock ward er herabgeworfen;
Der Gärtner hat bestochen werden sollen
5 Mit diesem Schmuck — Fluch über Weiberlist!
Trotz meiner Aufsicht, meinem scharfen Suchen
Noch Kostbarkeiten, noch geheime Schätze!
Sich über den Schrank machend.
Wo das gesteckt hat, liegt noch mehr!

Kennedy.

Zurück, Verwegner!
Hier liegen die Geheimnisse der Lady.

Paulet.

10 Die eben such' ich. Schriften hervorziehend.

Kennedy.

Unbedeutende

Papiere, bloße Übungen der Feder,
Des Kerkers traur'ge Weile zu verkürzen.

Paulet.

In müß'ger Weile schafft der böse Geist.

Kennedy.

Es sind französische Schriften.

Paulet.

Desto schlimmer!

15 Die Sprache redet Englands Feind.

Kennedy.

Konzepte

Von Briefen an die Königin von England.

Paulet.

Die überliefr' ich — Sieh! Was schimmert hier?

Er hat einen geheimen Ressort geöffnet und zieht aus einem verborgnen Fach Geschmeide hervor.

Ein königliches Stirnband, reich an Steinen,
Durchzogen mit den Lilien von Frankreich!

Er giebt es seinem Begleiter.

20 Verwahrt's, Drury. Legt's zu dem übrigen! Drury geht ab.

Kennedy.

O schimpfliche Gewalt, die wir erleiden!

Paulet.

Solang' sie noch besitzt, kann sie noch schaden
Denn alles wird Gewehr in ihrer Hand.

Kennedy.

Seid gütig, Sir! Nehmt nicht den letzten Schmuck
25 Aus unserm Leben weg! Die Jammervolle
Erfreut der Anblick alter Herrlichkeit,
Denn alles andre habt Ihr uns entrissen.

Paulet.

Es liegt in guter Hand. Gewissenhaft
Wird es zu seiner Zeit zurückgegeben!

Kennedy.

30 Wer sieht es diesen kahlen Wänden an,
Daß eine Königin hier wohnt? Wo ist
Die Himmeldecke über ihrem Sitz?
Muß sie den zärtlich weichgewöhnten Fuß
Nicht auf gemeinen rauhen Boden setzen?
35 Mit grobem Zinn — die schlechtste Edelfrau
Würd' es verschmähn — bedient man ihre Tafel.

Paulet.

So speiste sie zu Sterlyn ihren Gatten,
Da sie aus Gold mit ihrem Buhlen trank.

Kennedy.

Sogar des Spiegels kleine Notdurft mangelt.

Paulet.

40 Solang' sie noch ihr eitles Bild beschaut,
Hört sie nicht auf, zu hoffen und zu wagen.

Kennedy.

An Büchern fehlt's, den Geist zu unterhalten.

Paulet.

Die Bibel ließ man ihr, das Herz zu bessern.

Kennedy.

Selbst ihre Laute ward ihr weggenommen.

Paulet.

45 Weil sie verbuhlte Lieder drauf gespielt.

Kennedy.

Ist das ein Schicksal für die Weicherzogne,
Die in der Wiege Königin schon war,
Am üpp'gen Hof der Medicäerin
In jeder Freuden Fülle aufgewachsen?
50 Es sei genug, daß man die Macht ihr nahm;
Muß man die armen Flitter ihr mißgönnen?
In großes Unglück lehrt ein edles Herz

Sich endlich finden; aber wehe thut's,
Des Lebens kleine Zierden zu entbehren.

Paulet.

55 Sie wenden nur das Herz dem Eiteln zu,
Das in sich gehen und bereuen soll.
Ein üppig lastervolles Leben büßt sich
In Mangel und Erniedrigung allein.

Kennedy.

Wenn ihre zarte Jugend sich verging,
60 Mag sie's mit Gott abthun und ihrem Herzen,
In England ist kein Richter über sie.

Paulet.

Sie wird gerichtet, wo sie frevelte.

Kennedy.

Zum Freveln fesseln sie zu enge Bande.

Paulet.

Doch wußte sie aus diesen engen Banden
65 Den Arm zu strecken in die Welt, die Fackel
Des Bürgerkrieges in das Reich zu schleudern.
Und gegen unsre Königin, die Gott
Erhalte, Meuchelrotten zu bewaffnen.
Erregte sie aus diesen Mauern nicht
70 Den Böswicht Parry und den Babington
Zu der verfluchten That des Königsmords?
Hielt dieses Eisengitter sie zurück,
Das edle Herz des Norfolk zu umstricken?
Für sie geopfert fiel das beste Haupt
75 Auf dieser Insel unterm Henkerbeil —
Und schreckte dieses jammervolle Beispiel
Die Rasenden zurück, die sich wetteifernd
Um ihrentwillen in den Abgrund stürzen?

Die Blutgerüste füllen sich für sie
80 Mit immer neuen Todesopfern an,
Und das wird nimmer enden, bis sie selbst,
Die Schuldigste, darauf geopfert ist.
— O Fluch dem Tag, da dieses Landes Küste
Gastfreundlich diese Helena empfing.

Kennedy.

85 Gastfreundlich hätte England sie empfangen?
Die Unglückselige, die seit dem Tag,
Da sie den Fuß gesetzt in dieses Land,
Als eine Hilfeflehende, Vertriebne,
Bei der Verwandten Schutz zu suchen kam,
90 Sich wider Völkerrecht und Königswürde
Gefangen sieht, in enger Kerkerhaft
Der Jugend schöne Jahre muß vertrauern —
Die jetzt, nachdem sie alles hat erfahren,
Was das Gefängnis Bittres hat, gemeinen
95 Verbrechern gleich, vor des Gerichtes Schranken
Gefordert wird und schimpflich angeklagt
Auf Leib und Leben — eine Königin!

Paulet.

Sie kam ins Land als eine Mörderin,
Verjagt von ihrem Volk, des Throns entsetzt,
100 Den sie mit schwerer Greuelthat geschändet.
Verschworen kam sie gegen Englands Glück,
Der spanischen Maria blut'ge Zeiten
Zurück zu bringen, Engelland katholisch
Zu machen, an den Franzmann zu verraten.
105 Warum verschmähte sie's, den Edinburger
Vertrag zu unterschreiben, ihren Anspruch
An England aufzugeben und den Weg

Aus diesem Kerker schnell sich aufzuthun
Mit einem Federstrich? Sie wollte lieber
110 Gefangen bleiben, sich mißhandelt sehn,
Als dieses Titels leerem Prunk entsagen.
Weswegen that sie das? Weil sie den Ränken
Vertraut, den bösen Künsten der Verschwörung,
Und unheilspinnend diese ganze Insel
115 Aus ihrem Kerker zu erobern hofft.

Kennedy.

Ihr spottet, Sir. — Zur Härte fügt Ihr noch
Den bittern Hohn! Sie hegte solche Träume,
Die hier lebendig eingemauert lebt,
Zu der kein Schall des Trostes, keine Stimme
120 Der Freundschaft aus der lieben Heimat dringt,
Die längst kein Menschenangesicht mehr schaute,
Als ihrer Kerkermeister finstre Stirn,
Die erst seit kurzem einen neuen Wächter
Erhielt in Eurem rauhen Anverwandten,
125 Von neuen Stäben sich umgittert sieht —

Paulet.

Kein Eisengitter schützt vor ihrer List.
Weiß ich, ob diese Stäbe nicht durchfeilt,
Nicht dieses Zimmers Boden, diese Wände,
Von außen fest, nicht hohl von innen sind,
130 Und den Verrat einlassen, wenn ich schlafe?
Fluchvolles Amt, das mir geworden ist,
Die unheilbrütend Listige zu hüten.
Vom Schlummer jagt die Furcht mich auf; ich gehe
Nachts um, wie ein gequälter Geist, erprobe
135 Des Schlosses Riegel und der Wächter Treu'
Und sehe zitternd jeden Morgen kommen,

Der meine Furcht wahr machen kann. Doch wohl mir!
Wohl! Es ist Hoffnung, daß es bald nun endet.
Denn lieber möcht' ich der Verdammten Schar
140 Wachstehend an der Höllenpforte hüten,
Als diese ränkevolle Königin.

Kennedy.

Da kommt sie selbst!

Paulet.

Den Christus in der Hand,
Die Hoffart und die Weltlust in dem Herzen.

Zweiter Auftritt.

Maria im Schleier, ein Kruzifix in der Hand. Die Vorigen.

Kennedy ihr entgegeneilend.

O Königin! Man tritt uns ganz mit Füßen,
145 Der Tyrannei, der Härte wird kein Ziel,
Und jeder neue Tag häuft neue Leiden
Und Schmach auf dein gekröntes Haupt.

Maria.

Faß dich!
Sag' an, was neu geschehen ist?

Kennedy.

Sieh her!
Dein Pult ist aufgebrochen, deine Schriften,
150 Dein einz'ger Schatz, den wir mit Müh gerettet,
Der letzte Rest von deinem Brautgeschmeide

Aus Frankreich ist in seiner Hand. Du hast nun
Nichts Königliches mehr, bist ganz beraubt.

Maria.

Beruhige dich, Hanna! Diese Flitter machen
155 Die Königin nicht aus. Man kann uns niedrig
Behandeln, nicht erniedrigen. Ich habe
In England mich an viel gewöhnen lernen,
Ich kann auch das verschmerzen. Sir, Ihr habt Euch
Gewaltsam zugeeignet, was ich Euch
160 Noch heut zu übergeben willens war.
Bei diesen Schriften findet sich ein Brief,
Bestimmt für meine königliche Schwester
Von England — Gebt mir Euer Wort, daß Ihr
Ihn redlich an sie selbst wollt übergeben
165 Und nicht in Burleighs ungetreue Hand.

Paulet.

Ich werde mich bedenken, was zu thun ist.

Maria.

Ihr sollt den Inhalt wissen, Sir. Ich bitte
In diesem Brief um eine große Gunst —
— Um eine Unterredung mit ihr selbst,
170 Die ich mit Augen nie gesehn — Man hat mich
Vor ein Gericht von Männern vorgefordert,
Die ich als meinesgleichen nicht erkennen,
Zu denen ich kein Herz mir fassen kann.
Elisabeth ist meines Stammes, meines
175 Geschlechts und Ranges — Ihr allein, der Schwester,
Der Königin, der Frau kann ich mich öffnen.

Paulet.

Sehr oft, Mylady, habt Ihr Euer Schicksal

Und Eure Ehre Männern anvertraut,
Die Eurer Achtung minder würdig waren.

Maria.

180 Ich bitte noch um eine zweite Gunst,
Unmenschlichkeit allein kann mir sie weigern.
Schon lange Zeit entbehr' ich im Gefängnis
Der Kirche Trost, der Sakramente Wohlthat;
Und die mir Kron' und Freiheit hat geraubt,
185 Die meinem Leben selber droht, wird mir
Die Himmelsthüre nicht verschließen wollen.

Paulet.

Auf Euren Wunsch wird der Dechant des Orts —

Maria

unterbricht ihn lebhaft.

Ich will nichts vom Dechanten. Einen Priester
Von meiner eignen Kirche fordre ich.
190 — Auch Schreiber und Notarien verlang' ich,
Um meinen letzten Willen aufzusetzen.
Der Gram, das lange Kerkerelend nagt
An meinem Leben. Meine Tage sind
Gezählt, befürcht' ich, und ich achte mich
195 Gleich einer Sterbenden.

Paulet.

Da thut Ihr wohl;
Das sind Betrachtungen, die Euch geziemen.

Maria.

Und weiß ich, ob nicht eine schnelle Hand
Des Kummers langsames Geschäft beschleunigt?

Ich will mein Testament aufsetzen, will
200 Verfügung treffen über das, was mein ist.

Paulet.

Die Freiheit habt Ihr. Englands Königin
Will sich mit Eurem Raube nicht bereichern.

Maria.

Man hat von meinen treuen Kammerfrauen,
Von meinen Dienern mich getrennt — Wo sind sie?
205 Was ist ihr Schicksal? Ihrer Dienste kann ich
Entraten; doch beruhigt will ich sein,
Daß die Getreu'n nicht leiden und entbehren.

Paulet.

Für Eure Diener ist gesorgt. Er will gehen.

Maria.

Ihr geht, Sir? Ihr verlaßt mich abermals
210 Und ohne mein geängstigt fürchtend Herz
Der Qual der Ungewißheit zu entladen?
Ich bin, dank Eurer Späher Wachsamkeit,
Von aller Welt geschieden, keine Kunde
Gelangt zu mir durch diese Kerkermauern,
215 Mein Schicksal liegt in meiner Feinde Hand.
Ein peinlich langer Monat ist vorüber,
Seitdem die vierzig Kommissarien
In diesem Schloß mich überfallen, Schranken
Errichtet, schnell, mit unanständiger Eile,
220 Mich unbereitet, ohne Anwalts Hilfe,
Vor ein noch nie erhört Gericht gestellt,
Auf schlaugefaßte schwere Klagepunkte
Mich, die Betäubte, Überraschte, flugs
Aus dem Gedächtnis Rede stehen lassen —

225 Wie Geister kamen sie und schwanden wieder.
Seit diesem Tage schweigt mir jeder Mund,
Ich such' umsonst in Eurem Blick zu lesen,
Ob meine Unschuld, meiner Freunde Eifer,
Ob meiner Feinde böser Rat gesiegt.
230 Brecht endlich Euer Schweigen — Laßt mich wissen,
Was ich zu fürchten, was zu hoffen habe.

Paulet nach einer Pause.

Schließt Eure Rechnung mit dem Himmel ab!

Maria.

Ich hoff' auf seine Gnade, Sir — und hoffe
Auf strenges Recht von meinen ird'schen Richtern.

Paulet.

235 Recht soll Euch werden. Zweifelt nicht daran!

Maria.

Ist mein Prozeß entschieden, Sir?

Paulet.

Ich weiß nicht.

Maria.

Bin ich verurteilt?

Paulet.

Ich weiß nichts, Mylady.

Maria.

Man liebt hier, rasch zu Werk zu gehn. Soll mich
Der Mörder überfallen, wie die Richter?

Paulet.

240 Denkt immerhin, es sei so, und er wird Euch
In bess'rer Fassung dann als diese finden.

Maria.

Nichts soll mich in Erstaunen setzen, Sir,
Was ein Gerichtshof in Westminsterhall,
Den Burleighs Haß und Hattons Eifer lenkt,
245 Zu urteln sich erdreiste — Weiß ich doch,
Was Englands Königin wagen darf zu thun.

Paulet.

Englands Beherrscher brauchen nichts zu scheuen
Als ihr Gewissen und ihr Parlament.
Was die Gerechtigkeit gesprochen, furchtlos
250 Vor aller Welt wird es die Macht vollziehn.

Dritter Auftritt.

Die Vorigen. Mortimer, Paulets Neffe, tritt herein und ohne der Königin einige Aufmerksamkeit zu bezeugen, zu Paulet.

Mortimer.

Man sucht Euch, Oheim.

Er entfernt sich auf eben die Weise. Die Königin bemerkt es mit Unwillen und wendet sich zu Paulet, der ihm folgen will.

Maria.

Sir, noch eine Bitte.
Wenn Ihr mir was zu sagen habt — von Euch
Ertrag' ich viel, ich ehre Euer Alter.
Den Übermut des Jünglings trag' ich nicht;
255 Spart mir den Anblick seiner rohen Sitten!

Paulet.

Was ihn Euch widrig macht, macht mir ihn wert.
Wohl ist es keiner von den weichen Thoren,
Die eine falsche Weiberthräne schmelzt —
Er ist gereist, kommt aus Paris und Rheims
260 Und bringt sein treu altenglisch Herz zurück;
Lady, an dem ist Eure Kunst verloren! Geht ab.

Vierter Auftritt.

Maria. Kennedy.

Kennedy.

Darf Euch der Rohe das ins Antlitz sagen!
O, es ist hart!

Maria
in Nachdenken verloren.

Wir haben in den Tagen unsers Glanzes
265 Dem Schmeichler ein zu willig Ohr geliehn,
Gerecht ist's, gute Kennedy, daß wir
Des Vorwurfs ernste Stimme nun vernehmen.

Kennedy.

Wie? so gebeugt, so mutlos, teure Lady?
Wart Ihr doch sonst so froh, Ihr pflegtet mich zu trösten,
270 Und eher mußt' ich Euren Flattersinn,
Als Eure Schwermut schelten.

Maria.

Ich erkenn' ihn —
Es ist der blut'ge Schatten König Darnleys,

Der zürnend aus dem Gruftgewölbe steigt,
Und er wird nimmer Friede mit mir machen,
275 Bis meines Unglücks Maß erfüllet ist.

Kennedy.

Was für Gedanken —

Maria.

Du vergissest, Hanna —
Ich aber habe ein getreu Gedächtnis —
Der Jahrstag dieser unglückseligen That
Ist heute abermals zurückgekehrt,
280 Er ist's, den ich mit Buß' und Fasten feire.

Kennedy.

Schickt endlich diesen bösen Geist zur Ruh.
Ihr habt die That mit jahrelanger Reu',
Mit schweren Leidensproben abgebüßt.
Die Kirche, die den Löseschlüssel hat
285 Für jede Schuld, der Himmel hat vergeben.

Maria.

Frischblutend steigt die längst vergebne Schuld
Aus ihrem leichtbedeckten Grab empor!
Des Gatten racheforderndes Gespenst
Schickt keines Messedieners Glocke, kein
290 Hochwürdiges in Priesters Hand zur Gruft.

Kennedy.

Nicht Ihr habt ihn gemordet! Andre thaten's!

Maria.

Ich wußte drum. Ich ließ die That geschehn,
Und lockt' ihn schmeichelnd in das Todesnetz.

Kennedy.

Die Jugend mildert Eure Schuld. Ihr wart
So zarten Alters noch.

Maria.

295 So zart — und lud
Die schwere Schuld auf mein so junges Leben.

Kennedy.

Ihr wart durch blutige Beleidigung
Gereizt und durch des Mannes Übermut,
Den Eure Liebe aus der Dunkelheit
300 Wie eine Götterhand hervorgezogen,
Den Ihr durch Euer Brautgemach zum Throne
Geführt, mit Eurer blühenden Person
Beglückt und Eurer angestammten Krone.
Konnt' er vergessen, daß sein prangend Los
305 Der Liebe großmutsvolle Schöpfung war?
Und doch vergaß er's, der Unwürdige!
Beleidigte mit niedrigem Verdacht,
Mit rohen Sitten Eure Zärtlichkeit,
Und widerwärtig wurd' er Euren Augen.
310 Der Zauber schwand, der Euren Blick getäuscht;
Ihr floht erzürnt des Schändlichen Umarmung
Und gabt ihn der Verachtung preis — Und er —
Versucht' er's, Eure Gunst zurückzurufen?
Bat er um Gnade? Warf er sich bereuend
315 Zu Euren Füßen, Besserung versprechend?
Trotz bot Euch der Abscheuliche — Der Euer
Geschöpf war, Euren König wollt' er spielen,
Vor Euren Augen ließ er Euch den Liebling,
Den schönen Sänger Rizzio, durchbohren —
320 Ihr rächtet blutig nur die blut'ge That.

Maria.

Und blutig wird sie auch an mir sich rächen;
Du sprichst mein Urteil aus, da du mich tröstest.

Kennedy.

Da Ihr die That geschehn ließt, wart Ihr nicht
Ihr selbst, gehörtet Euch nicht selbst. Ergriffen
325 Hatt' Euch der Wahnsinn blinder Liebesglut,
Euch unterjocht dem furchtbaren Verführer,
Dem unglücksel'gen Bothwell — Über Euch
Mit übermüt'gem Männerwillen herrschte
Der Schreckliche, der Euch durch Zaubertränke,
330 Durch Höllenkünste das Gemüt verwirrend
Erhitzte —

Maria.

Seine Künste waren keine andre,
Als seine Männerkraft und meine Schwachheit.

Kennedy.

Nein, sag' ich. Alle Geister der Verdammnis
Mußt' er zu Hilfe rufen, der dies Band
335 Um Eure hellen Sinne wob. Ihr hattet
Kein Ohr mehr für der Freundin Warnungsstimme,
Kein Aug' für das, was wohlanständig war.
Verlassen hatte Euch die zarte Scheu
Der Menschen; Eure Wangen, sonst der Sitz
340 Schamhaft errötender Bescheidenheit,
Sie glühten nur vom Feuer des Verlangens.
Ihr warft den Schleier des Geheimnisses
Von Euch; des Mannes keckes Laster hatte
Auch Eure Blödigkeit besiegt; Ihr stelltet
345 Mit dreister Stirne Eure Schmach zur Schau.
Ihr ließt das königliche Schwert von Schottland

Durch ihn, den Mörder, dem des Volkes Flüche
Nachschallten, durch die Gassen Edinburgs
Vor Euch hertragen im Triumph, umringtet
350 Mit Waffen Euer Parlament, und hier,
Im eignen Tempel der Gerechtigkeit,
Zwangt Ihr mit frechem Possenspiel die Richter,
Den Schuldigen des Mordes loszusprechen —
Ihr gingt noch weiter — Gott!

Maria.

Vollende nur!
355 Und reicht' ihm meine Hand vor dem Altare!

Kennedy.

O, laßt ein ewig Schweigen diese That
Bedecken! Sie ist schauderhaft, empörend,
Ist einer ganz Verlornen wert — Doch Ihr seid keine
Verlorene — ich kenn' Euch ja, ich bin's,
360 Die Eure Kindheit auferzogen. Weich
Ist Euer Herz gebildet, offen ist's
Der Scham — der Leichtsinn nur ist Euer Laster.
Ich wiederhol' es, es giebt böse Geister,
Die in des Menschen unverwahrter Brust
365 Sich augenblicklich ihren Wohnplatz nehmen,
Die schnell in uns das Schreckliche begehn
Und, zu der Höll' entfliehend, das Entsetzen
In dem befleckten Busen hinterlassen.
Seit dieser That, die Euer Leben schwärzt,
370 Habt Ihr nichts Lasterhaftes mehr begangen,
Ich bin ein Zeuge Eurer Besserung.
Drum fasset Mut! Macht Friede mit Euch selbst!
Was Ihr auch zu bereuen habt, in England
Seid Ihr nicht schuldig; nicht Elisabeth,

375 Nicht Englands Parlament ist Euer Richter.
Macht ist's, die Euch hier unterdrückt; vor diesen
Anmaßlichen Gerichtshof dürft Ihr Euch
Hinstellen mit dem ganzen Mut der Unschuld.

Maria.

Wer kommt?

Mortimer zeigt sich an der Thüre.

Kennedy.

Es ist der Neffe. Geht hinein!

Fünfter Auftritt.

Die Vorigen. Mortimer scheu hereintretend.

Mortimer zur Amme.

380 Entfernt Euch, haltet Wache vor der Thür,
Ich habe mit der Königin zu reden.

Maria mit Ansehn.

Hanna, du bleibst.

Mortimer.

Habt keine Furcht, Mylady. Lernt mich kennen!

Er überreicht ihr eine Karte.

Maria

sieht sie an und fährt bestürzt zurück.

Ha! Was ist das?

Mortimer zur Amme.

Geht, Dame Kennedy!

385 Sorgt, daß mein Oheim uns nicht überfalle!

Maria

zur Amme, welche zaudert und die Königin fragend ansieht.

Geh, geh! Thu, was er sagt!

Die Amme entfernt sich mit Zeichen der Verwunderung.

Sechster Auftritt.

Mortimer. Maria.

Maria.

Von meinem Oheim,
Dem Kardinal von Lothringen aus Frankreich!

Liest.

„Traut dem Sir Mortimer, der Euch dies bringt,
Denn keinen treuern Freund habt Ihr in England."

Mortimern mit Erstaunen ansehend.

390 Ist's möglich? Ist's kein Blendwerk, das mich täuscht?
So nahe find' ich einen Freund und wähnte mich
Verlassen schon von aller Welt — find' ihn
In Euch, dem Neffen meines Kerkermeisters,
In dem ich meinen schlimmsten Feind —

Mortimer

sich ihr zu Füßen werfend.

Verzeihung
395 Für diese verhaßte Larve, Königin,
Die mir zu tragen Kampf genug gekostet,
Doch der ich's danke, daß ich mich Euch nahen,
Euch Hilfe und Errettung bringen kann.

Maria.

Steht auf — Ihr überrascht mich, Sir — Ich kann
400 So schnell nicht aus der Tiefe meines Elends
Zur Hoffnung übergehen — Redet, Sir —
Macht mir dies Glück begreiflich, daß ich's glaube.

Mortimer steht auf.

Die Zeit verrinnt. Bald wird mein Oheim hier sein,
Und ein verhaßter Mensch begleitet ihn.
405 Eh' Euch ihr Schreckensauftrag überrascht,
Hört an, wie Euch der Himmel Rettung schickt.

Maria.

Er schickt sie durch ein Wunder seiner Allmacht!

Mortimer.

Erlaubt, daß ich von mir beginne.

Maria.

Redet, Sir!

Mortimer.

Ich zählte zwanzig Jahre, Königin,
410 In strengen Pflichten war ich aufgewachsen,
In finsterm Haß des Papsttums aufgesäugt,
Als mich die unbezwingliche Begierde
Hinaus trieb auf das feste Land. Ich ließ
Der Puritaner dumpfe Predigtstuben,
415 Die Heimat hinter mir; in schnellem Lauf
Durchzog ich Frankreich, das gepriesene
Italien mit heißem Wunsche suchend.
Es war die Zeit des großen Kirchenfests
Von Pilgerscharen wimmelten die Wege,
420 Bekränzt war jedes Gottesbild, es war,
Als ob die Menschheit auf der Wandrung wäre,

Wallfahrend nach dem Himmelreich — Mich selbst
Ergriff der Strom der glaubenvollen Menge
Und riß mich in das Weichbild Roms —
425 Wie ward mir, Königin!
Als mir der Säulen Pracht und Siegesbogen
Entgegenstieg, des Kolosseums Herrlichkeit
Den Staunenden umfing, ein hoher Bildnergeist
In seine heitre Wunderwelt mich schloß!
430 Ich hatte nie der Künste Macht gefühlt;
Es haßt die Kirche, die mich auferzog,
Der Sinne Reiz, kein Abbild duldet sie,
Allein das körperlose Wort verehrend.
Wie wurde mir, als ich ins Innre nun
435 Der Kirchen trat, und die Musik der Himmel
Herunterstieg, und der Gestalten Fülle
Verschwenderisch aus Wand und Decke quoll,
Das Herrlichste und Höchste, gegenwärtig,
Vor den entzückten Sinnen sich bewegte,
440 Als ich sie selbst nun sah, die Göttlichen,
Den Gruß des Engels, die Geburt des Herrn,
Die heil'ge Mutter, die herabgestiegne
Dreifaltigkeit, die leuchtende Verklärung —
Als ich den Papst drauf sah in seiner Pracht
445 Das Hochamt halten und die Völker segnen!
O, was ist Goldes, was Juwelen Schein,
Womit der Erde Könige sich schmücken!
Nur er ist mit dem Göttlichen umgeben.
Ein wahrhaft Reich der Himmel ist sein Haus,
450 Denn nicht von dieser Welt sind diese Formen.

Maria.

O, schonet mein! Nicht weiter! Höret auf,

Den frischen Lebensteppich vor mir aus-
Zubreiten — Ich bin elend und gefangen.

Mortimer.

Auch ich war's, Königin! und mein Gefängnis
455 Sprang auf, und frei auf einmal fühlte sich
Der Geist, des Lebens schönen Tag begrüßend.
Haß schwur ich nun dem engen dumpfen Buch,
Mit frischem Kranz die Schläfe mir zu schmücken,
Mich fröhlich an die Fröhlichen zu schließen.
460 Viel edle Schotten drängten sich an mich
Und der Franzosen muntre Landsmannschaften.
Sie brachten mich zu Eurem edlen Oheim,
Dem Kardinal von Guise — Welch ein Mann!
Wie sicher, klar und männlich groß! — Wie ganz
465 Geboren, um die Geister zu regieren!
Das Muster eines königlichen Priesters,
Ein Fürst der Kirche, wie ich keinen sah!

Maria.

Ihr habt sein teures Angesicht gesehn,
Des vielgeliebten, des erhabnen Mannes,
470 Der meiner zarten Jugend Führer war.
O, redet mir von ihm! Denkt er noch mein?
Liebt ihn das Glück, blüht ihm das Leben noch,
Steht er noch herrlich da, ein Fels der Kirche?

Mortimer.

Der Treffliche ließ selber sich herab,
475 Die hohen Glaubenslehren mir zu deuten,
Und meines Herzens Zweifel zu zerstreun.
Er zeigte mir, daß grübelnde Vernunft
Den Menschen ewig in der Irre leitet,

Daß seine Augen sehen müssen, was
480 Das Herz soll glauben, daß ein sichtbar Haupt
Der Kirche not thut, daß der Geist der Wahrheit
Geruht hat auf den Sitzungen der Väter.
Die Wahnbegriffe meiner kind'schen Seele,
Wie schwanden sie vor seinem siegenden
485 Verstand und vor der Suada seines Mundes!
Ich kehrte in der Kirche Schoß zurück,
Schwur meinen Irrtum ab in seine Hände.

Maria.

So seid Ihr einer jener Tausende,
Die er mit seiner Rede Himmelskraft,
490 Wie der erhabne Prediger des Berges,
Ergriffen und zum ew'gen Heil geführt!

Mortimer.

Als ihn des Amtes Pflichten bald darauf
Nach Frankreich riefen, sandt' er mich nach Rheims,
Wo die Gesellschaft Jesu, fromm geschäftig,
495 Für Englands Kirche Priester auferzieht.
Den edlen Schotten Morgan fand ich hier,
Auch Euren treuen Leßley, den gelehrten
Bischof von Roße, die auf Frankreichs Boden
Freudlose Tage der Verbannung leben —
500 Eng schloß ich mich an diese Würdigen
Und stärkte mich im Glauben — Eines Tags,
Als ich mich umsah in des Bischofs Wohnung,
Fiel mir ein weiblich Bildnis in die Augen,
Von rührend wundersamem Reiz; gewaltig
505 Ergriff es mich in meiner tiefsten Seele,
Und des Gefühls nicht mächtig stand ich da.
Da sagte mir der Bischof: Wohl mit Recht

Mögt Ihr gerührt bei diesem Bilde weilen.
Die schönste aller Frauen, welche leben,
510 Ist auch die jammernswürdigste von allen;
Um unsers Glaubens willen duldet sie,
Und Euer Vaterland ist's, wo sie leidet.

Maria.

Der Redliche! Nein, ich verlor nicht alles,
Da solcher Freund im Unglück mir geblieben.

Mortimer.

515 Drauf fing er an, mit herzerschütternder
Beredsamkeit mir Euer Märtyrtum
Und Eurer Feinde Blutgier abzuschildern.
Auch Euren Stammbaum wies er mir, er zeigte
Mir Eure Abkunft von dem hohen Hause
520 Der Tudor, überzeugte mich, daß Euch
Allein gebührt, in Engelland zu herrschen,
Nicht dieser Afterkönigin, gezeugt
In ehebrecherischem Bett, die Heinrich,
Ihr Vater, selbst verwarf als Bastardtochter.
525 Nicht seinem einz'gen Zeugnis wollt' ich traun,
Ich holte Rat bei allen Rechtsgelehrten,
Viel alte Wappenbücher schlug ich nach,
Und alle Kundige, die ich befragte,
Bestätigten mir Eures Anspruchs Kraft.
530 Ich weiß nunmehr, daß Euer gutes Recht
An England Euer ganzes Unrecht ist,
Daß Euch dies Reich als Eigentum gehört,
Worin Ihr schuldlos als Gefangne schmachtet.

Maria.

O, dieses unglücksvolle Recht! Es ist
535 Die einz'ge Quelle aller meiner Leiden.

Mortimer.

Um diese Zeit kam mir die Kunde zu,
Daß Ihr aus Talbots Schloß hinweggeführt,
Und meinem Oheim übergeben worden —
Des Himmels wundervolle Rettungshand
540 Glaubt' ich in dieser Fügung zu erkennen.
Ein lauter Ruf des Schicksals war sie mir,
Das meinen Arm gewählt, Euch zu befreien.
Die Freunde stimmen freudig bei, es giebt
Der Kardinal mir seinen Rat und Segen,
545 Und lehrt mich der Verstellung schwere Kunst.
Schnell ward der Plan entworfen, und ich trete
Den Rückweg an ins Vaterland, wo ich,
Ihr wißt's, vor zehen Tagen bin gelandet. *Er hält inne.*
Ich sah Euch, Königin — Euch selbst!
550 Nicht Euer Bild! — O, welchen Schatz bewahrt
Dies Schloß! Kein Kerker! Eine Götterhalle,
Glanzvoller als der königliche Hof
Von England — O des Glücklichen, dem es
Vergönnt ist, eine Luft mit Euch zu atmen!
555 Wohl hat sie recht, die Euch so tief verbirgt!
Aufstehen würde Englands ganze Jugend,
Kein Schwert in seiner Scheide müßig bleiben,
Und die Empörung mit gigantischem Haupt
Durch diese Friedensinsel schreiten, sähe
560 Der Britte seine Königin!

Maria.

Wohl ihr,
Säh' jeder Britte sie mit Euren Augen!

Mortimer.

Wär' er, wie ich, ein Zeuge Eurer Leiden,

Der Sanftmut Zeuge und der edlen Fassung,
Womit Ihr das Unwürdige erduldet.
565 Denn geht Ihr nicht aus allen Leidensproben
Als eine Königin hervor? Raubt Euch
Des Kerkers Schmach von Eurem Schönheitsglanze?
Euch mangelt alles, was das Leben schmückt,
Und doch umfließt Euch ewig Licht und Leben.
570 Nie setz' ich meinen Fuß auf diese Schwelle,
Daß nicht mein Herz zerrissen wird von Qualen,
Nicht von der Lust entzückt, Euch anzuschauen! —
Doch furchtbar naht sich die Entscheidung, wachsend
Mit jeder Stunde dringet die Gefahr;
575 Ich darf nicht länger säumen — Euch nicht länger
Das Schreckliche verbergen —

Maria.

Ist mein Urteil
Gefällt? Entdeckt mir's frei! Ich kann es hören.

Mortimer.

Es ist gefällt. Die zweiundvierzig Richter haben
Ihr Schuldig ausgesprochen über Euch. Das Haus
580 Der Lords und der Gemeinen, die Stadt London
Bestehen heftig dringend auf des Urteils
Vollstreckung; nur die Königin säumt noch,
— Aus arger List, daß man sie nötige,
Nicht aus Gefühl der Menschlichkeit und Schonung.

Maria mit Fassung.

585 Sir Mortimer, Ihr überrascht mich nicht,
Erschreckt mich nicht. Auf solche Botschaft war ich
Schon längst gefaßt. Ich kenne meine Richter.
Nach den Mißhandlungen, die ich erlitten,

Begreif' ich wohl, daß man die Freiheit mir
590 Nicht schenken kann — Ich weiß, wo man hinaus will.
In ew'gem Kerker will man mich bewahren,
Und meine Rache, meinen Rechtsanspruch
Mit mir verscharren in Gefängnisnacht.

Mortimer.

Nein, Königin — o nein! nein! Dabei steht man
595 Nicht still. Die Tyrannei begnügt sich nicht,
Ihr Werk nur halb zu thun. Solang' Ihr lebt,
Lebt auch die Furcht der Königin von England.
Euch kann kein Kerker tief genug begraben;
Nur Euer Tod versichert ihren Thron.

Maria.

600 Sie könnt' es wagen, mein gekröntes Haupt
Schmachvoll auf einen Henkerblock zu legen?

Mortimer.

Sie wird es wagen. Zweifelt nicht daran!

Maria.

Sie könnte so die eigne Majestät
Und aller Könige im Staube wälzen?
605 Und fürchtet sie die Rache Frankreichs nicht?

Mortimer.

Sie schließt mit Frankreich einen ew'gen Frieden;
Dem Duc von Anjou schenkt sie Thron und Hand.

Maria.

Wird sich der König Spaniens nicht waffnen?

Mortimer.

Nicht eine Welt in Waffen fürchtet sie,
610 Solang' sie Frieden hat mit ihrem Volke.

Maria.

Den Britten wollte sie dies Schauspiel geben?

Mortimer.

Dies Land, Mylady, hat in letzten Zeiten
Der königlichen Frauen mehr vom Thron
Herab aufs Blutgerüste steigen sehn.
615 Die eigne Mutter der Elisabeth
Ging diesen Weg, und Katharina Howard;
Auch Lady Gray war ein gekröntes Haupt.

Maria nach einer Pause.

Nein, Mortimer! Euch blendet eitle Furcht.
Es ist die Sorge Eures treuen Herzens,
620 Die Euch vergebne Schrecknisse erschafft.
Nicht das Schafott ist's, das ich fürchte, Sir.
Es giebt noch andre Mittel, stillere,
Wodurch sich die Beherrscherin von England
Vor meinem Anspruch Ruhe schaffen kann.
625 Eh' sich ein Henker für mich findet, wird
Noch eher sich ein Mörder dingen lassen.
— Das ist's, wovor ich zittre, Sir! und nie
Setz' ich des Bechers Rand an meine Lippen,
Daß nicht ein Schauder mich ergreift, er könnte
630 Kredenzt sein von der Liebe meiner Schwester.

Mortimer.

Nicht offenbar noch heimlich soll's dem Mord
Gelingen, Euer Leben anzutasten.
Seid ohne Furcht! Bereitet ist schon alles.
Zwölf edle Jünglinge des Landes sind
635 In meinem Bündnis, haben heute früh
Das Sakrament darauf empfangen, Euch

Mit starkem Arm aus diesem Schloß zu führen.
Graf Aubespine, der Abgesandte Frankreichs,
Weiß um den Bund, er bietet selbst die Hände,
640 Und sein Palast ist's, wo wir uns versammeln.

Maria.

Ihr macht mich zittern, Sir — doch nicht vor Freude.
Mir fliegt ein böses Ahnen durch das Herz.
Was unternehmt Ihr? Wißt Ihr's? Schrecken Euch
Nicht Babingtons, nicht Tichburns blut'ge Häupter,
645 Auf Londons Brücke warnend aufgesteckt,
Nicht das Verderben der Unzähligen,
Die ihren Tod in gleichem Wagstück fanden
Und meine Ketten schwerer nur gemacht?
Unglücklicher, verführter Jüngling — flieht!
650 Flieht, wenn's noch Zeit ist — wenn der Späher Burleigh
Nicht jetzt schon Kundschaft hat von Euch, nicht schon
In eure Mitte den Verräter mischte.
Flieht aus dem Reiche schnell! Marien Stuart
Hat noch kein Glücklicher beschützt.

Mortimer.

Mich schrecken
655 Nicht Babingtons, nicht Tichburns blut'ge Häupter,
Auf Londons Brücke warnend aufgesteckt,
Nicht das Verderben der unzähl'gen andern,
Die ihren Tod in gleichem Wagstück fanden;
Sie fanden auch darin den ew'gen Ruhm,
660 Und Glück schon ist's, für Eure Rettung sterben.

Maria.

Umsonst! Mich rettet nicht Gewalt, nicht List.
Der Feind ist wachsam, und die Macht ist sein.

Nicht Paulet nur und seiner Wächter Schar,
Ganz England hütet meines Kerkers Thore.
665 Der freie Wille der Elisabeth allein
Kann sie mir aufthun.

Mortimer.

O, das hoffet nie!

Maria.

Ein einz'ger Mann lebt, der sie öffnen kann.

Mortimer.

O nennt mir diesen Mann —

Maria.

Graf Lester.

Mortimer
tritt erstaunt zurück.

Lester!

Graf Lester! — Euer blutigster Verfolger,
670 Der Günstling der Elisabeth — Von diesem —

Maria.

Bin ich zu retten, ist's allein durch ihn.
— Geht zu ihm! Öffnet Euch ihm frei,
Und zur Gewähr, daß ich's bin, die Euch sendet,
Bringt ihm dies Schreiben! Es enthält mein Bildnis.

Sie zieht ein Papier aus dem Busen, Mortimer tritt zurück und zögert, es anzunehmen.

675 Nehmt hin! Ich trag' es lange schon bei mir,
Weil Eures Oheims strenge Wachsamkeit
Mir jeden Weg zu ihm gehemmt — Euch sandte
Mein guter Engel —

Mortimer.

Königin — dies Rätsel —

Erklärt es mir —

Maria.

Graf Lester wird's Euch lösen.

680 Vertraut ihm, er wird Euch vertraun — Wer kommt?

Kennedy
eilfertig eintretend.

Sir Paulet naht mit einem Herrn vom Hofe.

Mortimer.

Es ist Lord Burleigh. Faßt Euch, Königin!
Hört es mit Gleichmut an, was er Euch bringt.

Er entfernt sich durch eine Seitenthür, Kennedy folgt ihm.

Siebenter Auftritt.

Maria. Lord Burleigh, Großschatzmeister von England, und Ritter Paulet.

Paulet.

Ihr wünschet heut Gewißheit Eures Schicksals,
685 Gewißheit bringt Euch Seine Herrlichkeit,
Mylord von Burleigh. Tragt sie mit Ergebung!

Maria.

Mit Würde, hoff' ich, die der Unschuld ziemt.

Burleigh.

Ich komme als Gesandter des Gerichts.

Maria.

Lord Burleigh leiht dienstfertig dem Gerichte,
690 Dem er den Geist geliehn, nun auch den Mund.

Paulet.

Ihr sprecht, als wüßtet Ihr bereits das Urteil.

Maria.

Da es Lord Burleigh bringt, so weiß ich es.
— Zur Sache, Sir!

Burleigh.

Ihr habt Euch dem Gericht
Der Zweiundvierzig unterworfen, Lady —

Maria.

695 Verzeiht, Mylord, daß ich Euch gleich zu Anfang
Ins Wort muß fallen — Unterworfen hätt' ich mich
Dem Richterspruch der Zweiundvierzig, sagt Ihr?
Ich habe keineswegs mich unterworfen.
Nie konnt' ich das — ich konnte meinem Rang,
700 Der Würde meines Volks und meines Sohnes
Und aller Fürsten nicht so viel vergeben.
Verordnet ist im englischen Gesetz,
Daß jeder Angeklagte durch Geschworne
Von seinesgleichen soll gerichtet werden.
705 Wer in der Committee ist meinesgleichen?
Nur Könige sind meine Peers.

Burleigh.

Ihr hörtet
Die Klagartikel an, ließt Euch darüber
Vernehmen vor Gerichte —

Maria.

Ja, ich habe mich
Durch Hattons arge List verleiten lassen,
710 Bloß meiner Ehre wegen, und im Glauben
An meiner Gründe siegende Gewalt,

Ein Ohr zu leihen jenen Klagepunkten
Und ihren Ungrund darzuthun — Das that ich
Aus Achtung für die würdigen Personen
715 Der Lords, nicht für ihr Amt, das ich verwerfe.

Burleigh.

Ob Ihr sie anerkennt, ob nicht, Mylady,
Das ist nur eine leere Förmlichkeit,
Die des Gerichtes Lauf nicht hemmen kann.
Ihr atmet Englands Luft, genießt den Schutz,
720 Die Wohlthat des Gesetzes, und so seid Ihr
Auch seiner Herrschaft unterthan!

Maria.

Ich atme
Die Luft in einem englischen Gefängnis.
Heißt das in England leben, der Gesetze
Wohlthat genießen? Kenn' ich sie doch kaum.
725 Nie hab' ich eingewilligt, sie zu halten.
Ich bin nicht dieses Reiches Bürgerin,
Bin eine freie Königin des Auslands.

Burleigh.

Und denkt Ihr, daß der königliche Name
Zum Freibrief dienen könne, blut'ge Zwietracht
730 In fremdem Lande straflos auszusäen?
Wie stünd' es um die Sicherheit der Staaten,
Wenn das gerechte Schwert der Themis nicht
Die schuld'ge Stirn des königlichen Gastes
Erreichen könnte, wie des Bettlers Haupt?

Maria.

735 Ich will mich nicht der Rechenschaft entziehn;
Die Richter sind es nur, die ich verwerfe.

Burleigh.

Die Richter! Wie, Mylady? Sind es etwa
Vom Pöbel aufgegriffene Verworfne,
Schamlose Zungendrescher, denen Recht
740 Und Wahrheit feil ist, die sich zum Organ
Der Unterdrückung willig dingen lassen?
Sind's nicht die ersten Männer dieses Landes,
Selbständig gnug, um wahrhaft sein zu dürfen,
Um über Fürstenfurcht und niedrige
745 Bestechung weit erhaben sich zu sehn?
Sind's nicht dieselben, die ein edles Volk
Frei und gerecht regieren, deren Namen
Man nur zu nennen braucht, um jeden Zweifel,
Um jeden Argwohn schleunig stumm zu machen?
750 An ihrer Spitze steht der Völkerhirte,
Der fromme Primas von Canterbury,
Der weise Talbot, der des Siegels wahret,
Und Howard, der des Reiches Flotten führt.
Sagt! Konnte die Beherrscherin von England
755 Mehr thun, als aus der ganzen Monarchie
Die Edelsten auslesen und zu Richtern
In diesem königlichen Streit bestellen?
Und wär's zu denken, daß Parteienhaß
Den einzelnen bestäche — können vierzig
760 Erlesne Männer sich in einem Spruche
Der Leidenschaft vereinigen?

Maria

nach einigem Stillschweigen.

Ich höre staunend die Gewalt des Mundes,
Der mir von je so unheilbringend war —
Wie werd' ich mich, ein ungelehrtes Weib,

765 Mit so kunstfert'gem Redner messen können! —
Wohl! Wären diese Lords, wie Ihr sie schildert,
Verstummen müßt' ich, hoffnungslos verloren
Wär' meine Sache, sprächen sie mich schuldig.
Doch diese Namen, die Ihr preisend nennt,
770 Die mich durch ihr Gewicht zermalmen sollen,
Mylord, ganz andre Rollen seh' ich sie
In den Geschichten dieses Landes spielen.
Ich sehe diesen hohen Adel Englands,
Des Reiches majestätischen Senat,
775 Gleich Sklaven des Serails den Sultanslaunen
Heinrichs des Achten, meines Großohms, schmeicheln —
Ich sehe dieses edle Oberhaus,
Gleich feil mit den erkäuflichen Gemeinen,
Gesetze prägen und verrufen, Ehen
780 Auflösen, binden, wie der Mächtige
Gebietet, Englands Fürstentöchter heute
Enterben, mit dem Bastardnamen schänden,
Und morgen sie zu Königinnen krönen.
Ich sehe diese würd'gen Peers mit schnell
785 Vertauschter Überzeugung unter vier
Regierungen den Glauben viermal ändern —

Burleigh.

Ihr nennt Euch fremd in Englands Reichsgesetzen;
In Englands Unglück seid Ihr sehr bewandert.

Maria.

Und das sind meine Richter! — Lord Schatzmeister!
790 Ich will gerecht sein gegen Euch! Seid Ihr's
Auch gegen mich — man sagt, Ihr meint es gut
Mit diesem Staat, mit Eurer Königin,
Seid unbestechlich, wachsam, unermüdet —

Ich will es glauben. Nicht der eigne Nutzen
795 Regiert Euch, Euch regiert allein der Vorteil
Des Souverains, des Landes. Eben darum
Mißtraut Euch, edler Lord, daß nicht der Nutzen
Des Staats Euch als Gerechtigkeit erscheine.
Nicht zweifl' ich dran, es sitzen neben Euch
800 Noch edle Männer unter meinen Richtern.
Doch sie sind Protestanten, Eiferer
Für Englands Wohl, und sprechen über mich,
Die Königin von Schottland, die Papistin!
Es kann der Britte gegen den Schotten nicht
805 Gerecht sein, ist ein uralt Wort — Drum ist
Herkömmlich seit der Väter grauen Zeit,
Daß vor Gericht kein Britte gegen den Schotten,
Kein Schotte gegen jenen zeugen darf.
Die Not gab dieses seltsame Gesetz;
810 Ein tiefer Sinn wohnt in den alten Bräuchen,
Man muß sie ehren, Mylord — die Natur
Warf diese beiden feur'gen Völkerschaften
Auf dieses Brett im Ocean; ungleich
Verteilte sie's, und hieß sie darum kämpfen,
815 Der Tweede schmales Bette trennt allein
Die heft'gen Geister; oft vermischte sich
Das Blut der Kämpfenden in ihren Wellen.
Die Hand am Schwerte, schauen sie sich drohend
Von beiden Ufern an, seit tausend Jahren.
820 Kein Feind bedränget Engelland, dem nicht
Der Schotte sich zum Helfer zugesellte;
Kein Bürgerkrieg entzündet Schottlands Städte,
Zu dem der Britte nicht den Zunder trug.
Und nicht erlöschen wird der Haß, bis endlich

825 Ein Parlament sie brüderlich vereint,
Ein Scepter waltet durch die ganze Insel.

Burleigh.

Und eine Stuart sollte dieses Glück
Dem Reich gewähren?

Maria.

Warum soll ich's leugnen?
Ja, ich gesteh's, daß ich die Hoffnung nährte,
830 Zwei edle Nationen unterm Schatten
Des Ölbaums frei und fröhlich zu vereinen.
Nicht ihres Völkerhasses Opfer glaubt' ich
Zu werden; ihre lange Eifersucht,
Der alten Zwietracht unglücksel'ge Glut
835 Hofft' ich auf ew'ge Tage zu ersticken,
Und, wie mein Ahnherr Richmond die zwei Rosen
Zusammenband nach blut'gem Streit, die Kronen
Schottland und England friedlich zu vermählen.

Burleigh.

Auf schlimmem Weg verfolgtet Ihr dies Ziel,
840 Da Ihr das Reich entzünden, durch die Flammen
Des Bürgerkriegs zum Throne steigen wolltet.

Maria.

Das wollt' ich nicht — beim großen Gott des Himmels!
Wann hätt' ich das gewollt? Wo sind die Proben?

Burleigh.

Nicht Streitens wegen kam ich her. Die Sache
845 Ist keinem Wortgefecht mehr unterworfen.
Es ist erkannt durch vierzig Stimmen gegen zwei,
Daß Ihr die Akte vom vergangnen Jahr
Gebrochen, dem Gesetz verfallen seid.

Es ist verordnet im vergangnen Jahr:
850 „Wenn sich Tumult im Königreich erhübe,
Im Namen und zum Nutzen irgend einer
Person, die Rechte vorgiebt an die Krone,
Daß man gerichtlich gegen sie verfahre,
Bis in den Tod die Schuldige verfolge“ —
855 Und da bewiesen ist —

Maria.

Mylord von Burleigh!
Ich zweifle nicht, daß ein Gesetz, ausdrücklich
Auf mich gemacht, verfaßt, mich zu verderben,
Sich gegen mich wird brauchen lassen — Wehe
Dem armen Opfer, wenn derselbe Mund,
860 Der das Gesetz gab, auch das Urteil spricht!
Könnt Ihr es leugnen, Lord, daß jene Akte
Zu meinem Untergang ersonnen ist?

Burleigh.

Zu Eurer Warnung sollte sie gereichen;
Zum Fallstrick habt Ihr selber sie gemacht.
865 Den Abgrund saht Ihr, der vor Euch sich aufthat
Und treu gewarnet stürztet Ihr hinein.
Ihr wart mit Babington, dem Hochverräter,
Und seinen Mordgesellen einverstanden,
Ihr hattet Wissenschaft von allem, lenktet
870 Aus Eurem Kerker planvoll die Verschwörung.

Maria.

Wann hätt' ich das gethan? Man zeige mir
Die Dokumente auf.

Burleigh.

Die hat man Euch
Schon neulich vor Gerichte vorgewiesen.

Maria.

Die Kopien, von fremder Hand geschrieben!
875 Man bringe die Beweise mir herbei,
Daß ich sie selbst diktiert, daß ich sie so
Diktiert, gerade so, wie man gelesen.

Burleigh.

Daß es dieselben sind, die er empfangen,
Hat Babington vor seinem Tod bekannt.

Maria.

880 Und warum stellte man ihn mir nicht lebend
Vor Augen? Warum eilte man so sehr,
Ihn aus der Welt zu fördern, eh' man ihn
Mir, Stirne gegen Stirne, vorgeführt?

Burleigh.

Auch Eure Schreiber, Kurl und Nau, erhärten
885 Mit einem Eid, daß es die Briefe seien,
Die sie aus Eurem Munde niederschrieben.

Maria.

Und auf das Zeugnis meiner Hausbedienten
Verdammt man mich? Auf Treu' und Glauben derer,
Die mich verraten, ihre Königin,
890 Die in demselben Augenblick die Treu'
Mir brachen, da sie gegen mich gezeugt?

Burleigh.

Ihr selbst erklärtet sonst den Schotten Kurl
Für einen Mann von Tugend und Gewissen.

Maria.

So kannt' ich ihn — doch eines Mannes Tugend
895 Erprobt allein die Stunde der Gefahr.
Die Folter konnt' ihn ängstigen, daß er

Aussagte und gestand, was er nicht wußte!
Durch falsches Zeugnis glaubt' er sich zu retten,
Und mir, der Königin, nicht viel zu schaden.

Burleigh.

900 Mit einem freien Eid hat er's beschworen.

Maria.

Vor meinem Angesichte nicht! — Wie, Sir?
Das sind zwei Zeugen, die noch beide leben!
Man stelle sie mir gegenüber, lasse sie
Ihr Zeugnis mir ins Antlitz wiederholen!
905 Warum mir eine Gunst, ein Recht verweigern,
Das man dem Mörder nicht versagt? Ich weiß
Aus Talbots Munde, meines vor'gen Hüters,
Daß unter dieser nämlichen Regierung
Ein Reichsschluß durchgegangen, der befiehlt,
910 Den Kläger dem Beklagten vorzustellen.
Wie? Oder hab' ich falsch gehört? — Sir Paulet!
Ich hab' Euch stets als Biedermann erfunden;
Beweist es jetzo! Sagt mir auf Gewissen,
Ist's nicht so? Giebt's kein solch Gesetz in England?

Paulet.

915 So ist's, Mylady. Das ist bei uns Rechtens.
Was wahr ist, muß ich sagen.

Maria.

Nun, Mylord!
Wenn man mich denn so streng nach englischem Recht
Behandelt, wo dies Recht mich unterdrückt,
Warum dasselbe Landesrecht umgehen,
920 Wenn es mir Wohlthat werden kann? — Antwortet!
Warum ward Babington mir nicht vor Augen

Gestellt, wie das Gesetz befiehlt? Warum
Nicht meine Schreiber, die noch beide leben?

Burleigh.

Ereifert Euch nicht, Lady. Euer Einverständnis
925 Mit Babington ist's nicht allein —

Maria.

Es ist's
Allein, was mich dem Schwerte des Gesetzes
Bloßstellt, wovon ich mich zu rein'gen habe.
Mylord! Bleibt bei der Sache! Beugt nicht aus!

Burleigh.

Es ist bewiesen, daß Ihr mit Mendoza,
930 Dem spanischen Botschafter, unterhandelt —

Maria lebhaft.

Bleibt bei der Sache, Lord!

Burleigh.

Daß Ihr Anschläge
Geschmiedet, die Religion des Landes
Zu stürzen, alle Könige Europens
Zum Krieg mit England aufgeregt —

Maria.

Und wenn ich's
935 Gethan? Ich hab' es nicht gethan — Jedoch
Gesetzt, ich that's! — Mylord, man hält mich hier
Gefangen wider alle Völkerrechte.
Nicht mit dem Schwerte kam ich in dies Land,
Ich kam herein als eine Bittende,
940 Das heil'ge Gastrecht fordernd, in den Arm
Der blutsverwandten Königin mich werfend —

Und so ergriff mich die Gewalt, bereitete
Mir Ketten, wo ich Schutz gehofft — Sagt an!
Ist mein Gewissen gegen diesen Staat
945 Gebunden? Hab' ich Pflichten gegen England?
Ein heilig Zwangsrecht üb' ich aus, da ich
Aus diesen Banden strebe, Macht mit Macht
Abwende, alle Staaten dieses Weltteils
Zu meinem Schutz aufrühre und bewege.
950 Was irgend nur in einem guten Krieg
Recht ist und ritterlich, das darf ich üben.
Den Mord allein, die heimlich blut'ge That,
Verbietet mir mein Stolz und mein Gewissen;
Mord würde mich beflecken und entehren.
955 Entehren, sag' ich — keineswegs mich
Verdammen, einem Rechtsspruch unterwerfen.
Denn nicht vom Rechte, von Gewalt allein
Ist zwischen mir und Engelland die Rede.

Burleigh bedeutend.

Nicht auf der Stärke schrecklich Recht beruft Euch,
960 Mylady! Es ist der Gefangenen nicht günstig.

Maria.

Ich bin die Schwache, sie die Mächt'ge. — Wohl,
Sie brauche die Gewalt, sie töte mich,
Sie bringe ihrer Sicherheit das Opfer.
Doch sie gestehe dann, daß sie die Macht
965 Allein, nicht die Gerechtigkeit geübt.
Nicht vom Gesetze borge sie das Schwert,
Sich der verhaßten Feindin zu entladen,
Und kleide nicht in heiliges Gewand
Der rohen Stärke blutiges Erkühnen.
970 Solch Gaukelspiel betrüge nicht die Welt!

Ermorden lassen kann sie mich, nicht richten!
Sie geb' es auf, mit des Verbrechens Früchten
Den heil'gen Schein der Tugend zu vereinen,
Und was sie ist, das wage sie zu scheinen! Sie geht ab.

Achter Auftritt.

Burleigh. Paulet.

Burleigh.

975 Sie trotzt uns — wird uns trotzen, Ritter Paulet,
Bis an die Stufen des Schafotts — Dies stolze Herz
Ist nicht zu brechen — Überraschte sie
Der Urtelspruch? Saht Ihr sie eine Thräne
Vergießen? ihre Farbe nur verändern?
980 Nicht unser Mitleid ruft sie an. Wohl kennt sie
Den Zweifelmut der Königin von England,
Und unsre Furcht ist's, was sie mutig macht.

Paulet.

Lord Großschatzmeister! Dieser eitle Trotz wird schnell
Verschwinden, wenn man ihm den Vorwand raubt.
985 Es sind Unziemlichkeiten vorgegangen
In diesem Rechtsstreit, wenn ich's sagen darf.
Man hätte diesen Babington und Tichburn
Ihr in Person vorführen, ihre Schreiber
Ihr gegenüberstellen sollen.

Burleigh schnell.

Nein!
990 Nein, Ritter Paulet! Das war nicht zu wagen.
Zu groß ist ihre Macht auf die Gemüter

Und ihrer Thränen weibliche Gewalt.
Ihr Schreiber Kurl, ständ' er ihr gegenüber,
Käm' es dazu, das Wort nun auszusprechen,
995 An dem ihr Leben hängt — er würde zaghaft
Zurückziehn, sein Geständnis widerrufen —

Paulet.

So werden Englands Feinde alle Welt
Erfüllen mit gehässigen Gerüchten,
Und des Prozesses festliches Gepräng
1000 Wird als ein kühner Frevel nur erscheinen.

Burleigh.

Dies ist der Kummer unsrer Königin —
Daß diese Stifterin des Unheils doch
Gestorben wäre, ehe sie den Fuß
Auf Englands Boden setzte!

Paulet.

Dazu sag' ich Amen.

Burleigh.

1005 Daß Krankheit sie im Kerker aufgerieben!

Paulet.

Viel Unglück hätt' es diesem Land erspart.

Burleigh.

Doch hätt' auch gleich ein Zufall der Natur
Sie hingerafft — wir hießen doch die Mörder.

Paulet.

Wohl wahr. Man kann den Menschen nicht verwehren,
1010 Zu denken, was sie wollen.

Burleigh.

Zu beweisen wär's
Doch nicht, und würde weniger Geräusch erregen —

Paulet.

Mag es Geräusch erregen! Nicht der laute,
Nur der gerechte Tadel kann verletzen.

Burleigh.

O! Auch die heilige Gerechtigkeit
1015 Entflieht dem Tadel nicht. Die Meinung hält es
Mit dem Unglücklichen; es wird der Neid
Stets den obsiegend Glücklichen verfolgen.
Das Richterschwert, womit der Mann sich ziert,
Verhaßt ist's in der Frauen Hand. Die Welt
1020 Glaubt nicht an die Gerechtigkeit des Weibes,
Sobald ein Weib das Opfer wird. Umsonst,
Daß wir, die Richter, nach Gewissen sprachen!
Sie hat der Gnade königliches Recht.
Sie muß es brauchen. Unerträglich ist's,
1025 Wenn sie den strengen Lauf läßt dem Gesetze!

Paulet.

Und also —

Burleigh rasch einfallend.

Also soll sie leben? Nein!
Sie darf nicht leben! Nimmermehr! Dies, eben
Dies ist's, was unsre Königin beängstigt —
Warum der Schlaf ihr Lager flieht — Ich lese
1030 In ihren Augen ihrer Seele Kampf,
Ihr Mund wagt ihre Wünsche nicht zu sprechen;
Doch vielbedeutend fragt ihr stummer Blick:
Ist unter allen meinen Dienern keiner,
Der die verhaßte Wahl mir spart, in ew'ger Furcht
1035 Auf meinem Thron zu zittern, oder grausam
Die Königin, die eigne Blutsverwandte,
Dem Beil zu unterwerfen?

Paulet.

Das ist nun die Notwendigkeit, steht nicht zu ändern.

Burleigh.

Wohl stünd's zu ändern, meint die Königin,
1040 Wenn sie nur aufmerksam're Diener hätte.

Paulet.

Aufmerksame?

Burleigh.

Die einen stummen Auftrag
Zu deuten wissen.

Paulet.

Einen stummen Auftrag!

Burleigh.

Die, wenn man ihnen eine gift'ge Schlange
Zu hüten gab, den anvertrauten Feind
1045 Nicht wie ein heilig teures Kleinod hüten.

Paulet bedeutungsvoll.

Ein hohes Kleinod ist der gute Name,
Der unbescholtne Ruf der Königin,
Den kann man nicht zu wohl bewachen, Sir!

Burleigh.

Als man die Lady von dem Shrewsbury
1050 Wegnahm und Ritter Paulets Hut vertraute,
Da war die Meinung —

Paulet.

Ich will hoffen, Sir,
Die Meinung war, daß man den schwersten Auftrag
Den reinsten Händen übergeben wollte.
Bei Gott! Ich hätte dieses Schergenamt
1055 Nicht übernommen, dächt' ich nicht, daß es

Den besten Mann in England forderte.
Laßt mich nicht denken, daß ich's etwas anderm
Als meinem reinen Rufe schuldig bin.

Burleigh.

Man breitet aus, sie schwinde, läßt sie kränker
1060 Und kränker werden, endlich still verscheiden;
So stirbt sie in der Menschen Angedenken —
Und Euer Ruf bleibt rein.

Paulet.

Nicht mein Gewissen.

Burleigh.

Wenn Ihr die eigne Hand nicht leihen wollt,
So werdet Ihr der fremden doch nicht wehren —

Paulet unterbricht ihn.

1065 Kein Mörder soll sich ihrer Schwelle nahn,
Solang' die Götter meines Dachs sie schützen.
Ihr Leben ist mir heilig, heil'ger nicht
Ist mir das Haupt der Königin von England.
Ihr seid die Richter! Richtet! Brecht den Stab!
1070 Und wenn es Zeit ist, laßt den Zimmerer
Mit Axt und Säge kommen, das Gerüst
Aufschlagen — für den Sherif und den Henker
Soll meines Schlosses Pforte offen sein.
Jetzt ist sie zur Bewahrung mir vertraut,
1075 Und seid gewiß, ich werde sie bewahren,
Daß sie nichts Böses thun soll, noch erfahren!

Gehen ab.

Zweiter Aufzug.

Der Palast zu Westminster.

Erster Auftritt.

Der Graf von Kent und Sir William Davison begegnen einander.

Davison.

Seid Ihr's, Mylord von Kent? Schon vom Turnierplatz
Zurück, und ist die Festlichkeit zu Ende?

Kent.

Wie? Wohntet Ihr dem Ritterspiel nicht bei?

Davison.

1080 Mich hielt mein Amt.

Kent.

Ihr habt das schönste Schauspiel
Verloren, Sir, das der Geschmack ersonnen,
Und edler Anstand ausgeführt — denn wißt!
Es wurde vorgestellt die keusche Festung
Der Schönheit, wie sie vom Verlangen
1085 Berennt wird — Der Lord Marschall, Oberrichter,
Der Seneschall nebst zehen andern Rittern
Der Königin verteidigten die Festung,
Und Frankreichs Kavaliere griffen an.
Voraus erschien ein Herold, der das Schloß
1090 Aufforderte in einem Madrigale,
Und von dem Wall antwortete der Kanzler.

Drauf spielte das Geschütz, und Blumensträuße,
Wohlriechend köstliche Essenzen wurden
Aus niedlichen Feldstücken abgefeuert.
1095 Umsonst! die Stürme wurden abgeschlagen,
Und das Verlangen mußte sich zurückziehn.

Davison.

Ein Zeichen böser Vorbedeutung, Graf,
Für die französische Brautwerbung.

Kent.

Nun, nun, das war ein Scherz — Im Ernste, denk' ich,
1100 Wird sich die Festung endlich doch ergeben.

Davison.

Glaubt Ihr? Ich glaub' es nimmermehr

Kent.

Die schwierigsten Artikel sind bereits
Berichtigt und von Frankreich zugestanden.
Monsieur begnügt sich, in verschlossener
1105 Kapelle seinen Gottesdienst zu halten,
Und öffentlich die Reichsreligion
Zu ehren und zu schützen — Hättet Ihr den Jubel
Des Volks gesehn, als diese Zeitung sich verbreitet!
Denn dieses war des Landes ew'ge Furcht,
1110 Sie möchte sterben ohne Leibeserben,
Und England wieder Papstes Fesseln tragen,
Wenn ihr die Stuart auf dem Throne folgte.

Davison.

Der Furcht kann es entledigt sein — Sie geht
Ins Brautgemach, die Stuart geht zum Tode.

Kent.

1115 Die Königin kommt!

Zweiter Auftritt.

Die Vorigen. Elisabeth, von Leicester geführt. Graf Aubespine, Bellievre, Graf Shrewsbury, Lord Burleigh mit noch andern französischen und englischen Herren treten auf.

Elisabeth zu Aubespine.

Graf! ich beklage diese edeln Herrn,
Die ihr galanter Eifer über Meer
Hieher geführt, daß sie die Herrlichkeit
Des Hofs von St. Germain bei mir vermissen.
1120 Ich kann so prächt'ge Götterfeste nicht
Erfinden als die königliche Mutter
Von Frankreich — Ein gesittet fröhlich Volk,
Das sich, so oft ich öffentlich mich zeige,
Mit Segnungen um meine Sänfte drängt,
1125 Dies ist das Schauspiel, das ich fremden Augen
Mit ein'gem Stolze zeigen kann. Der Glanz
Der Edelfräulein, die im Schönheitsgarten
Der Katharina blühn, verbärge nur
Mich selber und mein schimmerlos Verdienst.

Aubespine.

1130 Nur Eine Dame zeigt Westminsterhof
Dem überraschten Fremden — aber alles,
Was an dem reizenden Geschlecht entzückt,
Stellt sich versammelt dar in dieser einen.

Bellievre.

Erhabne Majestät von Engelland,
1135 Vergönne, daß wir unsern Urlaub nehmen,
Und Monsieur, unsern königlichen Herrn,

Mit der ersehnten Freudenpost beglücken.
Ihn hat des Herzens heiße Ungeduld
Nicht in Paris gelassen, er erwartet
1140 Zu Amiens die Boten seines Glücks,
Und bis nach Calais reichen seine Posten,
Das Jawort, das dein königlicher Mund
Aussprechen wird, mit Flügelschnelligkeit
Zu seinem trunknen Ohre hinzutragen.

Elisabeth.

1145 Graf Bellievre, dringt nicht weiter in mich!
Nicht Zeit ist's jetzt, ich wiederhol' es Euch,
Die freud'ge Hochzeitfackel anzuzünden.
Schwarz hängt der Himmel über diesem Land,
Und besser ziemte mir der Trauerflor
1150 Als das Gepränge bräutlicher Gewänder.
Denn nahe droht ein jammervoller Schlag
Mein Herz zu treffen und mein eignes Haus.

Bellievre.

Nur dein Versprechen gieb uns, Königin!
In frohern Tagen folge die Erfüllung.

Elisabeth.

1155 Die Könige sind nur Sklaven ihres Standes;
Dem eignen Herzen dürfen sie nicht folgen.
Mein Wunsch war's immer, unvermählt zu sterben,
Und meinen Ruhm hätt' ich darein gesetzt,
Daß man dereinst auf meinem Grabstein läse:
1160 „Hier ruht die jungfräuliche Königin."
Doch meine Unterthanen wollen's nicht;
Sie denken jetzt schon fleißig an die Zeit,
Wo ich dahin sein werde — Nicht genug,
Daß jetzt der Segen dieses Land beglückt;

1165 Auch ihrem künft'gen Wohl soll ich mich opfern,
Auch meine jungfräuliche Freiheit soll ich,
Mein höchstes Gut, hingeben für mein Volk,
Und der Gebieter wird mir aufgedrungen.
Es zeigt mir dadurch an, daß ich ihm nur
1170 Ein Weib bin, und ich meinte doch, regiert
Zu haben wie ein Mann und wie ein König.
Wohl weiß ich, daß man Gott nicht dient, wenn man
Die Ordnung der Natur verläßt, und Lob
Verdienen sie, die vor mir hier gewaltet,
1175 Daß sie die Klöster aufgethan, und tausend
Schlachtopfer einer falschverstandnen Andacht
Den Pflichten der Natur zurückgegeben.
Doch eine Königin, die ihre Tage
Nicht ungenützt in müßiger Beschauung
1180 Verbringt, die unverdrossen, unermüdet
Die schwerste aller Pflichten übt, die sollte
Von dem Naturzweck ausgenommen sein,
Der eine Hälfte des Geschlechts der Menschen
Der andern unterwürfig macht —

Aubespine.

1185 Jedwede Tugend, Königin, hast du,
Auf deinem Thron verherrlicht; nichts ist übrig,
Als dem Geschlechte, dessen Ruhm du bist,
Auch noch in seinen eigensten Verdiensten
Als Muster vorzuleuchten. Freilich lebt
1190 Kein Mann auf Erden, der es würdig ist,
Daß du die Freiheit ihm zum Opfer brächtest.
Doch wenn Geburt, wenn Hoheit, Heldentugend
Und Männerschönheit einen Sterblichen
Der Ehre würdig machen, so —

Elisabeth.

Kein Zweifel,

1195 Herr Abgesandter, daß ein Ehebündnis
Mit einem königlichen Sohne Frankreichs
Mich ehrt! Ja, ich gesteh' es unverhohlen,
Wenn es sein muß — wenn ich's nicht ändern kann,
Dem Dringen meines Volkes nachzugeben —
1200 Und es wird stärker sein als ich, befürcht' ich —
So kenn' ich in Europa keinen Fürsten,
Dem ich mein höchstes Kleinod, meine Freiheit,
Mit minderm Widerwillen opfern würde.
Laßt dies Geständnis Euch Genüge thun!

Bellievre.

1205 Es ist die schönste Hoffnung; doch es ist
Nur eine Hoffnung, und mein Herr wünscht mehr —

Elisabeth.

Was wünscht er?

Sie zieht einen Ring vom Finger und betrachtet ihn nachdenkend.

Hat die Königin doch nichts
Voraus vor dem gemeinen Bürgerweibe!
Das gleiche Zeichen weist auf gleiche Pflicht,
1210 Auf gleiche Dienstbarkeit — Der Ring macht Ehen,
Und Ringe sind's, die eine Kette machen.
— Bringt Seiner Hoheit dies Geschenk! Es ist
Noch keine Kette, bindet mich noch nicht;
Doch kann ein Reif draus werden, der mich bindet.

Bellievre

kniet nieder, den Ring empfangend.

1215 In seinem Namen, große Königin,
Empfang' ich knieend dies Geschenk, und drücke
Den Kuß der Huldigung auf meiner Fürstin Hand!

Elisabeth

zum Grafen Leicester, den sie während der letzten Rede unverwandt betrachtet hat.

Erlaubt, Mylord!

Sie nimmt ihm das blaue Band ab und hängt es dem Bellievre um.

Bekleidet Seine Hoheit
Mit diesem Schmuck, wie ich Euch hier damit
1220 Bekleide und in meines Ordens Pflichten nehme.
Honny soit qui mal y pense! — Es schwinde
Der Argwohn zwischen beiden Nationen,
Und ein vertraulich Band umschlinge fortan
Die Kronen Frankreich und Britannien!

Aubespine.

1225 Erhabne Königin, dies ist ein Tag
Der Freude! Möcht' er's allen sein, und möchte
Kein Leidender auf dieser Insel trauern!
Die Gnade glänzt auf deinem Angesicht.
O! daß ein Schimmer ihres heitern Lichts
1230 Auf eine unglücksvolle Fürstin fiele,
Die Frankreich und Britannien gleich nahe
Angeht —

Elisabeth.

Nicht weiter, Graf! Vermengen wir
Nicht zwei ganz unvereinbare Geschäfte.
Wenn Frankreich ernstlich meinen Bund verlangt,
1235 Muß es auch meine Sorgen mit mir teilen,
Und meiner Feinde Freund nicht sein —

Aubespine.

Unwürdig
In deinen eignen Augen würd' es handeln,
Wenn es die Unglückselige, die Glaubens-
Verwandte und die Witwe seines Königs

1240 In diesem Bund vergäße — Schon die Ehre,
Die Menschlichkeit verlangt —

Elisabeth.

In diesem Sinn
Weiß ich sein Fürwort nach Gebühr zu schätzen.
Frankreich erfüllt die Freundespflicht; mir wird
Verstattet sein, als Königin zu handeln.

Sie neigt sich gegen die französischen Herren, welche sich mit den übrigen Lords ehrfurchtsvoll entfernen.

Dritter Auftritt.

Elisabeth. Leicester. Burleigh. Talbot. Die Königin setzt sich.

Burleigh.

1245 Ruhmvolle Königin! Du krönest heut
Die heißen Wünsche deines Volks. Nun erst
Erfreun wir uns der segenvollen Tage,
Die du uns schenkst, da wir nicht zitternd mehr
In eine stürmevolle Zukunft schauen.
1250 Nur eine Sorge kümmert noch dies Land;
Ein Opfer ist's, das alle Stimmen fordern.
Gewähr' auch dieses, und der heut'ge Tag
Hat Englands Wohl auf immerdar gegründet.

Elisabeth.

Was wünscht mein Volk noch? Sprecht, Mylord!

Burleigh.

Es fordert
1255 Das Haupt der Stuart — Wenn du deinem Volk

Der Freiheit köstliches Geschenk, das teuer
Erworbne Licht der Wahrheit willst versichern,
So muß sie nicht mehr sein — Wenn wir nicht ewig
Für dein kostbares Leben zittern sollen,
1260 So muß die Feindin untergehn! — Du weißt es,
Nicht alle deine Britten denken gleich;
Noch viele heimliche Verehrer zählt
Der röm'sche Götzendienst auf dieser Insel.
Die alle nähren feindliche Gedanken;
1265 Nach dieser Stuart steht ihr Herz, sie sind
Im Bunde mit den lothringischen Brüdern,
Den unversöhnten Feinden deines Namens.
Dir ist von dieser wütenden Partei
Der grimmige Vertilgungskrieg geschworen,
1270 Den man mit falschen Höllenwaffen führt.
Zu Rheims, dem Bischofssitz des Kardinals,
Dort ist das Rüsthaus, wo sie Blitze schmieden;
Dort wird der Königsmord gelehrt — Von dort,
Geschäftig, senden sie nach deiner Insel
1275 Die Missionen aus, entschloss'ne Schwärmer,
In allerlei Gewand vermummt — Von dort
Ist schon der dritte Mörder ausgegangen,
Und unerschöpflich, ewig neu erzeugen
Verborgne Feinde sich aus diesem Schlunde.
1280 — Und in dem Schloß zu Fotheringhay sitzt
Die Ate dieses ew'gen Kriegs, die mit
Der Liebesfackel dieses Reich entzündet.
Für sie, die schmeichelnd jedem Hoffnung giebt,
Weiht sich die Jugend dem gewissen Tod —
1285 Sie zu befreien, ist die Losung; sie
Auf deinen Thron zu setzen, ist der Zweck.
Denn dies Geschlecht der Lothringer erkennt

Dein heilig Recht nicht an; du heißest ihnen
Nur eine Räuberin des Throns, gekrönt
1290 Vom Glück! Sie waren's, die die Thörichte
Verführt, sich Englands Königin zu schreiben.
Kein Friede ist mit ihr und ihrem Stamm!
Du mußt den Streich erleiden oder führen.
Ihr Leben ist dein Tod! Ihr Tod dein Leben!

Elisabeth.

1295 Mylord! Ein traurig Amt verwaltet Ihr.
Ich kenne Eures Eifers reinen Trieb,
Weiß, daß gediegne Weisheit aus Euch redet;
Doch diese Weisheit, welche Blut befiehlt,
Ich hasse sie in meiner tiefsten Seele.
1300 Sinnt einen mildern Rat aus — Edler Lord
Von Shrewsbury! Sagt Ihr uns Eure Meinung!

Talbot.

Du gabst dem Eifer ein gebührend Lob,
Der Burleighs treue Brust beseelt — Auch mir,
Strömt es mir gleich nicht so beredt vom Munde,
1305 Schlägt in der Brust kein minder treues Herz.
Mögst du noch lange leben, Königin,
Die Freude deines Volks zu sein, das Glück
Des Friedens diesem Reiche zu verlängern!
So schöne Tage hat dies Eiland nie
1310 Gesehn, seit eigne Fürsten es regieren.
Mög' es sein Glück mit seinem Ruhme nicht
Erkaufen! Möge Talbots Auge wenigstens
Geschlossen sein, wenn dies geschieht!

Elisabeth.

Verhüte Gott, daß wir den Ruhm befleckten!

Talbot.

1315 Nun dann, so wirst du auf ein ander Mittel sinnen,
Dies Reich zu retten — denn die Hinrichtung
Der Stuart ist ein ungerechtes Mittel.
Du kannst das Urteil über die nicht sprechen,
Die dir nicht unterthänig ist.

Elisabeth.

So irrt
1320 Mein Staatsrat und mein Parlament; im Irrtum
Sind alle Richterhöfe dieses Landes,
Die mir dies Recht einstimmig zuerkannt —

Talbot.

Nicht Stimmenmehrheit ist des Rechtes Probe;
England ist nicht die Welt, dein Parlament
1325 Nicht der Verein der menschlichen Geschlechter.
Dies heut'ge England ist das künft'ge nicht,
Wie's das vergangne nicht mehr ist — Wie sich
Die Neigung anders wendet, also steigt
Und fällt des Urteils wandelbare Woge.
1330 Sag' nicht, du müssest der Notwendigkeit
Gehorchen und dem Dringen deines Volks.
Sobald du willst, in jedem Augenblick
Kannst du erproben, daß dein Wille frei ist.
Versuch's! Erkläre, daß du Blut verabscheust,
1335 Der Schwester Leben willst gerettet sehn;
Zeig' denen, die dir anders raten wollen,
Die Wahrheit deines königlichen Zorns,
Schnell wirst du die Notwendigkeit verschwinden
Und Recht in Unrecht sich verwandeln sehn.
1340 Du selbst mußt richten, du allein. Du kannst dich
Auf dieses unstät schwanke Rohr nicht lehnen.

Der eignen Milde folge du getrost!
Nicht Strenge legte Gott ins weiche Herz
Des Weibes — Und die Stifter dieses Reichs,
1345 Die auch dem Weib die Herrscherzügel gaben,
Sie zeigten an, daß Strenge nicht die Tugend
Der Könige soll sein in diesem Lande.

Elisabeth.

Ein warmer Anwalt ist Graf Shrewsbury
Für meine Feindin und des Reichs. Ich ziehe
1350 Die Räte vor, die meine Wohlfahrt lieben.

Talbot.

Man gönnt ihr keinen Anwalt, niemand wagt's,
Zu ihrem Vorteil sprechend, deinem Zorn
Sich bloßzustellen — So vergönne mir,
Dem alten Manne, den am Grabesrand
1355 Kein irdisch Hoffen mehr verführen kann,
Daß ich die Aufgegebene beschütze.
Man soll nicht sagen, daß in deinem Staatsrat
Die Leidenschaft, die Selbstsucht eine Stimme
Gehabt, nur die Barmherzigkeit geschwiegen.
1360 Verbündet hat sich alles wider sie,
Du selber hast ihr Antlitz nie gesehn,
Nichts spricht in deinem Herzen für die Fremde.
— Nicht ihrer Schuld red' ich das Wort. Man sagt,
Sie habe den Gemahl ermorden lassen;
1365 Wahr ist's daß sie den Mörder ehlichte.
Ein schwer Verbrechen! — Aber es geschah
In einer finster unglücksvollen Zeit,
Im Angstgedränge bürgerlichen Kriegs,
Wo sie, die Schwache, sich umrungen sah

1370 Von heftigdringenden Vasallen, sich
Dem Mutvollstärksten in die Arme warf —
Wer weiß, durch welcher Künste Macht besiegt.
Denn ein gebrechlich Wesen ist das Weib.

Elisabeth.

Das Weib ist nicht schwach. Es giebt starke Seelen
1375 In dem Geschlecht — Ich will in meinem Beisein
Nichts von der Schwäche des Geschlechtes hören.

Talbot.

Dir war das Unglück eine strenge Schule.
Nicht seine Freudenseite kehrte dir
Das Leben zu. Du sahest keinen Thron
1380 Von ferne, nur das Grab zu deinen Füßen.
Zu Woodstock war's und in des Towers Nacht,
Wo dich der gnäd'ge Vater dieses Landes
Zur ernsten Pflicht durch Trübsal auferzog.
Dort suchte dich der Schmeichler nicht. Früh lernte,
1385 Vom eiteln Weltgeräusche nicht zerstreut,
Dein Geist sich sammeln, denkend in sich gehn
Und dieses Lebens wahre Güter schätzen.
— Die Arme rettete kein Gott. Ein zartes Kind
Ward sie verpflanzt nach Frankreich, an den Hof
1390 Des Leichtsinns, der gedankenlosen Freude.
Dort in der Feste ew'ger Trunkenheit
Vernahm sie nie der Wahrheit ernste Stimme.
Geblendet ward sie von der Laster Glanz,
Und fortgeführt vom Strome des Verderbens.
1395 Ihr ward der Schönheit eitles Gut zu teil,
Sie überstrahlte blühend alle Weiber,
Und durch Gestalt nicht minder als Geburt — —

Elisabeth.

Kommt zu Euch selbst, Mylord von Shrewsbury!
Denkt, daß wir hier im ernsten Rate sitzen.
1400 Das müssen Reize sondergleichen sein,
Die einen Greis in solches Feuer setzen.
— Mylord von Lester! Ihr allein schweigt still?
Was ihn beredt macht, bindet's Euch die Zunge?

Leicester.

Ich schweige vor Erstaunen, Königin,
1405 Daß man dein Ohr mit Schrecknissen erfüllt,
Daß diese Märchen, die in Londons Gassen
Den gläub'gen Pöbel ängsten, bis herauf
In deines Staatsrats heitre Mitte steigen
Und weise Männer ernst beschäftigen.
1410 Verwunderung ergreift mich, ich gesteh's,
Daß diese länderlose Königin
Von Schottland, die den eignen kleinen Thron
Nicht zu behaupten wußte, ihrer eignen
Vasallen Spott, der Auswurf ihres Landes,
1415 Dein Schrecken wird auf einmal im Gefängnis!
— Was, beim Allmächt'gen! machte sie dir furchtbar?
Daß sie dies Reich in Anspruch nimmt, daß dich
Die Guisen nicht als Königin erkennen?
Kann dieser Guisen Widerspruch das Recht
1420 Entkräften, das Geburt dir gab, der Schluß
Der Parlamente dir bestätigte?
Ist sie durch Heinrichs letzten Willen nicht
Stillschweigend abgewiesen, und wird England,
So glücklich im Genuß des neuen Lichts,
1425 Sich der Papistin in die Arme werfen?
Von dir, der angebeteten Monarchin,

Zu Darnleys Mörderin hinüberlaufen?
Was wollen diese ungestümen Menschen,
Die dich noch lebend mit der Erbin quälen,
1430 Dich nicht geschwind genug vermählen können,
Um Staat und Kirche von Gefahr zu retten?
Stehst du nicht blühend da in Jugendkraft,
Welkt jene nicht mit jedem Tag zum Grabe?
Bei Gott! du wirst, ich hoff's, noch viele Jahre
1435 Auf ihrem Grabe wandeln, ohne daß
Du selber sie hinabzustürzen brauchtest —

Burleigh.

Lord Lester hat nicht immer so geurteilt.

Leicester.

Wahr ist's, ich habe selber meine Stimme
Zu ihrem Tod gegeben im Gericht.
1440 — Im Staatsrat sprech' ich anders. Hier ist nicht
Die Rede von dem Recht, nur von dem Vorteil.
Ist's jetzt die Zeit, von ihr Gefahr zu fürchten,
Da Frankreich sie verläßt, ihr einz'ger Schutz,
Da du den Königssohn mit deiner Hand
1445 Beglücken willst, die Hoffnung eines neuen
Regentenstammes diesem Lande blüht?
Wozu sie also töten? Sie ist tot!
Verachtung ist der wahre Tod. Verhüte,
Daß nicht das Mitleid sie ins Leben rufe!
1450 Drum ist mein Rat: Man lasse die Sentenz,
Die ihr das Haupt abspricht, in voller Kraft
Bestehn! Sie lebe — aber unterm Beile
Des Henkers lebe sie, und schnell, wie sich
Ein Arm für sie bewaffnet, fall' es nieder.

Elisabeth steht auf.

1455 Mylords, ich hab' nun eure Meinungen
Gehört, und sag' euch Dank für euren Eifer.
Mit Gottes Beistand, der die Könige
Erleuchtet, will ich eure Gründe prüfen,
Und wählen, was das Bessere mir dünkt.

Vierter Auftritt.

Die Vorigen. Ritter Paulet mit Mortimer.

Elisabeth.

1460 Da kommt Amias Paulet. Edler Sir,
Was bringt Ihr uns?

Paulet.

Glorwürd'ge Majestät!
Mein Neffe, der ohnlängst von weiten Reisen
Zurückgekehrt, wirft sich zu deinen Füßen
Und leistet dir sein jugendlich Gelübde.
1465 Empfange du es gnadenvoll und laß
Ihn wachsen in der Sonne deiner Gunst.

Mortimer
läßt sich auf ein Knie nieder.

Lang' lebe meine königliche Frau,
Und Glück und Ruhm bekröne ihre Stirne!

Elisabeth.

Steht auf! Seid mir willkommen, Sir, in England!
1470 Ihr habt den großen Weg gemacht, habt Frankreich

Bereist und Rom und Euch zu Rheims verweilt.
Sagt mir denn an, was spinnen unsre Feinde?

Mortimer.

Ein Gott verwirre sie und wende rückwärts
Auf ihrer eignen Schützen Brust die Pfeile,
1475 Die gegen meine Königin gesandt sind!

Elisabeth.

Saht Ihr den Morgan und den ränkespinnenden
Bischof von Roße?

Mortimer.

Alle schottische
Verbannte lernt' ich kennen, die zu Rheims
Anschläge schmieden gegen diese Insel.
1480 In ihr Vertrauen stahl ich mich, ob ich
Etwa von ihren Ränken was entdeckte.

Paulet.

Geheime Briefe hat man ihm vertraut,
In Ziffern, für die Königin von Schottland,
Die er mit treuer Hand uns überliefert.

Elisabeth.

1485 Sagt, was sind ihre neuesten Entwürfe?

Mortimer.

Es traf sie alle wie ein Donnerstreich,
Daß Frankreich sie verläßt, den festen Bund
Mit England schließt; jetzt richten sie die Hoffnung
Auf Spanien.

Elisabeth.

So schreibt mir Walsingham.

Mortimer.

1490 Auch eine Bulle, die Papst Sixtus jüngst
Vom Vatikane gegen dich geschleudert,
Kam eben an zu Rheims, als ich's verließ;
Das nächste Schiff bringt sie nach dieser Insel.

Leicester.

Vor solchen Waffen zittert England nicht mehr.

Burleigh.

1495 Sie werden furchtbar in des Schwärmers Hand.

Elisabeth
Mortimern forschend ansehend.

Man gab Euch schuld, daß Ihr zu Rheims die Schulen
Besucht und Euren Glauben abgeschworen?

Mortimer.

Die Miene gab ich mir, ich leugn' es nicht,
So weit ging die Begierde, dir zu dienen!

Elisabeth
zu Paulet, der ihr Papiere überreicht.

1500 Was zieht Ihr da hervor?

Paulet.

Es ist ein Schreiben,
Das dir die Königin von Schottland sendet.

Burleigh
hastig darnach greifend.

Gebt mir den Brief!

Paulet
giebt das Papier der Königin.

Verzeiht, Lord Großschatzmeister!
In meiner Königin selbsteigne Hand

Befahl sie mir den Brief zu übergeben.
1505 Sie sagt mir stets, ich sei ihr Feind. Ich bin
Nur ihrer Laster Feind; was sich verträgt
Mit meiner Pflicht, mag ich ihr gern erweisen.

Die Königin hat den Brief genommen. Während sie ihn liest, sprechen Mortimer und Leicester einige Worte heimlich mit einander.

Burleigh zu Paulet.

Was kann der Brief enthalten? Eitle Klagen,
Mit denen man das mitleidsvolle Herz
1510 Der Königin verschonen soll.

Paulet.

Was er
Enthält, hat sie mir nicht verhehlt. Sie bittet
Um die Vergünstigung, das Angesicht
Der Königin zu sehen.

Burleigh schnell.

Nimmermehr!

Talbot.

Warum nicht? Sie erfleht nichts Ungerechtes.

Burleigh.

1515 Die Gunst des königlichen Angesichts
Hat sie verwirkt, die Mordanstifterin,
Die nach dem Blut der Königin gedürstet.
Wer's treu mit seiner Fürstin meint, der kann
Den falsch verräterischen Rat nicht geben.

Talbot.

1520 Wenn die Monarchin sie beglücken will,
Wollt Ihr der Gnade sanfte Regung hindern?

Burleigh.

Sie ist verurteilt! Unterm Beile liegt
Ihr Haupt. Unwürdig ist's der Majestät,
Das Haupt zu sehen, das dem Tod geweiht ist.
1525 Das Urteil kann nicht mehr vollzogen werden,
Wenn sich die Königin ihr genahet hat,
Denn Gnade bringt die königliche Nähe —

Elisabeth

nachdem sie den Brief gelesen, ihre Thränen trocknend.

Was ist der Mensch! Was ist das Glück der Erde!
Wie weit ist diese Königin gebracht,
1530 Die mit so stolzen Hoffnungen begann,
Die auf den ältsten Thron der Christenheit
Berufen worden, die in ihrem Sinn
Drei Kronen schon aufs Haupt zu setzen meinte!
Welch andre Sprache führt sie jetzt als damals,
1535 Da sie das Wappen Englands angenommen,
Und von den Schmeichlern ihres Hofs sich Königin
Der zwei britann'schen Inseln nennen ließ!
— Verzeiht, Mylords, es schneidet mir ins Herz,
Wehmut ergreift mich, und die Seele blutet,
1540 Daß Irdisches nicht fester steht, das Schicksal
Der Menschheit, das entsetzliche, so nahe
An meinem eignen Haupt vorüberzieht.

Talbot.

O Königin! Dein Herz hat Gott gerührt.
Gehorche dieser himmlischen Bewegung!
1545 Schwer büßte sie fürwahr die schwere Schuld,
Und Zeit ist's, daß die harte Prüfung ende!
Reich' ihr die Hand, der Tiefgefallenen!

Wie eines Engels Lichterscheinung steige
In ihres Kerkers Gräbernacht hinab —

Burleigh.

1550 Sei standhaft, große Königin! Laß nicht
Ein lobenswürdig menschliches Gefühl
Dich irre führen. Raube dir nicht selbst
Die Freiheit, das Notwendige zu thun.
Du kannst sie nicht begnadigen, nicht retten!
1555 So lade nicht auf dich verhaßten Tadel,
Daß du mit grausam höhnendem Triumph
Am Anblick deines Opfers dich geweidet.

Leicester.

Laßt uns in unsern Schranken bleiben, Lords.
Die Königin ist weise, sie bedarf
1560 Nicht unsers Rats, das Würdigste zu wählen.
Die Unterredung beider Königinnen
Hat nichts gemein mit des Gerichtes Gang.
Englands Gesetz, nicht der Monarchin Wille,
Verurteilt die Maria. Würdig ist's
1565 Der großen Seele der Elisabeth,
Daß sie des Herzens schönem Triebe folge,
Wenn das Gesetz den strengen Lauf behält.

Elisabeth.

Geht, meine Lords! Wir werden Mittel finden,
Was Gnade fordert, was Notwendigkeit
1570 Uns auferlegt, geziemend zu vereinen.
Jetzt — tretet ab!

Die Lords gehen. An der Thüre ruft sie den Mortimer zurück.

Sir Mortimer! Ein Wort!

Fünfter Auftritt.

Elisabeth. Mortimer.

Elisabeth

nachdem sie ihn einige Augenblicke forschend mit den Augen gemessen

Ihr zeigtet einen kecken Mut und seltne
Beherrschung Eurer selbst für Eure Jahre.
Wer schon so früh der Täuschung schwere Kunst
1575 Ausübte, der ist mündig vor der Zeit,
Und er verkürzt sich seine Prüfungsjahre.
— Auf eine große Bahn ruft Euch das Schicksal:
Ich prophezei' es Euch, und mein Orakel
Kann ich, zu Eurem Glücke! selbst vollziehn.

Mortimer.

1580 Erhabene Gebieterin, was ich
Vermag und bin, ist deinem Dienst gewidmet.

Elisabeth.

Ihr habt die Feinde Englands kennen lernen.
Ihr Haß ist unversöhnlich gegen mich,
Und unerschöpflich ihre Blutentwürfe.
1585 Bis diesen Tag zwar schützte mich die Allmacht;
Doch ewig wankt die Kron' auf meinem Haupt,
Solang' sie lebt, die ihrem Schwärmereifer
Den Vorwand leiht und ihre Hoffnung nährt.

Mortimer.

Sie lebt nicht mehr, sobald du es gebietest.

Elisabeth.

1590 Ach, Sir! Ich glaubte mich am Ziele schon
Zu sehn, und bin nicht weiter als am Anfang.

Ich wollte die Gesetze handeln lassen,
Die eigne Hand vom Blute rein behalten.
Das Urteil ist gesprochen. Was gewinn' ich?
1595 Es muß vollzogen werden, Mortimer!
Und ich muß die Vollziehung anbefehlen.
Mich immer trifft der Haß der That. Ich muß
Sie eingestehn, und kann den Schein nicht retten.
Das ist das Schlimmste!

Mortimer.

Was bekümmert dich
1600 Der böse Schein bei der gerechten Sache?

Elisabeth.

Ihr kennt die Welt nicht, Ritter. Was man scheint,
Hat jedermann zum Richter; was man ist, hat keinen.
Von meinem Rechte überzeug' ich niemand,
So muß ich Sorge tragen, daß mein Anteil
1605 An ihrem Tod in ew'gem Zweifel bleibe.
Bei solchen Thaten doppelter Gestalt
Giebt's keinen Schutz als in der Dunkelheit.
Der schlimmste Schritt ist, den man eingesteht;
Was man nicht aufgiebt, hat man nie verloren.

Mortimer ausforschend.

1610 Dann wäre wohl das Beste —

Elisabeth schnell.

Freilich wär's
Das Beste — O, mein guter Engel spricht
Aus Euch. Fahrt fort, vollendet, werter Sir!
Euch ist es Ernst, ihr dringet auf den Grund,
Seid ein ganz andrer Mann als Euer Oheim —

Mortimer betroffen.

1615 Entdecktest du dem Ritter deinen Wunsch?

Elisabeth.

Mich reuet, daß ich's that.

Mortimer.

Entschuldige

Den alten Mann. Die Jahre machen ihn

Bedenklich. Solche Wagestücke fordern

Den kecken Mut der Jugend —

Elisabeth schnell.

Darf ich Euch —

Mortimer.

1620 Die Hand will ich dir leihen; rette du

Den Namen, wie du kannst —

Elisabeth.

Ja, Sir! Wenn Ihr

Mich eines Morgens mit der Botschaft wecktet:

Maria Stuart, deine blut'ge Feindin,

Ist heute Nacht verschieden!

Mortimer.

Zählt auf mich!

Elisabeth.

1625 Wann wird mein Haupt sich ruhig schlafen legen?

Mortimer.

Der nächste Neumond ende deine Furcht.

Elisabeth.

— Gehabt Euch wohl, Sir! Laßt es Euch nicht leid thun,

Daß meine Dankbarkeit den Flor der Nacht

Entlehnen muß — Das Schweigen ist der Gott

1630 Der Glücklichen — Die engsten Bande sind's,

Die zärtesten, die das Geheimnis stiftet! Sie geht ab.

Sechster Auftritt.

Mortimer allein.

Geh, falsche, gleisnerische Königin!
Wie du die Welt, so täusch' ich dich. Recht ist's,
Dich zu verraten, eine gute That!
1635 Seh' ich aus wie ein Mörder? Lasest du
Ruchlose Fertigkeit auf meiner Stirn?
Trau' nur auf meinen Arm und halte deinen
Zurück! Gieb dir den frommen Heuchelschein
Der Gnade vor der Welt! Indessen du
1640 Geheim auf meine Mörderhilfe hoffst,
So werden wir zur Rettung Frist gewinnen!
Erhöhen willst du mich — zeigst mir von ferne
Bedeutend einen kostbarn Preis — und wärst
Du selbst der Preis und deine Frauengunst!
1645 Wer bist du, Ärmste, und was kannst du geben?
Mich locket nicht des eiteln Ruhmes Geiz!
Bei ihr nur ist des Lebens Reiz —
Um sie, in ew'gem Freudenchore, schweben
Der Anmut Götter und der Jugendlust,
1650 Das Glück der Himmel ist an ihrer Brust,
Du hast nur tote Güter zu vergeben!
Das eine Höchste, was das Leben schmückt,
Wenn sich ein Herz, entzückend und entzückt,
Dem Herzen schenkt in süßem Selbstvergessen,
1655 Die Frauenkrone hast du nie besessen,
Nie hast du liebend einen Mann beglückt!
— Ich muß den Lord erwarten, ihren Brief

Ihm übergeben. Ein verhaßter Auftrag!
Ich habe zu dem Höflinge kein Herz,
1660 Ich selber kann sie retten, ich allein;
Gefahr und Ruhm und auch der Preis sei mein!

Indem er gehen will, begegnet ihm Paulet.

Siebenter Auftritt.

Mortimer. Paulet.

Paulet.

Was sagte dir die Königin?

Mortimer.

Nichts, Sir.

Nichts — von Bedeutung.

Paulet

fixiert ihn mit ernstem Blick.

Höre, Mortimer!

Es ist ein schlüpfrig glatter Grund, auf den
1665 Du dich begeben. Lockend ist die Gunst
Der Könige, nach Ehre geizt die Jugend.
— Laß dich den Ehrgeiz nicht verführen!

Mortimer.

Wart Ihr's nicht selbst, der an den Hof mich brachte?

Paulet.

Ich wünschte, daß ich's nicht gethan. Am Hofe
1670 Ward unsers Hauses Ehre nicht gesammelt.

Steht fest, mein Neffe! Kaufe nicht zu teuer!
Verletze dein Gewissen nicht!

Mortimer.

Was fällt Euch ein? Was für Besorgnisse!

Paulet.

Wie groß dich auch die Königin zu machen
1675 Verspricht — trau' ihrer Schmeichelrede nicht!
Verleugnen wird sie dich, wenn du gehorcht,
Und, ihren eignen Namen rein zu waschen,
Die Blutthat rächen, die sie selbst befahl.

Mortimer.

Die Blutthat, sagt Ihr? —

Paulet.

Weg mit der Verstellung!
1680 Ich weiß, was dir die Königin angesonnen;
Sie hofft, daß deine ruhmbegier'ge Jugend
Willfähr'ger sein wird als mein starres Alter.
Hast du ihr zugesagt? Hast du?

Mortimer.

Mein Oheim!

Paulet.

Wenn du's gethan hast, so verfluch' ich dich,
1685 Und dich verwerfe —

Leicester kommt.

Werter Sir, erlaubt
Ein Wort mit Eurem Neffen. Die Monarchin
Ist gnadenvoll gesinnt für ihn; sie will,
Daß man ihm die Person der Lady Stuart
Uneingeschränkt vertraue — Sie verläßt sich
1690 Auf seine Redlichkeit —

Paulet.

Verläßt sich — Gut!

Leicester.

Was sagt Ihr, Sir?

Paulet.

Die Königin verläßt sich
Auf ihn, und ich, Mylord, verlasse mich
Auf mich und meine beiden offnen Augen. Er geht ab.

Achter Auftritt.

Leicester. Mortimer.

Leicester verwundert.

Was wandelte den Ritter an?

Mortimer.

1695 Ich weiß es nicht — Das unerwartete
Vertrauen, das die Königin mir schenkt —

Leicester
ihn forschend ansehend.

Verdient Ihr, Ritter, daß man Euch vertraut?

Mortimer ebenso.

Die Frage thu' ich Euch, Mylord von Lester.

Leicester.

Ihr hattet mir was ingeheim zu sagen.

Mortimer.

1700 Versichert mir erst, daß ich's wagen darf.

Leicester.

Wer giebt mir die Versicherung für Euch?
— Laßt Euch mein Mißtraun nicht beleidigen!
Ich seh' Euch zweierlei Gesichter zeigen
An diesem Hofe — Eins darunter ist
1705 Notwendig falsch; doch welches ist das wahre?

Mortimer.

Es geht mir ebenso mit Euch, Graf Lester.

Leicester.

Wer soll nun des Vertrauens Anfang machen?

Mortimer.

Wer das Geringere zu wagen hat.

Leicester.

Nun! Der seid Ihr!

Mortimer.

Ihr seid es! Euer Zeugnis,
1710 Des vielbedeutenden, gewalt'gen Lords,
Kann mich zu Boden schlagen; meins vermag
Nichts gegen Euren Rang und Eure Gunst.

Leicester.

Ihr irrt Euch, Sir. In allem andern bin ich
Hier mächtig, nur in diesem zarten Punkt,
1715 Den ich jetzt Eurer Treu' preisgeben soll,
Bin ich der schwächste Mann an diesem Hof,
Und ein verächtlich Zeugnis kann mich stürzen.

Mortimer.

Wenn sich der allvermögende Lord Lester
So tief zu mir herunterläßt, ein solch
1720 Bekenntnis mir zu thun, so darf ich wohl

Ein wenig höher denken von mir selbst,
Und ihm in Großmut ein Exempel geben.

Leicester.

Geht mir voran im Zutraun, ich will folgen.

Mortimer

den Brief schnell hervorziehend.

Dies sendet Euch die Königin von Schottland.

Leicester

schrickt zusammen und greift hastig darnach.

1725 Sprecht leise, Sir — Was seh' ich! Ach! Es ist
Ihr Bild!

Küßt es und betrachtet es mit stummem Entzücken.

Mortimer

der ihn während des Lesens scharf beobachtet.

Mylord, nun glaub' ich Euch.

Leicester

nachdem er den Brief schnell durchlaufen.

Sir Mortimer! Ihr wißt des Briefes Inhalt?

Mortimer.

Nichts weiß ich.

Leicester.

Nun! Sie hat Euch ohne Zweifel
Vertraut —

Mortimer.

Sie hat mir nichts vertraut. Ihr würdet
1730 Dies Rätsel mir erklären, sagte sie.
Ein Rätsel ist es mir, daß Graf von Lester,
Der Günstling der Elisabeth, Mariens
Erklärter Feind und ihrer Richter einer,
Der Mann sein soll, von dem die Königin

1735 In ihrem Unglück Rettung hofft — Und dennoch
Muß dem so sein, denn Eure Augen sprechen
Zu deutlich aus, was Ihr für sie empfindet.

Leicester.

Entdeckt mir selbst erst, wie es kommt, daß Ihr
Den feur'gen Anteil nehmt an ihrem Schicksal,
1740 Und was Euch ihr Vertraun erwarb.

Mortimer.

Mylord,
Das kann ich Euch mit wenigem erklären.
Ich habe meinen Glauben abgeschworen
Zu Rom, und steh' im Bündnis mit den Guisen.
Ein Brief des Erzbischofs zu Rheims hat mich
1745 Beglaubigt bei der Königin von Schottland.

Leicester.

Ich weiß von Eurer Glaubensänderung;
Sie ist's, die mein Vertrauen zu Euch weckte.
Gebt mir die Hand. Verzeiht mir meinen Zweifel.
Ich kann der Vorsicht nicht zu viel gebrauchen,
1750 Denn Walsingham und Burleigh hassen mich;
Ich weiß, daß sie mir lauernd Netze stellen.
Ihr konntet ihr Geschöpf und Werkzeug sein,
Mich in das Garn zu ziehn —

Mortimer.

Wie kleine Schritte
Geht ein so großer Lord an diesem Hof!
1755 Graf! Ich beklag' Euch.

Leicester.

Freudig werf' ich mich
An die vertraute Freundesbrust, wo ich

Des langen Zwangs mich endlich kann entladen.
Ihr seid verwundert, Sir, daß ich so schnell
Das Herz geändert gegen die Maria.
1760 Zwar in der That haßt' ich sie nie — der Zwang
Der Zeiten machte mich zu ihrem Gegner.
Sie war mir zugedacht seit langen Jahren,
Ihr wißt's, eh' sie die Hand dem Darnley gab,
Als noch der Glanz der Hoheit sie umlachte.
1765 Kalt stieß ich damals dieses Glück von mir;
Jetzt im Gefängnis, an des Todes Pforten
Such' ich sie auf, und mit Gefahr des Lebens.

Mortimer.

Das heißt großmütig handeln!

Leicester.

— Die Gestalt
Der Dinge, Sir, hat sich indes verändert.
1770 Mein Ehrgeiz war es, der mich gegen Jugend
Und Schönheit fühllos machte. Damals hielt ich
Mariens Hand für mich zu klein; ich hoffte
Auf den Besitz der Königin von England.

Mortimer.

Es ist bekannt, daß sie Euch allen Männern
1775 Vorzog —

Leicester.

So schien es, edler Sir — und nun, nach zehn
Verlornen Jahren unverdross'nen Werbens,
Verhaßten Zwangs — O Sir, mein Herz geht auf!
Ich muß des langen Unmuts mich entladen —
Man preist mich glücklich — Wüßte man, was es
1780 Für Ketten sind, um die man mich beneidet —
Nachdem ich zehen bittre Jahre lang

Dem Götzen ihrer Eitelkeit geopfert,
Mich jedem Wechsel ihrer Sultanslaunen
Mit Sklavendemut unterwarf, das Spielzeug
1785 Des kleinen grillenhaften Eigensinns,
Geliebkost jetzt von ihrer Zärtlichkeit,
Und jetzt mit sprödem Stolz zurückgestoßen,
Von ihrer Gunst und Strenge gleich gepeinigt,
Wie ein Gefangener vom Argusblick
1790 Der Eifersucht gehütet, ins Verhör
Genommen wie ein Knabe, wie ein Diener
Gescholten — O, die Sprache hat kein Wort
Für diese Hölle!

Mortimer.

Ich beklag' Euch, Graf.

Leicester.

Täuscht mich am Ziel der Preis! Ein andrer kommt,
1795 Die Frucht des teuren Werbens mir zu rauben.
An einen jungen blühenden Gemahl
Verlier' ich meine lang' besess'nen Rechte!
Heruntersteigen soll ich von der Bühne,
Wo ich so lange als der Erste glänzte.
1800 Nicht ihre Hand allein, auch ihre Gunst
Droht mir der neue Ankömmling zu rauben.
Sie ist ein Weib, und er ist liebenswert.

Mortimer.

Er ist Kathrinens Sohn. In guter Schule
Hat er des Schmeichelns Künste ausgelernt.

Leicester.

1805 So stürzen meine Hoffnungen — Ich suche
In diesem Schiffbruch meines Glücks ein Brett

Zu fassen — und mein Auge wendet sich
Der ersten schönen Hoffnung wieder zu.
Mariens Bild, in ihrer Reize Glanz,
1810 Stand neu vor mir, Schönheit und Jugend traten
In ihre vollen Rechte wieder ein;
Nicht kalter Ehrgeiz mehr, das Herz verglich,
Und ich empfand, welch Kleinod ich verloren.
Mit Schrecken seh' ich sie in tiefes Elend
1815 Herabgestürzt, gestürzt durch mein Verschulden.
Da wird in mir die Hoffnung wach, ob ich
Sie jetzt noch retten könnte und besitzen.
Durch eine treue Hand gelingt es mir,
Ihr mein verändert Herz zu offenbaren,
1820 Und dieser Brief, den Ihr mir überbracht,
Versichert mir, daß sie verzeiht, sich mir
Zum Preise schenken will, wenn ich sie rette.

Mortimer.

Ihr thatet aber nichts zu ihrer Rettung!
Ihr ließt geschehn, daß sie verurteilt wurde,
1825 Gabt Eure Stimme selbst zu ihrem Tod!
Ein Wunder muß geschehn — Der Wahrheit Licht
Muß mich, den Neffen ihres Hüters, rühren,
Im Vatikan zu Rom muß ihr der Himmel
Den unverhofften Retter zubereiten,
1830 Sonst fand sie nicht einmal den Weg zu Euch!

Leicester.

Ach, Sir, es hat mir Qualen gnug gekostet!
Um selbe Zeit ward sie von Talbots Schloß
Nach Fotheringhay weggeführt, der strengen
Gewahrsam Eures Oheims anvertraut.
1835 Gehemmt ward jeder Weg zu ihr; ich mußte

Fortfahren vor der Welt, sie zu verfolgen.
Doch denket nicht, daß ich sie leidend hätte
Zum Tode gehen lassen! Nein, ich hoffte,
Und hoffe noch, das Äußerste zu hindern,
1840 Bis sich ein Mittel zeigt, sie zu befrein.

Mortimer.

Das ist gefunden — Lester, Euer edles
Vertraun verdient Erwiderung. Ich will sie
Befreien, darum bin ich hier, die Anstalt
Ist schon getroffen, Euer mächt'ger Beistand
1845 Versichert uns den glücklichen Erfolg.

Leicester.

Was sagt Ihr? Ihr erschreckt mich. Wie? Ihr wolltet —

Mortimer.

Gewaltsam aufthun will ich ihren Kerker;
Ich hab' Gefährten, alles ist bereit —

Leicester.

Ihr habt Mitwisser und Vertraute! Weh mir!
1850 In welches Wagnis reißt Ihr mich hinein!
Und diese wissen auch um mein Geheimnis?

Mortimer.

Sorgt nicht! Der Plan ward ohne Euch entworfen;
Ohn' Euch wär' er vollstreckt, bestünde sie
Nicht drauf, Euch ihre Rettung zu verdanken.

Leicester.

1855 So könnt Ihr mich für ganz gewiß versichern,
Daß in dem Bund mein Name nicht genannt ist?

Mortimer.

Verlaßt Euch drauf! Wie? So bedenklich, Graf,

Bei einer Botschaft, die Euch Hilfe bringt!
Ihr wollt die Stuart retten und besitzen,
1860 Ihr findet Freunde, plötzlich, unerwartet,
Vom Himmel fallen Euch die nächsten Mittel —
Doch zeigt Ihr mehr Verlegenheit als Freude?

Leicester.

Es ist nichts mit Gewalt. Das Wagestück
Ist zu gefährlich.

Mortimer.

Auch das Säumen ist's!

Leicester.

1865 Ich sag' Euch, Ritter, es ist nicht zu wagen.

Mortimer bitter.

Nein, nicht für Euch, der sie besitzen will!
Wir wollen sie bloß retten, und sind nicht so
Bedenklich —

Leicester.

Junger Mann, Ihr seid zu rasch
In so gefährlich dornenvoller Sache.

Mortimer.

1870 Ihr — sehr bedacht in solchem Fall der Ehre.

Leicester.

Ich seh' die Netze, die uns rings umgeben

Mortimer.

Ich fühle Mut, sie alle zu durchreißen.

Leicester.

Tollkühnheit, Raserei ist dieser Mut.

Mortimer.

Nicht Tapferkeit ist diese Klugheit, Lord.

Leicester.

1875 Euch lüstet's wohl, wie Babington zu enden?

Mortimer.

Euch nicht, des Norfolks Großmut nachzuahmen.

Leicester.

Norfolk hat seine Braut nicht heimgeführt.

Mortimer.

Er hat bewiesen, daß er's würdig war.

Leicester.

Wenn wir verderben, reißen wir sie nach.

Mortimer.

1880 Wenn wir uns schonen, wird sie nicht gerettet.

Leicester.

Ihr überlegt nicht, hört nicht, werdet alles
Mit heftig blindem Ungestüm zerstören,
Was auf so guten Weg geleitet war.

Mortimer.

Wohl auf den guten Weg, den Ihr gebahnt?
1885 Was habt Ihr denn gethan, um sie zu retten?
— Und wie? Wenn ich nun Bube gnug gewesen,
Sie zu ermorden, wie die Königin
Mir anbefahl, wie sie zu dieser Stunde
Von mir erwartet — Nennt mir doch die Anstalt,
1890 Die Ihr gemacht, ihr Leben zu erhalten.

Leicester erstaunt.

Gab Euch die Königin diesen Blutbefehl?

Mortimer.

Sie irrte sich in mir, wie sich Maria
In Euch.

Leicester.

Und Ihr habt zugesagt? Habt Ihr?

Mortimer.

Damit sie andre Hände nicht erkaufe,
1895 Bot ich die meinen an.

Leicester.

Ihr thatet wohl.
Dies kann uns Raum verschaffen. Sie verläßt sich
Auf Euren blut'gen Dienst, das Todesurteil
Bleibt unvollstreckt, und wir gewinnen Zeit —

Mortimer ungeduldig.

Nein, wir verlieren Zeit!

Leicester.

Sie zählt auf Euch;
1900 So minder wird sie Anstand nehmen, sich
Den Schein der Gnade vor der Welt zu geben.
Vielleicht, daß ich durch List sie überrede,
Das Angesicht der Gegnerin zu sehn,
Und dieser Schritt muß ihr die Hände binden.
1905 Burleigh hat recht. Das Urteil kann nicht mehr
Vollzogen werden, wenn sie sie gesehn.
— Ja, ich versuch' es, alles biet' ich auf —

Mortimer.

Und was erreicht Ihr dadurch? Wenn sie sich
In mir getäuscht sieht, wenn Maria fortfährt,
1910 Zu leben — Ist nicht alles wie zuvor?
Frei wird sie niemals! Auch das Mildeste,
Was kommen kann, ist ewiges Gefängnis.
Mit einer kühnen That müßt Ihr doch enden.

Warum wollt Ihr nicht gleich damit beginnen?
1915 In Euren Händen ist die Macht, Ihr bringt
Ein Heer zusammen, wenn Ihr nur den Adel
Auf Euren vielen Schlössern waffnen wollt!
Maria hat noch viel verborgne Freunde;
Der Howard und der Percy edle Häuser,
1920 Ob ihre Häupter gleich gestürzt, sind noch
An Helden reich, sie harren nur darauf,
Daß ein gewalt'ger Lord das Beispiel gebe!
Weg mit Verstellung! Handelt öffentlich!
Verteidigt als ein Ritter die Geliebte,
1925 Kämpft einen edlen Kampf um sie! Ihr seid
Herr der Person der Königin von England,
Sobald Ihr wollt. Lockt sie auf Eure Schlösser,
Sie ist Euch oft dahin gefolgt. Dort zeigt ihr
Den Mann! Sprecht als Gebieter! Haltet sie
1930 Verwahrt, bis sie die Stuart freigegeben!

Leicester.

Ich staune, ich entsetze mich — Wohin
Reißt Euch der Schwindel? — Kennt Ihr diesen Boden?
Wißt Ihr, wie's steht an diesem Hof, wie eng
Dies Frauenreich die Geister hat gebunden?
1935 Sucht nach dem Heldengeist, der ehmals wohl
In diesem Land sich regte — Unterworfen
Ist alles unterm Schlüssel eines Weibes,
Und jedes Mutes Federn abgespannt.
Folgt meiner Leitung! Wagt nichts unbedachtsam!
1940 — Ich höre kommen, geht!

Mortimer.

Maria hofft!
Kehr' ich mit leerem Trost zu ihr zurück?

Leicester.

Bringt ihr die Schwüre meiner ew'gen Liebe!

Mortimer.

Bringt ihr die selbst! Zum Werkzeug ihrer Rettung
Bot ich mich an, nicht Euch zum Liebesboten!

Er geht ab.

Neunter Auftritt.

Elisabeth. Leicester.

Elisabeth.

1945 Wer ging da von Euch weg? Ich hörte sprechen.

Leicester

sich auf ihre Rede schnell und erschrocken umwendend.

Es war Sir Mortimer.

Elisabeth.

Was ist Euch, Lord?
So ganz betreten?

Leicester faßt sich.

— Über deinen Anblick!
Ich habe dich so reizend nie gesehn.
Geblendet steh' ich da von deiner Schönheit.
1950 — Ach!

Elisabeth.

Warum seufzt Ihr?

Leicester.

Hab' ich keinen Grund
Zu seufzen? Da ich deinen Reiz betrachte,
Erneut sich mir der namenlose Schmerz
Des drohenden Verlustes.

Elisabeth.

Was verliert Ihr?

Leicester.

Dein Herz, dein liebenswürdig Selbst verlier' ich.
1955 Bald wirst du in den jugendlichen Armen
Des feurigen Gemahls dich glücklich fühlen,
Und ungeteilt wird er dein Herz besitzen.
Er ist von königlichem Blut, das bin
Ich nicht; doch Trotz sei aller Welt geboten,
1960 Ob einer lebt auf diesem Erdenrund,
Der mehr Anbetung für dich fühlt als ich.
Der Duc von Anjou hat dich nie gesehn,
Nur deinen Ruhm und Schimmer kann er lieben.
Ich liebe dich. Wärst du die ärmste Hirtin,
1965 Ich als der größte Fürst der Welt geboren,
Zu deinem Stand würd' ich heruntersteigen,
Mein Diadem zu deinen Füßen legen.

Elisabeth.

Beklag' mich, Dudley, schilt mich nicht! — Ich darf ja
Mein Herz nicht fragen. Ach! das hätte anders
1970 Gewählt. Und wie beneid' ich andre Weiber,
Die das erhöhen dürfen, was sie lieben.
So glücklich bin ich nicht, daß ich dem Manne,
Der mir vor allen teuer ist, die Krone
Aufsetzen kann! — Der Stuart ward's vergönnt,

1975 Die Hand nach ihrer Neigung zu verschenken;
Die hat sich jegliches erlaubt, sie hat
Den vollen Kelch der Freuden ausgetrunken.

Leicester.

Jetzt trinkt sie auch den bittern Kelch des Leidens.

Elisabeth.

Sie hat der Menschen Urteil nichts geachtet.
1980 Leicht wurd' es ihr zu leben, nimmer lud sie
Das Joch sich auf, dem ich mich unterwarf.
Hätt' ich doch auch Ansprüche machen können,
Des Lebens mich, der Erde Lust zu freun;
Doch zog ich strenge Königspflichten vor.
1985 Und doch gewann sie aller Männer Gunst,
Weil sie sich nur befliß, ein Weib zu sein,
Und um sie buhlt die Jugend und das Alter.
So sind die Männer. Lüstlinge sind alle!
Dem Leichtsinn eilen sie, der Freude zu,
1990 Und schätzen nichts, was sie verehren müssen.
Verjüngte sich nicht dieser Talbot selbst,
Als er auf ihren Reiz zu reden kam!

Leicester.

Vergieb es ihm! Er war ihr Wächter einst;
Die List'ge hat mit Schmeicheln ihn bethört.

Elisabeth.

1995 Und ist's denn wirklich wahr, daß sie so schön ist?
So oft mußt' ich die Larve rühmen hören;
Wohl möcht' ich wissen, was zu glauben ist.
Gemälde schmeicheln, Schilderungen lügen,
Nur meinen eignen Augen würd' ich traun.
2000 — Was schaut Ihr mich so seltsam an?

Leicester.

Ich stellte
Dich in Gedanken neben die Maria.
—Die Freude wünscht' ich mir, ich berg' es nicht,
Wenn es ganz in geheim geschehen könnte,
Der Stuart gegenüber dich zu sehn!
2005 Dann solltest du erst deines ganzen Siegs
Genießen! Die Beschämung gönnt' ich ihr,
Daß sie mit eignen Augen—denn der Neid
Hat scharfe Augen — überzeugt sich sähe,
Wie sehr sie auch an Adel der Gestalt
2010 Von dir besiegt wird, der sie so unendlich
In jeder andern würd'gen Tugend weicht.

Elisabeth.

Sie ist die Jüngere an Jahren.

Leicester.

Jünger!
Man sieht's ihr nicht an. Freilich, ihre Leiden!
Sie mag wohl vor der Zeit gealtert haben.
2015 Ja, und was ihre Kränkung bittrer machte,
Das wäre, dich als Braut zu sehn! Sie hat
Des Lebens schöne Hoffnung hinter sich,
Dich sähe sie dem Glück entgegenschreiten!
Und als die Braut des Königssohns von Frankreich,
2020 Da sie sich stets so viel gewußt, so stolz
Gethan mit der französischen Vermählung,
Noch jetzt auf Frankreichs mächt'ge Hilfe pocht!

Elisabeth nachlässig hinwerfend.

Man peinigt mich ja, sie zu sehn.

Leicester lebhaft.

Sie fordert's
Als eine Gunst, gewähr' es ihr als Strafe!
2025 Du kannst sie auf das Blutgerüste führen,
Es wird sie minder peinigen, als sich
Von deinen Reizen ausgelöscht zu sehn.
Dadurch ermordest du sie, wie sie dich
Ermorden wollte — Wenn sie deine Schönheit
2030 Erblickt, durch Ehrbarkeit bewacht, in Glorie
Gestellt durch einen unbefleckten Tugendruf,
Den sie, leichtsinnig buhlend, von sich warf,
Erhoben durch der Krone Glanz, und jetzt
Durch zarte Bräutlichkeit geschmückt — dann hat
2035 Die Stunde der Vernichtung ihr geschlagen.
Ja — wenn ich jetzt die Augen auf dich werfe —
Nie warst du, nie zu einem Sieg der Schönheit
Gerüsteter als eben jetzt — Mich selbst
Hast du umstrahlt wie eine Lichterscheinung,
2040 Als du vorhin ins Zimmer tratest — Wie?
Wenn du gleich jetzt, jetzt wie du bist, hinträtest
Vor sie, du findest keine schönre Stunde —

Elisabeth.

Jetzt — Nein — Nein — Jetzt nicht, Lester — Nein, das
muß ich
Erst wohl bedenken — mich mit Burleigh —

Leicester lebhaft einfallend.

Burleigh!
2045 Der denkt allein auf deinen Staatsvorteil;
Auch deine Weiblichkeit hat ihre Rechte;
Der zarte Punkt gehört vor dein Gericht,
Nicht vor des Staatsmanns — ja, auch Staatskunst will es,

Daß du sie siehst, die öffentliche Meinung
2050 Durch eine That der Großmut dir gewinnest!
Magst du nachher dich der verhaßten Feindin,
Auf welche Weise dir's gefällt, entladen.

Elisabeth.

Nicht wohlanständig wär' mir's, die Verwandte
Im Mangel und in Schmach zu sehn. Man sagt,
2055 Daß sie nicht königlich umgeben sei,
Vorwerfend wär' mir ihres Mangels Anblick.

Leicester.

Nicht ihrer Schwelle brauchst du dich zu nahn.
Hör' meinen Rat! Der Zufall hat es eben
Nach Wunsch gefügt. Heut ist das große Jagen,
2060 An Fotheringhay führt der Weg vorbei,
Dort kann die Stuart sich im Park ergehn,
Du kommst ganz wie von ohngefähr dahin,
Es darf nichts als vorher bedacht erscheinen,
Und wenn es dir zuwider, redest du
2065 Sie gar nicht an —

Elisabeth.

Begeh' ich eine Thorheit,
So ist es Eure, Lester, nicht die meine.
Ich will Euch heute keinen Wunsch versagen,
Weil ich von meinen Unterthanen allen
Euch heut am wehesten gethan. Ihn zärtlich ansehend.
2070 Sei's eine Grille nur von Euch. Dadurch
Giebt Neigung sich ja kund, daß sie bewilligt
Aus freier Gunst, was sie auch nicht gebilligt.

Leicester stürzt zu ihren Füßen, der Vorhang fällt.

Dritter Aufzug.

Gegend in einem Park. Vorn mit Bäumen besetzt, hinten eine weite Aussicht.

Erster Auftritt.

Maria tritt in schnellem Lauf hinter Bäumen hervor. Hanna Kennedy folgt langsam.

Kennedy.

Ihr eilet ja, als wenn Ihr Flügel hättet,
So kann ich Euch nicht folgen, wartet doch!

Maria.

2075 Laß mich der neuen Freiheit genießen,
Laß mich ein Kind sein, sei es mit!
Und auf dem grünen Teppich der Wiesen
Prüfen den leichten, geflügelten Schritt.
Bin ich dem finstern Gefängnis entstiegen?
2080 Hält sie mich nicht mehr, die traurige Gruft?
Laß mich in vollen, in durstigen Zügen
Trinken die freie, die himmlische Luft.

Kennedy.

O meine teure Lady! Euer Kerker
Ist nur um ein klein Weniges erweitert.
2085 Ihr seht nur nicht die Mauer, die uns einschließt,
Weil sie der Bäume dicht Gesträuch versteckt.

Maria.

O Dank, Dank diesen freundlich grünen Bäumen,
Die meines Kerkers Mauern mir verstecken!
Ich will mich frei und glücklich träumen,
2090 Warum aus meinem süßen Wahn mich wecken?
Umfängt mich nicht der weite Himmelsschoß?
Die Blicke, frei und fessellos,
Ergehen sich in ungemess'nen Räumen.
Dort, wo die grauen Nebelberge ragen,
2095 Fängt meines Reiches Grenze an,
Und diese Wolken, die nach Mittag jagen,
Sie suchen Frankreichs fernen Ocean.
Eilende Wolken! Segler der Lüfte!
Wer mit euch wanderte, mit euch schiffte!
2100 Grüßet mir freundlich mein Jugendland!
Ich bin gefangen, ich bin in Banden,
Ach, ich hab' keinen andern Gesandten!
Frei in Lüften ist eure Bahn,
Ihr seid nicht dieser Königin unterthan.

Kennedy.

2105 Ach, teure Lady! Ihr seid außer Euch,
Die langentbehrte Freiheit macht Euch schwärmen.

Maria.

Dort legt ein Fischer den Nachen an!
Dieses elende Werkzeug könnte mich retten,
Brächte mich schnell zu befreundeten Städten.
2110 Spärlich nährt es den dürftigen Mann.
Beladen wollt' ich ihn reich mit Schätzen,
Einen Zug sollt' er thun, wie er keinen gethan,
Das Glück sollt' er finden in seinen Netzen,
Nähm' er mich ein in den rettenden Kahn.

Kennedy.

2115 Verlorne Wünsche! Seht Ihr nicht, daß uns
Von ferne dort die Spähertritte folgen?
Ein finster grausames Verbot scheucht jedes
Mitleidige Geschöpf aus unserm Wege.

Maria.

Nein, gute Hanna. Glaub' mir, nicht umsonst
2120 Ist meines Kerkers Thor geöffnet worden.
Die kleine Gunst ist mir des größern Glücks
Verkünderin. Ich irre nicht. Es ist
Der Liebe thät'ge Hand, der ich sie danke;
Lord Lesters mächt'gen Arm erkenn' ich drin.
2125 Allmählich will man mein Gefängnis weiten,
Durch Kleineres zum Größern mich gewöhnen,
Bis ich das Antlitz dessen endlich schaue,
Der mir die Bande löst auf immerdar.

Kennedy.

Ach, ich kann diesen Widerspruch nicht reimen!
2130 Noch gestern kündigt man den Tod Euch an,
Und heute wird Euch plötzlich solche Freiheit.
Auch denen, hört' ich sagen, wird die Kette
Gelöst, auf die die ew'ge Freiheit wartet.

Maria.

Hörst du das Hifthorn? Hörst du's klingen,
2135 Mächtigen Rufes, durch Feld und Hain?
Ach, auf das mutige Roß mich zu schwingen,
An den fröhlichen Zug mich zu reihn!
Noch mehr! O die bekannte Stimme,
Schmerzlich süßer Erinnerung voll.
2140 Oft vernahm sie mein Ohr mit Freuden
Auf des Hochlands bergichten Heiden,
Wenn die tobende Jagd erscholl.

Zweiter Auftritt.

Paulet. Die Vorigen.

Paulet.

Nun! Hab' ich's endlich recht gemacht, Mylady?
Verdien' ich einmal Euren Dank?

Maria.

Wie, Ritter?
2145 Seid Ihr's, der diese Gunst mir ausgewirkt?
Ihr seid's?

Paulet.

Warum soll ich's nicht sein? Ich war
Am Hof, ich überbrachte Euer Schreiben —

Maria.

Ihr übergabt es? Wirklich, thatet Ihr's?
Und diese Freiheit, die ich jetzt genieße,
2150 Ist eine Frucht des Briefs —

Paulet mit Bedeutung.

Und nicht die einz'ge!
Macht Euch auf eine größre noch gefaßt!

Maria.

Auf eine größre, Sir? Was meint Ihr damit?

Paulet.

Ihr hörtet doch die Hörner —

Maria

zurückfahrend, mit Ahnung.

Ihr erschreckt mich!

Paulet.

Die Königin jagt in dieser Gegend.

Maria.

Was?

Paulet.

In wenig Augenblicken steht sie vor Euch.

Kennedy

auf Maria zueilend, welche zittert und hinzusinken droht.

Wie wird Euch, teure Lady! Ihr verblaßt.

Paulet.

Nun! ist's nun nicht recht? War's nicht Eure Bitte?
Sie wird Euch früher gewährt, als Ihr gedacht.
Ihr wart sonst immer so geschwinder Zunge,
2160 Jetzt bringet Eure Worte an, jetzt ist
Der Augenblick, zu reden!

Maria.

O, warum hat man mich nicht vorbereitet!
Jetzt bin ich nicht darauf gefaßt, jetzt nicht.
Was ich mir als die höchste Gunst erbeten,
2165 Dünkt mir jetzt schrecklich, fürchterlich — Komm, Hanna,
Führ' mich ins Haus, daß ich mich fasse, mich
Erhole —

Paulet.

Bleibt! Ihr müßt sie hier erwarten.
Wohl, wohl mag's Euch beängstigen, ich glaub's,
Vor Eurem Richter zu erscheinen.

Dritter Auftritt.

Graf Shrewsbury zu den Vorigen.

Maria.

2170 Es ist nicht darum! Gott, mir ist ganz anders
Zu Mut — Ach; edler Shrewsbury! Ihr kommt,
Vom Himmel mir ein Engel zugesendet!
— Ich kann sie nicht sehn! Rettet, rettet mich
Von dem verhaßten Anblick —

Shrewsbury.

2175 Kommt zu Euch, Königin! Faßt Euren Mut
Zusammen! Das ist die entscheidungsvolle Stunde.

Maria.

Ich habe drauf geharret — Jahre lang
Mich drauf bereitet, alles hab' ich mir
Gesagt und ins Gedächtnis eingeschrieben,
2180 Wie ich sie rühren wollte und bewegen!
Vergessen plötzlich, ausgelöscht ist alles,
Nichts lebt in mir in diesem Augenblick,
Als meiner Leiden brennendes Gefühl.
In blut'gen Haß gewendet wider sie
2185 Ist mir das Herz, es fliehen alle guten
Gedanken, und die Schlangenhaare schüttelnd
Umstehen mich die finstern Höllengeister.

Shrewsbury.

Gebietet Eurem wild empörten Blut,
Bezwingt des Herzens Bitterkeit! Es bringt
2190 Nicht gute Frucht, wenn Haß dem Haß begegnet.
Wie sehr auch Euer Innres widerstrebe,

Gehorcht der Zeit und dem Gesetz der Stunde!
Sie ist die Mächtige — Demütigt Euch!

Maria.

Vor ihr! Ich kann es nimmermehr.

Shrewsbury.

Thut's dennoch!
2195 Sprecht ehrerbietig, mit Gelassenheit!
Ruft ihre Großmut an, trotzt nicht, jetzt nicht
Auf Euer Recht, jetzo ist nicht die Stunde.

Maria.

Ach, mein Verderben hab' ich mir erfleht,
Und mir zum Fluche wird mein Flehn erhört!
2200 Nie hätten wir uns sehen sollen, niemals!
Daraus kann nimmer, nimmer Gutes kommen!
Eh' mögen Feu'r und Wasser sich in Liebe
Begegnen, und das Lamm den Tiger küssen —
Ich bin zu schwer verletzt — sie hat zu schwer
2205 Beleidigt — Nie ist zwischen uns Versöhnung!

Shrewsbury.

Seht sie nur erst von Angesicht!
Ich sah es ja, wie sie von Eurem Brief
Erschüttert war, ihr Auge schwamm in Thränen.
Nein, sie ist nicht gefühllos, hegt Ihr selbst
2210 Nur besseres Vertrauen — Darum eben
Bin ich vorausgeeilt, damit ich Euch
In Fassung setzen und ermahnen möchte.

Maria seine Hand ergreifend.

Ach, Talbot! Ihr wart stets mein Freund — Daß ich
In Eurer milden Haft geblieben wäre!
2215 Es ward mir hart begegnet, Shrewsbury!

Shrewsbury.

Vergeßt jetzt alles! Darauf denkt allein,
Wie Ihr sie unterwürfig wollt empfangen.

Maria.

Ist Burleigh auch mit ihr, mein böser Engel?

Shrewsbury.

Niemand begleitet sie, als Graf von Lester.

Maria.

2220 Lord Lester!

Shrewsbury.

Fürchtet nichts von ihm! Nicht er
Will Euren Untergang — Sein Werk ist es,
Daß Euch die Königin die Zusammenkunft
Bewilligt.

Maria.

Ach! Ich wußt' es wohl!

Shrewsbury.

Was sagt Ihr?

Paulet.

Die Königin kommt!

Alles weicht auf die Seite, nur Maria bleibt, auf die Kennedy gelehnt.

Vierter Auftritt.

Die Vorigen. Elisabeth. Graf Leicester. Gefolge.

Elisabeth zu Leicester.

2225 Wie heißt der Landsitz?

Leicester.

Fotheringhayschloß.

Elisabeth zu Shrewsbury.

Schickt unser Jagdgefolg voraus nach London!
Das Volk drängt allzu heftig in den Straßen,
Wir suchen Schutz in diesem stillen Park.

Talbot entfernt das Gefolge. Sie fixiert mit den Augen die Maria, indem sie zu Paulet weiter spricht.

Mein gutes Volk liebt mich zu sehr. Unmäßig,
2230 Abgöttisch sind die Zeichen seiner Freude,
So ehrt man einen Gott, nicht einen Menschen.

Maria

welche diese Zeit über halb ohnmächtig auf die Amme gelehnt war, erhebt sich jetzt, und ihr Auge begegnet dem gespannten Blick der Elisabeth. Sie schaudert zusammen und wirft sich wieder an der Amme Brust.

O Gott, aus diesen Zügen spricht kein Herz!

Elisabeth.

Wer ist die Lady?

Ein allgemeines Schweigen.

Leicester.

— Du bist zu Fotheringhay, Königin.

Elisabeth

stellt sich überrascht und erstaunt, einen finstern Blick auf Leicestern richtend.

2235 Wer hat mir das gethan? Lord Lester!

Leicester.

Es ist geschehen, Königin — und nun
Der Himmel deinen Schritt hierher gelenkt,
So laß die Großmut und das Mitleid siegen!

Shrewsbury.

Laß dich erbitten, königliche Frau,
2240 Dein Aug' auf die Unglückliche zu richten,
Die hier vergeht vor deinem Anblick.

Maria rafft sich zusammen und will auf die Elisabeth zugehen, steht aber auf halbem Weg schaudernd still; ihre Gebärden drücken den heftigsten Kampf aus.

Elisabeth.

Wie, Mylords?
Wer war es denn, der eine Tiefgebeugte
Mir angekündigt? Eine Stolze find' ich,
Vom Unglück keineswegs geschmeidigt.

Maria.

Sei's!
2245 Ich will mich auch noch diesem unterwerfen.
Fahr hin, ohnmächt'ger Stolz der edeln Seele!
Ich will vergessen, wer ich bin, und was
Ich litt; ich will vor ihr mich niederwerfen,
Die mich in diese Schmach herunterstieß.

Sie wendet sich gegen die Königin.

2250 Der Himmel hat für Euch entschieden, Schwester!
Gekrönt vom Sieg ist Euer glücklich Haupt;
Die Gottheit bet' ich an, die Euch erhöhte!

Sie fällt vor ihr nieder.

Doch seid auch Ihr nun edelmütig, Schwester
Laßt mich nicht schmachvoll liegen! Eure Hand
2255 Streckt aus, reicht mir die königliche Rechte,
Mich zu erheben von dem tiefen Fall!

Elisabeth zurücktretend.

Ihr seid an Eurem Platz, Lady Maria!
Und dankend preis' ich meines Gottes Gnade.

Der nicht gewollt, daß ich zu Euren Füßen
2260 So liegen sollte, wie Ihr jetzt zu meinen.

Maria mit steigendem Affekt.

Denkt an den Wechsel alles Menschlichen!
Es leben Götter, die den Hochmut rächen!
Verehret, fürchtet sie, die schrecklichen,
Die mich zu Euren Füßen niederstürzen —
2265 Um dieser fremden Zeugen willen, ehrt
In mir Euch selbst! entweihet, schändet nicht
Das Blut der Tudor, das in meinen Adern,
Wie in den Euren, fließt — O Gott im Himmel!
Steht nicht da, schroff und unzugänglich wie
2270 Die Felsenklippe, die der Strandende
Vergeblich ringend zu erfassen strebt.
Mein Alles hängt, mein Leben, mein Geschick,
An meiner Worte, meiner Thränen Kraft;
Löst mir das Herz, daß ich das Eure rühre!
2275 Wenn Ihr mich anschaut mit dem Eisesblick,
Schließt sich das Herz mir schaudernd zu, der Strom
Der Thränen stockt, und kaltes Grausen fesselt
Die Flehensworte mir im Busen an.

Elisabeth kalt und streng.

Was habt Ihr mir zu sagen, Lady Stuart?
2280 Ihr habt mich sprechen wollen. Ich vergesse
Die Königin, die schwer beleidigte,
Die fromme Pflicht der Schwester zu erfüllen,
Und meines Anblicks Trost gewähr' ich Euch.
Dem Trieb der Großmut folg' ich, setze mich
2285 Gerechtem Tadel aus, daß ich so weit
Heruntersteige — denn Ihr wißt,
Daß Ihr mich habt ermorden lassen wollen.

Maria.

Womit soll ich den Anfang machen, wie
Die Worte klüglich stellen, daß sie Euch
2290 Das Herz ergreifen, aber nicht verletzen!
O Gott, gieb meiner Rede Kraft, und nimm
Ihr jeden Stachel, der verwunden könnte!
Kann ich doch für mich selbst nicht sprechen, ohne Euch
Schwer zu verklagen, und das will ich nicht.
2295 — Ihr habt an mir gehandelt, wie nicht recht ist,
Denn ich bin eine Königin wie Ihr,
Und Ihr habt als Gefangne mich gehalten.
Ich kam zu Euch als eine Bittende,
Und Ihr, des Gastrechts heilige Gesetze,
2300 Der Völker heilig Recht in mir verhöhnend,
Schloßt mich in Kerkermauern ein; die Freunde,
Die Diener werden grausam mir entrissen,
Unwürd'gem Mangel werd' ich preisgegeben,
Man stellt mich vor ein schimpfliches Gericht —
2305 Nichts mehr davon! Ein ewiges Vergessen
Bedecke, was ich Grausames erlitt.
— Seht! Ich will alles eine Schickung nennen;
Ihr seid nicht schuldig, ich bin auch nicht schuldig;
Ein böser Geist stieg aus dem Abgrund auf,
2310 Den Haß in unsern Herzen zu entzünden,
Der unsre zarte Jugend schon entzweit.
Er wuchs mit uns, und böse Menschen fachten
Der unglücksel'gen Flamme Atem zu.
Wahnsinn'ge Eiferer bewaffneten
2315 Mit Schwert und Dolch die unberufne Hand —
Das ist das Fluchgeschick der Könige
Daß sie, entzweit, die Welt in Haß zerreißen

Und jeder Zwietracht Furien entfesseln.
— Jetzt ist kein fremder Mund mehr zwischen uns,

nähert sich ihr zutraulich und mit schmeichelndem Ton.

2320 Wir stehn einander selbst nun gegenüber.
Jetzt, Schwester, redet! Nennt mir meine Schuld;
Ich will Euch völliges Genügen leisten.
Ach, daß Ihr damals mir Gehör geschenkt,
Als ich so dringend Euer Auge suchte!
2325 Es wäre nie so weit gekommen, nicht
An diesem traur'gen Ort geschähe jetzt
Die unglückselig traurige Begegnung.

Elisabeth.

Mein guter Stern bewahrte mich davor,
Die Natter an den Busen mir zu legen.
2330 — Nicht die Geschicke, Euer schwarzes Herz
Klagt an, die wilde Ehrsucht Eures Hauses.
Nichts Feindliches war zwischen uns geschehn,
Da kündigte mir Euer Ohm, der stolze,
Herrschwüt'ge Priester, der die freche Hand
2335 Nach allen Kronen streckt, die Fehde an,
Bethörte Euch, mein Wappen anzunehmen,
Euch meine Königstitel zuzueignen,
Auf Tod und Leben in den Kampf mit mir
Zu gehn — Wen rief er gegen mich nicht auf?
2340 Der Priester Zungen und der Völker Schwert,
Des frommen Wahnsinns fürchterliche Waffen;
Hier selbst, im Friedenssitze meines Reichs,
Blies er mir der Empörung Flammen an —
Doch Gott ist mit mir, und der stolze Priester
2345 Behält das Feld nicht — meinem Haupte war
Der Streich gedrohet, und das Eure fällt!

Maria.

Ich steh' in Gottes Hand. Ihr werdet Euch
So blutig Eurer Macht nicht überheben —

Elisabeth.

Wer soll mich hindern? Euer Oheim gab
2350 Das Beispiel allen Königen der Welt,
Wie man mit seinen Feinden Frieden macht.
Die Sankt Barthelemi sei meine Schule!
Was ist mir Blutsverwandtschaft, Völkerrecht?
Die Kirche trennet aller Pflichten Band,
2355 Den Treubruch heiligt sie, den Königsmord;
Ich übe nur, was Eure Priester lehren.
Sagt! Welches Pfand gewährte mir für Euch,
Wenn ich großmütig Eure Bande löste?
Mit welchem Schloß verwahr' ich Eure Treue,
2360 Das nicht Sankt Peters Schlüssel öffnen kann?
Gewalt nur ist die einz'ge Sicherheit;
Kein Bündnis ist mit dem Gezücht der Schlangen,

Maria.

O, das ist Euer traurig finstrer Argwohn!
Ihr habt mich stets als eine Feindin nur
2365 Und Fremdlingin betrachtet. Hättet Ihr
Zu Eurer Erbin mich erklärt, wie mir
Gebührt, so hätten Dankbarkeit und Liebe
Euch eine treue Freundin und Verwandte
In mir erhalten.

Elisabeth.

Draußen, Lady Stuart,
2370 Ist Eure Freundschaft, Euer Haus das Papsttum,
Der Mönch ist Euer Bruder — Euch zur Erbin

Erklären! Der verräterische Fallstrick!
Daß Ihr bei meinem Leben noch mein Volk
Verführtet, eine listige Armida,
2375 Die edle Jugend meines Königreichs
In Eurem Buhlernetze schlau verstricktet —
Daß alles sich der neu aufgeh'nden Sonne
Zuwendete, und ich —

Maria.

Regiert in Frieden!
Jedwedem Anspruch auf dies Reich entsag' ich.
2380 Ach, meines Geistes Schwingen sind gelähmt;
Nicht Größe lockt mich mehr — Ihr habt's erreicht,
Ich bin nur noch der Schatten der Maria.
Gebrochen ist in langer Kerkerschmach
Der edle Mut — Ihr habt das Äußerste an mir
2385 Gethan, habt mich zerstört in meiner Blüte!
— Jetzt macht ein Ende, Schwester! Sprecht es aus
Das Wort, um dessentwillen Ihr gekommen,
Denn nimmer will ich glauben, daß Ihr kamt,
Um Euer Opfer grausam zu verhöhnen.
2390 Sprecht dieses Wort aus! Sagt mir: „Ihr seid frei,
Maria! Meine Macht habt Ihr gefühlt,
Jetzt lernet meinen Edelmut verehren!"
Sagt's, und ich will mein Leben, meine Freiheit
Als ein Geschenk aus Eurer Hand empfangen.
2395 — Ein Wort macht alles ungeschehn. Ich warte
Darauf. O, laßt mich's nicht zu lang' erharren!
Weh Euch, wenn Ihr mit diesem Wort nicht endet!
Denn wenn Ihr jetzt nicht segenbringend, herrlich,
Wie eine Gottheit von mir scheidet — Schwester!
2400 Nicht um dies ganze reiche Eiland, nicht

Um alle Länder, die das Meer umfaßt,
Möcht' ich vor Euch so stehn, wie Ihr vor mir!

Elisabeth.

Bekennt Ihr endlich Euch für überwunden?
Ist's aus mit Euren Ränken? Ist kein Mörder
2405 Mehr unterweges? Will kein Abenteurer
Für Euch die traur'ge Ritterschaft mehr wagen?
— Ja, es ist aus, Lady Maria. Ihr verführt
Mir keinen mehr. Die Welt hat andre Sorgen.
Es lüstet keinen, Euer — vierter Mann
2410 Zu werden, denn Ihr tötet Eure Freier,
Wie Eure Männer!

Maria auffahrend.

Schwester! Schwester!
O Gott! Gott! Gieb mir Mäßigung!

Elisabeth
sieht sie lange mit einem Blick stolzer Verachtung an.

Das also sind die Reizungen, Lord Lester,
Die ungestraft kein Mann erblickt, daneben
2415 Kein andres Weib sich wagen darf zu stellen!
Fürwahr! Der Ruhm war wohlfeil zu erlangen,
Es kostet nichts, die allgemeine Schönheit
Zu sein, als die gemeine sein für alle!

Maria.

Das ist zu viel!

Elisabeth höhnisch lachend.

Jetzt zeigt Ihr Euer wahres
2420 Gesicht, bis jetzt war's nur die Larve.

Maria

von Zorn glühend, doch mit einer edlen Würde.

Ich habe menschlich, jugendlich gefehlt,
Die Macht verführte mich, ich hab' es nicht
Verheimlicht und verborgen, falschen Schein
Hab' ich verschmäht mit königlichem Freimut.
2425 Das Ärgste weiß die Welt von mir, und ich
Kann sagen, ich bin besser als mein Ruf.
Weh Euch, wenn sie von Euren Thaten einst
Den Ehrenmantel zieht, womit Ihr gleißend
Die wilde Glut verstohlner Lüste deckt.
2430 Nicht Ehrbarkeit habt Ihr von Eurer Mutter
Geerbt; man weiß, um welcher Tugend willen
Anna von Boulen das Schafott bestiegen.

Shrewsbury

tritt zwischen beide Königinnen.

O Gott des Himmels! Muß es dahin kommen!
Ist das die Mäßigung, die Unterwerfung,
2435 Lady Maria?

Maria.

Mäßigung! Ich habe
Ertragen, was ein Mensch ertragen kann.
Fahr hin, lammherzige Gelassenheit!
Zum Himmel fliehe, leidende Geduld!
Spreng' endlich deine Bande, tritt hervor
2440 Aus deiner Höhle, langverhaltner Groll! —
Und du, der dem gereizten Basilisk
Den Mordblick gab, leg' auf die Zunge mir
Den gift'gen Pfeil —

Shrewsbury.

O, sie ist außer sich!
Verzeih der Rasenden, der schwer Gereizten!

Elisabeth, vor Zorn sprachlos, schießt wütende Blicke auf Marien.

Leicester
in der heftigsten Unruhe, sucht die Elisabeth hinweg zu führen.

Höre
2445 Die Wütende nicht an! Hinweg, hinweg
Von diesem unglücksel'gen Ort!

Maria.

Der Thron von England ist durch einen Bastard
Entweiht, der Britten edelherzig Volk
Durch eine list'ge Gauklerin betrogen.
2450 — Regierte Recht, so läget Ihr vor mir
Im Staube jetzt, denn ich bin Euer König.

Elisabeth geht schnell ab, die Lords folgen ihr in der höchsten Bestürzung.

Fünfter Auftritt.

Maria. Kennedy.

Kennedy.

O, was habt Ihr gethan! Sie geht in Wut!
Jetzt ist es aus, und alle Hoffnung schwindet.

Maria noch ganz außer sich.

Sie geht in Wut! Sie trägt den Tod im Herzen!

Der Kennedy um den Hals fallend.

2455 O, wie mir wohl ist, Hanna! Endlich, endlich,
Nach Jahren der Erniedrigung, der Leiden,

Maria Stuart. — Kaulbach.

(Die Unterredung der beiden Königinnen.)

Ein Augenblick der Rache, des Triumphs!
Wie Bergeslasten fällt's von meinem Herzen,
Das Messer stieß ich in der Feindin Brust.

Kennedy.

2460 Unglückliche! Der Wahnsinn reißt Euch hin,
Ihr habt die Unversöhnliche verwundet.
Sie führt den Blitz, sie ist die Königin,
Vor ihrem Buhlen habt ihr sie verhöhnt!

Maria.

Vor Lesters Augen hab' ich sie erniedrigt!
2465 Er sah es, er bezeugte meinen Sieg!
Wie ich sie niederschlug von ihrer Höhe,
Er stand dabei, mich stärkte seine Nähe!

Sechster Auftritt.

Mortimer zu den Vorigen.

Kennedy.

O Sir! Welch ein Erfolg —

Mortimer.

Ich hörte alles.

Giebt der Amme ein Zeichen, sich auf ihren Posten zu begeben, und tritt näher. Sein ganzes Wesen drückt eine heftige, leidenschaftliche Stimmung aus.

Du hast gesiegt! Du tratst sie in den Staub,
2470 Du warst die Königin, sie der Verbrecher.
Ich bin entzückt von deinem Mut, ich bete
Dich an, wie eine Göttin groß und herrlich
Erscheinst du mir in diesem Augenblick.

Maria.

Ihr spracht mit Lestern, überbrachtet ihm
2475 Mein Schreiben, mein Geschenk — O redet, Sir!

Mortimer
mit glühenden Blicken sie betrachtend.

Wie dich der edle königliche Zorn
Umglänzte, deine Reize mir verklärte!
Du bist das schönste Weib auf dieser Erde!

Maria.

Ich bitt' Euch, Sir! Stillt meine Ungeduld!
2480 Was spricht Mylord? O sagt, was darf ich hoffen?

Mortimer.

Wer? Er? Das ist ein Feiger, Elender!
Hofft nichts von ihm, verachtet ihn, vergeßt ihn!

Maria.

Was sagt Ihr?

Mortimer.

Er Euch retten und besitzen!
Er Euch! Er soll es wagen! Er! Mit mir
2485 Muß er auf Tod und Leben darum kämpfen!

Maria.

Ihr habt ihm meinen Brief nicht übergeben?
— O, dann ist's aus!

Mortimer.

Der Feige liebt das Leben.
Wer dich will retten und die Seine nennen,
Der muß den Tod beherzt umarmen können!

Maria.

2490 Er will nichts für mich thun?

Mortimer.

Nichts mehr von ihm!
Was kann er thun, und was bedarf man sein?
Ich will dich retten, ich allein!

Maria.

Ach, was vermögt Ihr!

Mortimer.

Täuschet Euch nicht mehr,
Als ob es noch wie gestern mit Euch stünde!
2495 So wie die Königin jetzt von Euch ging,
Wie dies Gespräch sich wendete, ist alles
Verloren, jeder Gnadenweg gesperrt.
Der That bedarf's jetzt, Kühnheit muß entscheiden,
Für alles werde alles frisch gewagt,
2500 Frei müßt Ihr sein, noch eh der Morgen tagt!

Maria.

Was sprecht Ihr? Diese Nacht! Wie ist das möglich?

Mortimer.

Hört, was beschlossen ist. Versammelt hab' ich
In heimlicher Kapelle die Gefährten;
Ein Priester hörte unsre Beichte an,
2505 Ablaß ist uns erteilt für alle Schulden,
Die wir begingen, Ablaß im voraus
Für alle, die wir noch begehen werden.
Das letzte Sakrament empfingen wir,
Und fertig sind wir zu der letzten Reise.

Maria.

2510 O welche fürchterliche Vorbereitung!

Mortimer.

Dies Schloß ersteigen wir in dieser Nacht,
Der Schlüssel bin ich mächtig. Wir ermorden
Die Hüter, reißen dich aus deiner Kammer
Gewaltsam, sterben muß von unsrer Hand,
2515 Daß niemand überbleibe, der den Raub
Verraten könne, jede lebende Seele.

Maria.

Und Drury, Paulet, meine Kerkermeister?
O, eher werden sie ihr letztes Blut —

Mortimer.

Von meinem Dolche fallen sie zuerst!

Maria.

2520 Was? Euer Oheim, Euer zweiter Vater?

Mortimer.

Von meinen Händen stirbt er. Ich ermord' ihn.

Maria.

O blut'ger Frevel!

Mortimer.

Alle Frevel sind
Vergeben im voraus. Ich kann das Ärgste
Begehen, und ich will's.

Maria.

O schrecklich, schrecklich!

Mortimer.

2525 Und müßt' ich auch die Königin durchbohren,
Ich hab' es auf die Hostie geschworen.

Maria.

Nein, Mortimer! Eh so viel Blut um mich —

Mortimer.

Was ist mir alles Leben gegen dich
Und meine Liebe! Mag der Welten Band
2530 Sich lösen, eine zweite Wasserflut
Herwogend alles Atmende verschlingen!
— Ich achte nichts mehr! Eh ich dir entsage,
Eh nahe sich das Ende aller Tage!

Maria zurücktretend.

Gott! welche Sprache, Sir, und — welche Blicke!
2535 — Sie schrecken, sie verscheuchen mich.

Mortimer
mit irren Blicken und im Ausdruck des stillen Wahnsinns.

Das Leben ist
Nur ein Moment, der Tod ist auch nur einer!
— Man schleife mich nach Tyburn, Glied für Glied
Zerreiße man mit glüh'nder Eisenzange,

Indem er heftig auf sie zugeht, mit ausgebreiteten Armen.

Wenn ich dich, Heißgeliebte, umfange —

Maria zurücktretend.

2540 Unsinniger, zurück! —

Mortimer.

An dieser Brust,
Auf diesem liebeatmenden Munde —

Maria.

Um Gottes willen, Sir! Laßt mich hineingehn!

Mortimer.

Der ist ein Rasender, der nicht das Glück
Festhält in unauflöslicher Umarmung,
2545 Wenn es ein Gott in seine Hand gegeben.

Ich will dich retten, kost' es tausend Leben;
Ich rette dich, ich will es; doch, so wahr
Gott lebt! ich schwör's, ich will dich auch besitzen.

Maria.

O, will kein Gott, kein Engel mich beschützen!
2550 Furchtbares Schicksal! Grimmig schleuderst du
Von einem Schrecknis mich dem andern zu.
Bin ich geboren, nur die Wut zu wecken?
Verschwört sich Haß und Liebe, mich zu schrecken?

Mortimer.

Ja, glühend, wie sie hassen, lieb' ich dich!
2555 Sie wollen dich enthaupten, diesen Hals,
Den blendend weißen, mit dem Beil durchschneiden.
O, weihe du dem Lebensgott der Freuden,
Was du dem Hasse blutig opfern mußt!
Mit diesen Reizen, die nicht dein mehr sind,
2560 Beselige den glücklichen Geliebten!
Die schöne Locke, dieses seidne Haar,
Verfallen schon den finstern Todesmächten,
Gebrauch's, den Sklaven ewig zu umflechten!

Maria.

O, welche Sprache muß ich hören! Sir!
2565 Mein Unglück sollt' Euch heilig sein, mein Leiden,
Wenn es mein königliches Haupt nicht ist.

Mortimer.

Die Krone ist von deinem Haupt gefallen,
Du hast nichts mehr von ird'scher Majestät;
Versuch' es, laß dein Herrscherwort erschallen,
2570 Ob dir ein Freund, ein Retter aufersteht.
Nichts blieb dir als die rührende Gestalt,

Der hohen Schönheit göttliche Gewalt,
Die läßt mich alles wagen und vermögen,
Die treibt dem Beil des Henkers mich entgegen —

Maria.

2575 O, wer errettet mich von seiner Wut!

Mortimer.

Verwegner Dienst belohnt sich auch verwegen!
Warum verspritzt der Tapfere sein Blut?
Ist Leben doch des Lebens höchstes Gut!
Ein Rasender, der es umsonst verschleudert!
2580 Erst will ich ruhn an seiner wärmsten Brust —

Er preßt sie heftig an sich.

Maria.

O, muß ich Hilfe rufen gegen den Mann,
Der mein Erretter —

Mortimer.

Du bist nicht gefühllos;
Nicht kalter Strenge klagt die Welt dich an,
Dich kann die heiße Liebesbitte rühren,
2585 Du hast den Sänger Rizzio beglückt,
Und jener Bothwell durfte dich entführen.

Maria.

Vermessener!

Mortimer.

Er war nur dein Tyrann!
Du zittertest vor ihm, da du ihn liebtest!
Wenn nur der Schrecken dich gewinnen kann,
2590 Beim Gott der Hölle! —

Maria.

Laßt mich! Raset Ihr?

Mortimer.

Erzittern sollst du auch vor mir!

Kennedy hereinstürzend.

Man naht. Man kommt. Bewaffnet Volk erfüllt
Den ganzen Garten.

Mortimer.

auffahrend und zum Degen greifend.

Ich beschütze dich!

Maria.

O Hanna! rette mich aus seinen Händen!
2595 Wo find' ich Ärmste einen Zufluchtsort?
Zu welchem Heiligen soll ich mich wenden?
Hier ist Gewalt, und drinnen ist der Mord.

Sie flieht dem Hause zu, Kennedy folgt.

Siebenter Auftritt.

Mortimer. Paulet und Drury, welche außer sich hereinstürzen. Gefolge eilt über die Scene.

Paulet.

Verschließt die Pforten! Zieht die Brücken auf!

Mortimer.

Oheim, was ist's?

Paulet.

Wo ist die Mörderin?
2600 Hinab mit ihr ins finsterste Gefängnis!

Mortimer.

Was giebt's, was ist geschehn?

Paulet.

Die Königin!

Verfluchte Hände! Teuflisches Erkühnen!

Mortimer.

Die Königin! Welche Königin?

Paulet.

Von England!

Sie ist ermordet auf der Londner Straßen!

Eilt ins Haus.

Achter Auftritt.

Mortimer. Gleich darauf Okelly.

Mortimer.

2605 Bin ich im Wahnwitz? Kam nicht eben jemand
Vorbei und rief, die Königin sei ermordet?
Nein, nein, mir träumte nur. Ein Fieberwahn
Bringt mir als wahr und wirklich vor den Sinn,
Was die Gedanken gräßlich mir erfüllt.
2610 Wer kommt? Es ist Okell'. So schreckenvoll!

Okelly hereinstürzend.

Flieht, Mortimer! Flieht! Alles ist verloren.

Mortimer.

Was ist verloren?

Okelly.

Fragt nicht lange! Denkt

Auf schnelle Flucht!

Mortimer.

Was giebt's denn?

Okelly.

Sauvage führte

Den Streich, der Rasende.

Mortimer.

So ist es wahr?

Okelly.

2615 Wahr, wahr! O, rettet Euch!

Mortimer.

Sie ist ermordet,

Und auf den Thron von England steigt Maria!

Okelly.

Ermordet! Wer sagt das?

Mortimer.

Ihr selbst!

Okelly.

Sie lebt!

Und ich und Ihr, wir alle sind des Todes.

Mortimer.

Sie lebt!

Okelly.

2620 Der Stoß ging fehl, der Mantel fing ihn auf,
Und Shrewsbury entwaffnete den Mörder.

Mortimer.

Sie lebt!

Okelly.

Lebt, um uns alle zu verderben!
Kommt, man umzingelt schon den Park.

Mortimer.

Wer hat
Das Rasende gethan?

Okelly.

Der Barnabit'
2625 Aus Toulon war's, den Ihr in der Kapelle
Tiefsinnig sitzen saht, als uns der Mönch
Das Anathem' ausdeutete, worin
Der Papst die Königin mit dem Fluch belegt.
Das Nächste, Kürzeste wollt' er ergreifen,
2630 Mit einem kecken Streich die Kirche Gottes
Befrein, die Martyrkrone sich erwerben;
Dem Priester nur vertraut er seine That,
Und auf dem Londner Weg ward sie vollbracht.

Mortimer
nach einem langen Stillschweigen.

O, dich verfolgt ein grimmig wütend Schicksal,
2635 Unglückliche! Jetzt — ja, jetzt mußt du sterben,
Dein Engel selbst bereitet deinen Fall.

Okelly.

Sagt, wohin wendet Ihr die Flucht? Ich gehe,
Mich in des Nordens Wäldern zu verbergen.

Mortimer.

Flieht hin, und Gott geleite Eure Flucht!
2640 Ich bleibe. Noch versuch' ich's, sie zu retten,
Wo nicht, auf ihrem Sarge mir zu betten.

Gehen ab zu verschiedenen Seiten.

Vierter Aufzug.

Vorzimmer.

Erster Auftritt.

Graf Aubespine. Kent und Leicester.

Aubespine.

Wie steht's um Ihro Majestät? Mylords,
Ihr seht mich noch ganz außer mir vor Schrecken.
Wie ging das zu? Wie konnte das in Mitte
2645 Des allertreusten Volks geschehen?

Leicester.

Es geschah
Durch keinen aus dem Volke. Der es that,
War Eures Königs Unterthan, ein Franke.

Aubespine.

Ein Rasender gewißlich.

Kent.

Ein Papist,
Graf Aubespine!

Zweiter Auftritt.

Vorige. Burleigh im Gespräch mit Davison.

Burleigh.

Sogleich muß der Befehl
2650 Zur Hinrichtung verfaßt und mit dem Siegel
Versehen werden — Wenn er ausgefertigt,
Wird er der Königin zur Unterschrift
Gebracht. Geht! Keine Zeit ist zu verlieren.

Davison.

Es soll geschehn.

Geht ab.

Aubespine Burleigh entgegen.

Mylord, mein treues Herz
2655 Teilt die gerechte Freude dieser Insel.
Lob sei dem Himmel, der den Mörderstreich
Gewehrt von diesem königlichen Haupt!

Burleigh.

Er sei gelobt, der unsrer Feinde Bosheit
Zu Schanden machte!

Aubespine.

Mög' ihn Gott verdammen,
2660 Den Thäter dieser fluchenswerten That!

Burleigh.

Den Thäter und den schändlichen Erfinder.

Aubespine zu Kent.

Gefällt es Eurer Herrlichkeit, Lordmarschall
Bei Ihro Majestät mich einzuführen,

Daß ich den Glückwunsch meines Herrn und Königs
2665 Zu ihren Füßen schuldigst niederlege —

Burleigh.

Bemüht Euch nicht, Graf Aubespine.

Aubespine offiziös.

Ich weiß,
Lord Burleigh, was mir obliegt.

Burleigh.

Euch liegt ob,
Die Insel auf das schleunigste zu räumen.

Aubespine tritt erstaunt zurück.

Was! Wie ist das!

Burleigh.

Der heilige Charakter
2670 Beschützt Euch heute noch, und morgen nicht mehr.

Aubespine.

Und was ist mein Verbrechen?

Burleigh.

Wenn ich es
Genannt, so ist es nicht mehr zu vergeben.

Aubespine.

Ich hoffe, Lord, das Recht der Abgesandten —

Burleigh.

Schützt — Reichsverräter nicht.

Leicester und **Kent.**

Ha! Was ist das!

Aubespine.

Mylord,
2675 Bedenkt Ihr wohl —

Burleigh.

Ein Paß, von Eurer Hand
Geschrieben, fand sich in des Mörders Tasche.

Kent.

Ist's möglich?

Aubespine.

Viele Pässe teil' ich aus,
Ich kann der Menschen Innres nicht erforschen.

Burleigh.

In Eurem Hause beichtete der Mörder.

Aubespine.

2680 Mein Haus ist offen.

Burleigh.

Jedem Feinde Englands.

Aubespine.

Ich fordre Untersuchung.

Burleigh.

Fürchtet sie!

Aubespine.

In meinem Haupt ist mein Monarch verletzt;
Zerreißen wird er das geschloss'ne Bündnis.

Burleigh.

Zerrissen schon hat es die Königin;
2685 England wird sich mit Frankreich nicht vermählen.
Mylord von Kent! Ihr übernehmet es,
Den Grafen sicher an das Meer zu bringen.
Das aufgebrachte Volk hat sein Hotel
Gestürmt, wo sich ein ganzes Arsenal
2690 Von Waffen fand; es droht ihn zu zerreißen,

Wie er sich zeigt; verberget ihn, bis sich
Die Wut gelegt — Ihr haftet für sein Leben!

Aubespine.

Ich gehe, ich verlasse dieses Land,
Wo man der Völker Recht mit Füßen tritt
2695 Und mit Verträgen spielt — doch mein Monarch
Wird blut'ge Rechenschaft —

Burleigh.

Er hole sie!

Kent und Aubespine gehen ab.

Dritter Auftritt.

Leicester und Burleigh.

Leicester.

So löst Ihr selbst das Bündnis wieder auf,
Das Ihr geschäftig unberufen knüpftet.
Ihr habt um England wenig Dank verdient,
2700 Mylord, die Mühe konntet Ihr Euch sparen.

Burleigh.

Mein Zweck war gut. Gott leitete es anders.
Wohl dem, der sich nichts Schlimmeres bewußt ist!

Leicester.

Man kennt Cecils geheimnisreiche Miene,
Wenn er die Jagd auf Staatsverbrechen macht.
2705 — Jetzt, Lord, ist eine gute Zeit für Euch.
Ein ungeheurer Frevel ist geschehn,

Und noch umhüllt Geheimnis seine Thäter.
Jetzt wird ein Inquisitionsgericht
Eröffnet. Wort und Blicke werden abgewogen,
2710 Gedanken selber vor Gericht gestellt.
Da seid Ihr der allwicht'ge Mann, der Atlas
Des Staats; ganz England liegt auf Euren Schultern.

Burleigh.

In Euch, Mylord, erkenn' ich meinen Meister,
Denn solchen Sieg, als Eure Redekunst
2715 Erfocht, hat meine nie davongetragen.

Leicester.

Was meint Ihr damit, Lord?

Burleigh.

Ihr wart es doch, der hinter meinem Rücken
Die Königin nach Fotheringhayschloß
Zu locken wußte?

Leicester.

Hinter Eurem Rücken!
2720 Wann scheuten meine Thaten Eure Stirn?

Burleigh.

Die Königin hättet Ihr nach Fotheringhay
Geführt? Nicht doch! Ihr habt die Königin
Nicht hingeführt! — Die Königin war es,
Die so gefällig war, Euch hinzuführen.

Leicester.

2725 Was wollt Ihr damit sagen, Lord?

Burleigh.

Die edle
Person, die Ihr die Königin dort spielen ließt!

Der herrliche Triumph, den Ihr der arglos
Vertrauenden bereitet! — Güt'ge Fürstin!
So schamlos frech verspottete man dich,
2730 So schonungslos wardst du dahingegeben!
— Das also ist die Großmut und die Milde,
Die Euch im Staatsrat plötzlich angewandelt!
Darum ist diese Stuart ein so schwacher,
Verachtungswerter Feind, daß es der Müh
2735 Nicht lohnt, mit ihrem Blut sich zu beflecken!
Ein feiner Plan! Fein zugespitzt! Nur schade,
Zu fein geschärfet, daß die Spitze brach!

Leicester.

Nichtswürdiger! Gleich folgt mir! An dem Throne
Der Königin sollt Ihr mir Rede stehn.

Burleigh.

2740 Dort trefft Ihr mich — Und sehet zu, Mylord,
Daß Euch dort die Beredsamkeit nicht fehle.

Geht ab.

Vierter Auftritt.

Leicester allein, darauf Mortimer.

Leicester.

Ich bin entdeckt, ich bin durchschaut — Wie kam
Der Unglückselige auf meine Spuren!
Weh mir, wenn er Beweise hat! Erfährt
2745 Die Königin, daß zwischen mir und der Maria

Verständnisse gewesen — Gott! Wie schuldig
Steh' ich vor ihr! Wie hinterlistig treulos
Erscheint mein Rat, mein unglückseliges
Bemühn, nach Fotheringhay sie zu führen!
2750 Grausam verspottet sieht sie sich von mir,
An die verhaßte Feindin sich verraten!
O, nimmer, nimmer kann sie das verzeihn!
Vorherbedacht wird alles nun erscheinen,
Auch diese bittre Wendung des Gesprächs,
2755 Der Gegnerin Triumph und Hohngelächter,
Ja, selbst die Mörderhand, die blutig, schrecklich,
Ein unerwartet ungeheures Schicksal,
Dazwischen kam, werd' ich bewaffnet haben!
Nicht Rettung seh' ich, nirgends! Ha! Wer kommt?

Mortimer
kommt in der heftigsten Unruhe und blickt scheu umher.

2760 Graf Lester! Seid Ihr's? Sind wir ohne Zeugen?

Leicester.

Unglücklicher, hinweg! Was sucht Ihr hier?

Mortimer.

Man ist auf unsrer Spur, auf Eurer auch;
Nehmt Euch in acht!

Leicester.

Hinweg, hinweg!

Mortimer.

Man weiß,
Daß bei dem Grafen Aubespine geheime
2765 Versammlung war —

Leicester.

Was kümmert's mich!

Mortimer.

Daß sich der Mörder
Dabei befunden —

Leicester.

Das ist Eure Sache!
Verwegener! Was unterfangt Ihr Euch,
In Euren blut'gen Frevel mich zu flechten?
Verteidigt Eure bösen Händel selbst!

Mortimer.

2770 So hört mich doch nur an!

Leicester in heftigem Zorn.

Geht in die Hölle!
Was hängt Ihr Euch, gleich einem bösen Geist,
An meine Fersen! Fort! Ich kenn' Euch nicht,
Ich habe nichts gemein mit Meuchelmördern.

Mortimer.

Ihr wollt nicht hören. Euch zu warnen komm' ich;
2775 Auch Eure Schritte sind verraten —

Leicester.

Ha!

Mortimer.

Der Großschatzmeister war zu Fotheringhay,
Sogleich nachdem die Unglücksthat geschehn war,
Der Königin Zimmer wurde streng durchsucht,
Da fand sich —

Leicester.

Was?

Mortimer.

Ein angefangner Brief
2780 Der Königin an Euch --

Leicester.

Die Unglücksel'ge!

Mortimer.

Worin sie Euch auffordert, Wort zu halten,
Euch das Versprechen ihrer Hand erneuert,
Des Bildnisses gedenkt —

Leicester.

Tod und Verdammnis!

Mortimer.

Lord Burleigh hat den Brief.

Leicester.

Ich bin verloren!

Er geht während der folgenden Rede Mortimers verzweiflungsvoll auf und nieder.

Mortimer.

2785 Ergreift den Augenblick! Kommt ihm zuvor!
Errettet Euch, errettet sie — Schwört Euch
Heraus, ersinnt Entschuldigungen, wendet
Das Ärgste ab! Ich selbst kann nichts mehr thun.
Zerstreut sind die Gefährten, auseinander
2790 Gesprengt ist unser ganzer Bund. Ich eile
Nach Schottland, neue Freunde dort zu sammeln.
An Euch ist's jetzt; versucht, was Euer Ansehn,
Was eine kecke Stirn vermag!

Leicester

steht still, plötzlich besonnen.

Das will ich.

Er geht nach der Thüre, öffnet sie und ruft:

He da! Trabanten!

Zu dem Offizier, der mit Bewaffneten hereintritt.

Diesen Staatsverräter
2795 Nehmt in Verwahrung und bewacht ihn wohl!
Die schändlichste Verschwörung ist entdeckt;
Ich bringe selbst der Königin die Botschaft.

Er geht ab.

Mortimer

steht anfangs starr vor Erstaunen, faßt sich aber bald und sieht Leicestern mit einem Blick der tiefsten Verachtung nach.

Ha, Schändlicher! — Doch ich verdiene das.
Wer hieß mich auch dem Elenden vertrauen?
2800 Weg über meinen Nacken schreitet er;
Mein Fall muß ihm die Rettungsbrücke bauen.
— So rette dich! Verschlossen bleibt mein Mund,
Ich will dich nicht in mein Verderben flechten.
Auch nicht im Tode mag ich deinen Bund;
2805 Das Leben ist das einz'ge Gut des Schlechten.

Zu dem Offizier der Wache, der hervortritt, um ihn gefangen zu nehmen.

Was willst du, feiler Sklav' der Tyrannei?
Ich spotte deiner, ich bin frei!

Einen Dolch ziehend.

Offizier.

Er ist bewehrt — Entreißt ihm seinen Dolch!

Sie dringen auf ihn ein, er erwehrt sich ihrer.

Mortimer.

Und frei im letzten Augenblicke soll
2810 Mein Herz sich öffnen, meine Zunge lösen!
Fluch und Verderben euch, die ihren Gott
Und ihre wahre Königin verraten!
Die von der irdischen Maria sich

Treulos wie von der himmlischen gewendet,
2815 Sich dieser Bastardkönigin verkauft —

Offizier.

Hört Ihr die Lästrung! Auf! Ergreifet ihn!

Mortimer.

Geliebte! Nicht erretten konnt' ich dich,
So will ich dir ein männlich Beispiel geben.
Maria, heil'ge, bitt' für mich!
2820 Und nimm mich zu dir in dein himmlisch Leben!

Er durchsticht sich mit dem Dolch und fällt der Wache in die Arme.

Fünfter Auftritt.

Zimmer der Königin.

Elisabeth, einen Brief in der Hand. Burleigh.

Elisabeth.

Mich hinzuführen! Solchen Spott mit mir
Zu treiben! Der Verräter! Im Triumph
Vor seiner Buhlerin mich aufzuführen!
O, so ward noch kein Weib betrogen, Burleigh!

Burleigh.

2825 Ich kann es noch nicht fassen, wie es ihm,
Durch welche Macht, durch welche Zauberkünste
Gelang, die Klugheit meiner Königin
So sehr zu überraschen.

Elisabeth.

O, ich sterbe
Vor Scham! Wie mußt' er meiner Schwäche spotten!
2830 Sie glaubt' ich zu erniedrigen und war,
Ich selber, ihres Spottes Ziel!

Burleigh.

Du siehst nun ein, wie treu ich dir geraten!

Elisabeth.

O, ich bin schwer dafür gestraft, daß ich
Von Eurem weisen Rate mich entfernt!
2835 Und sollt' ich ihm nicht glauben? In den Schwüren
Der treusten Liebe einen Fallstrick fürchten?
Wem darf ich traun, wenn er mich hinterging?
Er, den ich groß gemacht vor allen Großen,
Der mir der Nächste stets am Herzen war,
2840 Dem ich verstattete, an diesem Hof
Sich wie der Herr, der König zu betragen!

Burleigh.

Und zu derselben Zeit verriet er dich
An diese falsche Königin von Schottland!

Elisabeth.

O, sie bezahle mir's mit ihrem Blut!
2845 — Sagt! Ist das Urteil abgefaßt?

Burleigh.

Es liegt
Bereit, wie du befohlen.

Elisabeth.

Sterben soll sie!
Er soll sie fallen sehn, und nach ihr fallen.

Verstoßen hab' ich ihn aus meinem Herzen,
Fort ist die Liebe, Rache füllt es ganz.
2850 So hoch er stand, so tief und schmählich sei
Sein Sturz! Er sei ein Denkmal meiner Strenge,
Wie er ein Beispiel meiner Schwäche war.
Man führ' ihn nach dem Tower; ich werde Peers
Ernennen, die ihn richten. Hingegeben
2855 Sei er der ganzen Strenge des Gesetzes.

Burleigh.

Er wird sich zu dir drängen, sich rechtfert'gen —

Elisabeth.

Wie kann er sich rechtfert'gen? Überführt
Ihn nicht der Brief? O, sein Verbrechen ist
Klar wie der Tag!

Burleigh.

Doch du bist mild und gnädig;
2860 Sein Anblick, seine mächt'ge Gegenwart —

Elisabeth.

Ich will ihn nicht sehn. Niemals, niemals wieder!
Habt Ihr Befehl gegeben, daß man ihn
Zurückweist, wenn er kommt?

Burleigh.

So ist's befohlen!

Page tritt ein.

Mylord von Lester!

Königin.

Der Abscheuliche!
2865 Ich will ihn nicht sehn. Sagt ihm, daß ich ihn
Nicht sehen will.

Page.

Das wag' ich nicht dem Lord
Zu sagen, und er würde mir's nicht glauben.

Königin.

So hab' ich ihn erhöht, daß meine Diener
Vor seinem Ansehn mehr als meinem zittern!

Burleigh zum Pagen.

2870 Die Königin verbiet' ihm, sich zu nahn!

Page geht zögernd ab.

Königin nach einer Pause.

Wenn's dennoch möglich wäre — Wenn er sich
Rechtfert'gen könnte! — Sagt mir, könnt' es nicht
Ein Fallstrick sein, den mir Maria legte,
Mich mit dem treusten Freunde zu entzwei'n?
2875 O, sie ist eine abgefeimte Bübin.
Wenn sie den Brief nur schrieb, mir gift'gen Argwohn
Ins Herz zu streun, ihn, den sie haßt, ins Unglück
Zu stürzen —

Burleigh.

Aber, Königin, erwäge —

Sechster Auftritt.

Vorige. Leicester.

Leicester
reißt die Thür mit Gewalt auf und tritt mit gebieterischem Wesen herein.

Den Unverschämten will ich sehn, der mir
2880 Das Zimmer meiner Königin verbietet.

Elisabeth.

Ha, der Verwegene!

Leicester.

Mich abzuweisen!
Wenn sie für einen Burleigh sichtbar ist,
So ist sie's auch für mich!

Burleigh.

Ihr seid sehr kühn, Mylord,
Hier wider die Erlaubnis einzustürmen.

Leicester.

2885 Ihr seid sehr frech, Lord, hier das Wort zu nehmen.
Erlaubnis? Was? Es ist an diesem Hofe
Niemand, durch dessen Mund Graf Lester sich
Erlauben und verbieten lassen kann!

Indem er sich der Elisabeth demütig nähert.

Aus meiner Königin eignem Mund will ich —

Elisabeth ohne ihn anzusehen.

2890 Aus meinem Angesicht, Nichtswürdiger!

Leicester.

Nicht meine gütige Elisabeth,
Den Lord vernehm' ich, meinen Feind, in diesen
Unholden Worten — Ich berufe mich auf meine
Elisabeth — Du liehest ihm dein Ohr;
2895 Das Gleiche fordr' ich.

Elisabeth.

Redet, Schändlicher!
Vergrößert Euren Frevel! Leugnet ihn!

Leicester.

Laßt diesen Überlästigen sich erst
Entfernen — Tretet ab, Mylord — Was ich
Mit meiner Königin zu verhandeln habe,
2900 Braucht keinen Zeugen. Geht!

Elisabeth zu Burleigh.

Bleibt! Ich befehl' es!

Leicester.

Was soll der dritte zwischen dir und mir!
Mit meiner angebeteten Monarchin
Hab' ich's zu thun — Die Rechte meines Platzes
Behaupt' ich — Es sind heil'ge Rechte!
2905 Und ich bestehe drauf, daß sich der Lord
Entferne!

Elisabeth.

Euch geziemt die stolze Sprache!

Leicester.

Wohl ziemt sie mir, denn ich bin der Beglückte,
Dem deine Gunst den hohen Vorzug gab;
Das hebt mich über ihn und über alle!
2910 Dein Herz verlieh mir diesen stolzen Rang,
Und was die Liebe gab, werd' ich, bei Gott!
Mit meinem Leben zu behaupten wissen.
Er geh' — und zweier Augenblicke nur
Bedarf's, mich mit dir zu verständigen.

Elisabeth.

2915 Ihr hofft umsonst, mich listig zu beschwatzen.

Leicester.

Beschwatzen konnte dich der Plauderer;
Ich aber will zu deinem Herzen reden,
Und was ich im Vertraun auf deine Gunst
Gewagt, will ich auch nur vor deinem Herzen
2920 Rechtfertigen — Kein anderes Gericht
Erkenn' ich über mir, als deine Neigung!

Elisabeth.

Schamloser! Eben diese ist's, die Euch zuerst
Verdammt — Zeigt ihm den Brief, Mylord!

Burleigh.

Hier ist er!

Leicester

durchläuft den Brief, ohne die Fassung zu verändern.

Das ist der Stuart Hand!

Elisabeth.

Lest und verstummt!

Leicester

nachdem er gelesen, ruhig.

2925 Der Schein ist gegen mich; doch darf ich hoffen,
Daß ich nicht nach dem Schein gerichtet werde!

Elisabeth.

Könnt Ihr es leugnen, daß Ihr mit der Stuart
In heimlichem Verständnis wart, ihr Bildnis
Empfingt, ihr zur Befreiung Hoffnung machtet?

Leicester.

2930 Leicht wäre mir's, wenn ich mich schuldig fühlte,
Das Zeugnis einer Feindin zu verwerfen!
Doch frei ist mein Gewissen; ich bekenne,
Daß sie die Wahrheit schreibt!

Elisabeth.

Nun denn,
Unglücklicher!

Burleigh.

Sein eigner Mund verdammt ihn.

Elisabeth.

2935 Aus meinen Augen! In den Tower — Verräter!

Leicester.

Der bin ich nicht. Ich hab' gefehlt, daß ich
Aus diesem Schritt dir ein Geheimnis machte;
Doch redlich war die Absicht, es geschah,
Die Feindin zu erforschen, zu verderben.

Elisabeth.

2940 Elende Ausflucht! —

Burleigh.

Wie, Mylord? Ihr glaubt —

Leicester.

Ich habe ein gewagtes Spiel gespielt,
Ich weiß, und nur Graf Lester durfte sich
An diesem Hofe solcher That erkühnen.
Wie ich die Stuart hasse, weiß die Welt.
2945 Der Rang, den ich bekleide, das Vertrauen,
Wodurch die Königin mich ehrt, muß jeden Zweifel
In meine treue Meinung niederschlagen.
Wohl darf der Mann, den deine Gunst vor allen
Auszeichnet, einen eignen kühnen Weg
2950 Einschlagen, seine Pflicht zu thun.

Burleigh.

Warum,
Wenn's eine gute Sache war, verschwiegt Ihr?

Leicester.

Mylord! Ihr pflegt zu schwatzen, eh Ihr handelt,
Und seid die Glocke Eurer Thaten. Das
Ist Eure Weise, Lord. Die meine ist,
2955 Erst handeln und dann reden!

Burleigh.

Ihr redet jetzo, weil Ihr müßt.

Leicester
ihn stolz und höhnisch mit den Augen messend.

Und Ihr
Berühmt Euch, eine wundergroße That
Ins Werk gerichtet, Eure Königin
Gerettet, die Verräterei entlarvt
2960 Zu haben — Alles wißt Ihr, Eurem Scharfblick
Kann nichts entgehen, meint Ihr — Armer Prahler!
Trotz Eurer Spürkunst war Maria Stuart
Noch heute frei, wenn ich es nicht verhindert.

Burleigh.

Ihr hättet —

Leicester.

Ich, Mylord. Die Königin
2965 Vertraute sich dem Mortimer, sie schloß
Ihr Innerstes ihm auf, sie ging so weit,
Ihm einen blut'gen Auftrag gegen die Maria
Zu geben, da der Oheim sich mit Abscheu
Von einem gleichen Antrag abgewendet —
2970 Sagt! Ist es nicht so?

Königin und Burleigh sehen einander betroffen an.

Burleigh.

Wie gelangtet Ihr
Dazu? —

Leicester.

Ist's nicht so? — Nun, Mylord! Wo hatte
Ihr Eure tausend Augen, nicht zu sehn,
Daß dieser Mortimer Euch hinterging?
Daß er ein wütender Papist, ein Werkzeug
2975 Der Guisen, ein Geschöpf der Stuart war,
Ein keck entschloss'ner Schwärmer, der gekommen,

Die Stuart zu befrein, die Königin
Zu morden —

Elisabeth
mit dem äußersten Erstaunen.

Dieser Mortimer!

Leicester.

Er war's, durch den
Maria Unterhandlung mit mir pflog,
2980 Den ich auf diesem Wege kennen lernte.
Noch heute sollte sie aus ihrem Kerker
Gerissen werden; diesen Augenblick
Entdeckte mir's sein eigner Mund; ich ließ ihn
Gefangen nehmen, und in der Verzweiflung,
2985 Sein Werk vereitelt, sich entlarvt zu sehn,
Gab er sich selbst den Tod!

Elisabeth.

O, ich bin unerhört
Betrogen — Dieser Mortimer!

Burleigh.

Und jetzt
Geschah das? Jetzt, nachdem ich Euch verlassen!

Leicester.

Ich muß um meinetwillen sehr beklagen,
2990 Daß es dies Ende mit ihm nahm. Sein Zeugnis,
Wenn er noch lebte, würde mich vollkommen
Gereinigt, aller Schuld entledigt haben.
Drum übergab ich ihn des Richters Hand.
Die strengste Rechtsform sollte meine Unschuld
2995 Vor aller Welt bewähren und besiegeln.

Burleigh.

Er tötete sich, sagt Ihr. Er sich selber? Oder
Ihr ihn?

Leicester.

Unwürdiger Verdacht! Man höre
Die Wache ab, der ich ihn übergab!

Er geht an die Thür und ruft hinaus. Der Offizier der Leibwache tritt herein.

Erstattet Ihrer Majestät Bericht,
3000 Wie dieser Mortimer umkam!

Offizier.

Ich hielt die Wache
Im Vorsaal, als Mylord die Thüre schnell
Eröffnete und mir befahl, den Ritter
Als einen Staatsverräter zu verhaften.
Wir sahen ihn hierauf in Wut geraten,
3005 Den Dolch ziehn, unter heftiger Verwünschung
Der Königin, und eh wir's hindern konnten,
Ihn in die Brust sich stoßen, daß er tot
Zu Boden stürzte —

Leicester.

Es ist gut. Ihr könnt
Abtreten, Sir! Die Königin weiß genug!

Offizier geht ab.

Elisabeth.

3010 O, welcher Abgrund von Abscheulichkeiten!

Leicester.

Wer war's nun, der dich rettete? War es
Mylord von Burleigh? Wußt' er die Gefahr,
Die dich umgab? War er's, der sie von dir
Gewandt? — Dein treuer Lester war dein Engel!

Burleigh.

3015 Graf! Dieser Mortimer starb Euch sehr gelegen. conveniently

Elisabeth.

Ich weiß nicht, was ich sagen soll. Ich glaub' Euch,
Und glaub' Euch nicht. Ich denke, Ihr seid schuldig
Und seid es nicht! O die Verhaßte, die
Mir all dies Weh bereitet!

Leicester.

Sie muß sterben.
3020 Jetzt stimm' ich selbst für ihren Tod. Ich riet
Dir an, das Urteil unvollstreckt zu lassen,
Bis sich aufs neu ein Arm für sie erhübe.
Dies ist geschehn — und ich bestehe drauf,
Daß man das Urteil ungesäumt vollstrecke.

Burleigh.

3025 Ihr rietet dazu! Ihr!

Leicester.

So sehr es mich
Empört, zu einem Äußersten zu greifen,
Ich sehe nun und glaube, daß die Wohlfahrt
Der Königin dies blut'ge Opfer heischt;
Drum trag' ich darauf an, daß der Befehl
3030 Zur Hinrichtung gleich ausgefertigt werde!

Burleigh zur Königin.

Da es Mylord so treu und ernstlich meint,
So trag' ich darauf an, daß die Vollstreckung
Des Richterspruchs ihm übertragen werde.

Leicester.

Mir!

Burleigh.

Euch. Nicht besser könnt Ihr den Verdacht,
3035 Der jetzt noch auf Euch lastet, widerlegen,
Als wenn Ihr sie, die Ihr geliebt zu haben
Beschuldigt werdet, selbst enthaupten lasset.

Elisabeth

Leicestern mit den Augen fixierend.

Mylord rät gut. So sei's, und dabei bleib' es.

Leicester.

Mich sollte billig meines Ranges Höh'
3040 Von einem Auftrag dieses traur'gen Inhalts
Befrein, der sich in jedem Sinne besser
Für einen Burleigh ziemen mag als mich.
Wer seiner Königin so nahe steht,
Der sollte nichts Unglückliches vollbringen.
3045 Jedoch um meinen Eifer zu bewähren,
Um meiner Königin genug zu thun,
Begeb' ich mich des Vorrechts meiner Würde
Und übernehme die verhaßte Pflicht.

Elisabeth.

Lord Burleigh teile sie mit Euch!

Zu diesem.

Tragt Sorge,
3050 Daß der Befehl gleich ausgefertigt werde!

Burleigh geht. Man hört draußen ein Getümmel.

Siebenter Auftritt.

Graf von Kent zu den Vorigen.

Elisabeth.

Was giebt's, Mylord von Kent? Was für ein Auflauf
Erregt die Stadt — Was ist es?

Kent.

Königin,
Es ist das Volk, das den Palast umlagert;
Es fordert heftig dringend, dich zu sehn.

Elisabeth.

3055 Was will mein Volk?

Kent.

Der Schrecken geht durch London,
Dein Leben sei bedroht, es gehen Mörder
Umher, vom Papste wider dich gesendet.
Verschworen seien die Katholischen,
Die Stuart aus dem Kerker mit Gewalt
3060 Zu reißen und zur Königin auszurufen.
Der Pöbel glaubt's und wütet. Nur das Haupt
Der Stuart, das noch heute fällt, kann ihn
Beruhigen.

Elisabeth.

Wie? Soll mir Zwang geschehn?

Kent.

Sie sind entschlossen, eher nicht zu weichen,
3065 Bis du das Urteil unterzeichnet hast.

Achter Auftritt.

Burleigh und Davison mit einer Schrift. Die Vorigen.

Elisabeth.

Was bringt Ihr, Davison?

Davison nähert sich, ernsthaft.

Du hast befohlen,

O Königin —

Elisabeth.

Was ist's?

Indem sie die Schrift ergreifen will, schauert sie zusammen und fährt zurück.

O Gott!

Burleigh.

Gehorche

Der Stimme des Volks, sie ist die Stimme Gottes.

Elisabeth
unentschlossen mit sich selbst kämpfend.

O meine Lords! Wer sagt mir, ob ich wirklich
3070 Die Stimme meines ganzen Volks, die Stimme
Der Welt vernehme! Ach, wie sehr befürcht' ich,
Wenn ich dem Wunsch der Menge nun gehorcht,
Daß eine ganz verschiedne Stimme sich
Wird hören lassen — ja, daß eben die,
3075 Die jetzt gewaltsam zu der That mich treiben,
Mich, wenn's vollbracht ist, strenge tadeln werden!

Neunter Auftritt.

Graf Shrewsbury zu den Vorigen.

Shrewsbury

kommt in großer Bewegung.

Man will dich übereilen, Königin!
O, halte fest, sei standhaft!

Indem er Davison mit der Schrift gewahr wird.

Oder ist es
Geschehen? Ist es wirklich? Ich erblicke
3080 Ein unglückselig Blatt in dieser Hand.
Das komme meiner Königin jetzt nicht
Vor Augen.

Elisabeth.

Edler Shrewsbury! Man zwingt mich.

Shrewsbury.

Wer kann dich zwingen? Du bist Herrscherin,
Hier gilt es, deine Majestät zu zeigen!
3085 Gebiete Schweigen jenen rohen Stimmen,
Die sich erdreisten, deinem Königswillen
Zwang anzuthun, dein Urteil zu regieren.
Die Furcht, ein blinder Wahn bewegt das Volk,
Du selbst bist außer dir, bist schwer gereizt,
3090 Du bist ein Mensch, und jetzt kannst du nicht richten.

Burleigh.

Gerichtet ist schon längst. Hier ist kein Urteil
Zu fällen, zu vollziehen ist's.

Kent.

der sich bei Shrewsburys Eintritt entfernt hat, kommt zurück.

Der Auflauf wächst, das Volk ist länger nicht
Zu bändigen.

Elisabeth zu Shrewsbury.

Ihr seht, wie sie mich drängen!

Shrewsbury.

3095 Nur Aufschub fordr' ich. Dieser Federzug
Entscheidet deines Lebens Glück und Frieden.
Du hast es Jahre lang bedacht, soll dich
Der Augenblick im Sturme mit sich führen?
Nur kurzen Aufschub! Sammle dein Gemüt,
3100 Erwarte eine ruhigere Stunde!

Burleigh heftig.

Erwarte, zögre, säume, bis das Reich
In Flammen steht, bis es der Feindin endlich
Gelingt, den Mordstreich wirklich zu vollführen.
Dreimal hat ihn ein Gott von dir entfernt.
3105 Heut hat er nahe dich berührt; noch einmal
Ein Wunder hoffen, hieße Gott versuchen.

Shrewsbury.

Der Gott, der dich durch seine Wunderhand
Viermal erhielt, der heut dem schwachen Arm
Des Greisen Kraft gab, einen Wütenden
3110 Zu überwält'gen — er verdient Vertrauen!
Ich will die Stimme der Gerechtigkeit
Jetzt nicht erheben, jetzt ist nicht die Zeit,
Du kannst in diesem Sturme sie nicht hören.
Dies eine nur vernimm! Du zitterst jetzt

3115 Vor dieser lebenden Maria. Nicht
Die Lebende hast du zu fürchten. Zittre vor
Der Toten, der Enthaupteten! Sie wird
Vom Grab' erstehen, eine Zwietrachtsgöttin,
Ein Rachegeist in deinem Reich herumgehn,
3120 Und deines Volkes Herzen von dir wenden.
Jetzt haßt der Britte die Gefürchtete,
Er wird sie rächen, wenn sie nicht mehr ist.
Nicht mehr die Feindin seines Glaubens, nur
Die Enkeltochter seiner Könige,
3125 Des Hasses Opfer und der Eifersucht
Wird er in der Bejammerten erblicken!
Schnell wirst du die Veränderung erfahren.
Durchziehe London, wenn die blut'ge That
Geschehen, zeige dich dem Volk, das sonst
3130 Sich jubelnd um dich her ergoß, du wirst
Ein andres England sehn, ein andres Volk,
Denn dich umgiebt nicht mehr die herrliche
Gerechtigkeit, die alle Herzen dir
Besiegte! Furcht, die schreckliche Begleitung
3135 Der Tyrannei, wird schaudernd vor dir herziehn,
Und jede Straße, wo du gehst, veröden.
Du hast das Letzte, Äußerste gethan,
Welch Haupt steht fest, wenn dieses heil'ge fiel!

Elisabeth.

Ach, Shrewsbury! Ihr habt mir heut das Leben
3140 Gerettet, habt des Mörders Dolch von mir
Gewendet — Warum ließet Ihr ihm nicht
Den Lauf? So wäre jeder Streit geendigt,
Und alles Zweifels ledig, rein von Schuld,
Läg' ich in meiner stillen Gruft! Fürwahr!

3145 Ich bin des Lebens und des Herrschens müd'.
Muß eine von uns Königinnen fallen,
Damit die andre lebe — und es ist
Nicht anders, das erkenn' ich — kann denn ich
Nicht die sein, welche weicht? Mein Volk mag wählen,
3150 Ich geb' ihm seine Majestät zurück.
Gott ist mein Zeuge, daß ich nicht für mich,
Nur für das Beste meines Volks gelebt.
Hofft es von dieser schmeichlerischen Stuart,
Der jüngern Königin, glücklichere Tage,
3155 So steig' ich gern von diesem Thron, und kehre
In Woodstocks stille Einsamkeit zurück,
Wo meine anspruchlose Jugend lebte,
Wo ich, vom Tand der Erdengröße fern,
Die Hoheit in mir selber fand — Bin ich
3160 Zur Herrscherin doch nicht gemacht! Der Herrscher
Muß hart sein können, und mein Herz ist weich.
Ich habe diese Insel lange glücklich
Regiert, weil ich nur brauchte zu beglücken.
Es kommt die erste schwere Königspflicht,
3165 Und ich empfinde meine Ohnmacht —

Burleigh.

Nun bei Gott!
Wenn ich so ganz unkönigliche Worte
Aus meiner Königin Mund vernehmen muß,
So wär's Verrat an meiner Pflicht, Verrat
Am Vaterlande, länger still zu schweigen.
3170 — Du sagst, du liebst dein Volk, mehr als dich selbst,
Das zeige jetzt! Erwähle nicht den Frieden
Für dich und überlaß das Reich den Stürmen.
— Denk' an die Kirche! Soll mit dieser Stuart

Der alte Aberglaube wiederkehren?
3175 Der Mönch aufs neu' hier herrschen, der Legat
Aus Rom gezogen kommen, unsre Kirchen
Verschließen, unsre Könige entthronen?
— Die Seelen aller deiner Unterthanen,
Ich fordre sie von dir — Wie du jetzt handelst,
3180 Sind sie gerettet oder sind verloren.
Hier ist nicht Zeit zu weichlichem Erbarmen,
Des Volkes Wohlfahrt ist die höchste Pflicht;
Hat Shrewsbury das Leben dir gerettet,
So will ich England retten — das ist mehr!

Elisabeth.

3185 Man überlasse mich mir selbst! Bei Menschen ist
Nicht Rat noch Trost in dieser großen Sache.
Ich trage sie dem höhern Richter vor.
Was der mich lehrt, das will ich thun — Entfernt euch,
Mylords!

Zu Davison.

Ihr, Sir, könnt in der Nähe bleiben!

Die Lords gehen ab. Shrewsbury allein bleibt noch einige Augenblicke vor der Königin stehen, mit bedeutungsvollem Blick, dann entfernt er sich langsam, mit einem Ausdruck des tiefsten Schmerzes.

Zehnter Auftritt.

Elisabeth allein.

3190 O Sklaverei des Volksdiensts! Schmähliche
Knechtschaft — Wie bin ich's müde, diesem Götzen
Zu schmeicheln, den mein Innerstes verachtet!

Wann soll ich frei auf diesem Throne stehn!
Die Meinung muß ich ehren, um das Lob
3195 Der Menge buhlen, einem Pöbel muß ich's
Recht machen, dem der Gaukler nur gefällt.
O, der ist noch nicht König, der der Welt
Gefallen muß! Nur der ist's, der bei seinem Thun
Nach keines Menschen Beifall braucht zu fragen. –

3200 Warum hab' ich Gerechtigkeit geübt,
Willkür gehaßt mein Leben lang, daß ich
Für diese erste unvermeidliche
Gewaltthat selbst die Hände mir gefesselt!
Das Muster, das ich selber gab, verdammt mich!
3205 War ich tyrannisch, wie die spanische
Maria war, mein Vorfahr auf dem Thron, ich könnte
Jetzt ohne Tadel Königsblut verspritzen!
Doch war's denn meine eigne freie Wahl,
Gerecht zu sein? Die allgewaltige
3210 Notwendigkeit, die auch das freie Wollen
Der Könige zwingt, gebot mir diese Tugend.

Umgeben rings von Feinden, hält mich nur
Die Volksgunst auf dem angefochtnen Thron.
Mich zu vernichten streben alle Mächte
3215 Des festen Landes. Unversöhnlich schleudert
Der röm'sche Papst den Bannfluch auf mein Haupt;
Mit falschem Bruderkuß verrät mich Frankreich,
Und offnen, wütenden Vertilgungskrieg
Bereitet mir der Spanier auf den Meeren.
3220 So steh' ich kämpfend gegen eine Welt,
Ein wehrlos Weib! Mit hohen Tugenden
Muß ich die Blöße meines Rechts bedecken,

Den Flecken meiner fürstlichen Geburt,
Wodurch der eigne Vater mich geschändet.
3225 Umsonst bedeck' ich ihn — Der Gegner Haß
Hat ihn entblößt, und stellt mir diese Stuart,
Ein ewig drohendes Gespenst, entgegen.

Nein, diese Furcht soll endigen!
Ihr Haupt soll fallen. Ich will Frieden haben!
3230 — Sie ist die Furie meines Lebens! mir
Ein Plagegeist vom Schicksal angeheftet.
Wo ich mir eine Freude, eine Hoffnung
Gepflanzt, da liegt die Höllenschlange mir
Im Wege. Sie entreißt mir den Geliebten,
3235 Den Bräut'gam raubt sie mir! Maria Stuart
Heißt jedes Unglück, das mich niederschlägt!
Ist sie aus den Lebendigen vertilgt,
Frei bin ich, wie die Luft auf den Gebirgen.

Stillschweigen.

Mit welchem Hohn sie auf mich niedersah,
3240 Als sollte mich der Blick zu Boden blitzen!
Ohnmächtige! Ich führe beſſ're Waffen;
Sie treffen tödlich, und du bist nicht mehr!

Mit raschem Schritt nach dem Tische gehend und die Feder ergreifend.

Ein Bastard bin ich dir? — Unglückliche!
Ich bin es nur, solang' du lebst und atmest.
3245 Der Zweifel meiner fürstlichen Geburt,
Er ist getilgt, sobald ich dich vertilge.
Sobald dem Britten keine Wahl mehr bleibt,
Bin ich im echten Ehebett geboren!

Sie unterschreibt mit einem raschen, festen Federzug, läßt dann die Feder fallen und tritt mit einem Ausdruck des Schreckens zurück. Nach einer Pause klingelt sie.

Elfter Auftritt.

Elisabeth. Davison.

Elisabeth.

Wo sind die andern Lords?

Davison.

Sie sind gegangen,
3250 Das aufgebrachte Volk zur Ruh zu bringen.
Das Toben war auch augenblicks gestillt,
Sobald der Graf von Shrewsbury sich zeigte.
„Der ist's, das ist er!" riefen hundert Stimmen;
„Der rettete die Königin! Hört ihn,
3255 Den bravsten Mann in England!" Nun begann
Der edle Talbot und verwies dem Volk
In sanften Worten sein gewaltsames
Beginnen, sprach so kraftvoll überzeugend,
Daß alles sich besänftigte und still
3260 Vom Platze schlich.

Elisabeth.

Die wankelmüt'ge Menge,
Die jeder Wind herumtreibt! Wehe dem,
Der auf dies Rohr sich lehnet! — Es ist gut,
Sir Davison. Ihr könnt nun wieder gehn.

Wie sich jener nach der Thüre gewendet.

Und dieses Blatt — Nehmt es zurück — Ich leg's
3265 In Eure Hände.

Davison
wirft einen Blick in das Papier und erschrickt.

Königin! Dein Name!
Du hast entschieden?

Elisabeth.

— Unterschreiben sollt' ich.
Ich hab's gethan. Ein Blatt Papier entscheidet
Noch nicht, ein Name tötet nicht.

Davison.

Dein Name, Königin, unter dieser Schrift
3270 Entscheidet alles, tötet, ist ein Strahl
Des Donners, der geflügelt trifft — Dies Blatt
Befiehlt den Kommissarien, dem Sherif,
Nach Fotheringhayschloß sich steh'nden Fußes
Zur Königin von Schottland zu verfügen,
3275 Den Tod ihr anzukündigen, und schnell,
Sobald der Morgen tagt, ihn zu vollziehn.
Hier ist kein Aufschub! Jene hat gelebt,
Wenn ich dies Blatt aus meinen Händen gebe.

Elisabeth.

Ja, Sir! Gott legt ein wichtig groß Geschick
3280 In Eure schwachen Hände. Fleht ihn an,
Daß er mit seiner Weisheit Euch erleuchte!
Ich geh' und überlass' Euch Eurer Pflicht.

Sie will gehen.

Davison tritt ihr in den Weg.

Nein, meine Königin! Verlaß mich nicht,
Eh du mir deinen Willen kund gethan.
3285 Bedarf es hier noch einer andern Weisheit,
Als dein Gebot buchstäblich zu befolgen?
— Du legst dies Blatt in meine Hand, daß ich
Zu schleuniger Vollziehung es befördre?

Elisabeth.

Das werdet Ihr nach Eurer Klugheit —

Davison

schnell und erschrocken einfallend.

Nicht

3290 Nach meiner! Das verhüte Gott! Gehorsam
Ist meine ganze Klugheit. Deinem Diener
Darf hier nichts zu entscheiden übrig bleiben.
Ein klein Versehn wär' hier ein Königsmord,
Ein unabsehbar, ungeheures Unglück.
3295 Vergönne mir, in dieser großen Sache
Dein blindes Werkzeug willenlos zu sein!
In klare Worte fasse deine Meinung,
Was soll mit diesem Blutbefehl geschehn?

Elisabeth.

— Sein Name spricht es aus.

Davison.

3300 So willst du, daß er gleich vollzogen werde?

Elisabeth zögernd.

Das sag' ich nicht, und zittre, es zu denken.

Davison.

Du willst, daß ich ihn länger noch bewahre?

Elisabeth schnell.

Auf Eure Gefahr! Ihr haftet für die Folgen.

Davison.

Ich? Heil'ger Gott! — Sprich, Königin! Was willst du?

Elisabeth ungeduldig.

3305 Ich will, daß dieser unglücksel'gen Sache
Nicht mehr gedacht soll werden, daß ich endlich
Will Ruhe davor haben und auf ewig.

Davison.

Es kostet dir ein einzig Wort. O, sage,
Bestimme, was mit dieser Schrift soll werden!

Elisabeth.

3310 Ich hab's gesagt, und quält mich nun nicht weiter!

Davison.

Du hättest es gesagt? Du hast mir nichts
Gesagt — O, es gefalle meiner Königin,
Sich zu erinnern.

Elisabeth stampft auf den Boden.

Unerträglich!

Davison.

Habe Nachsicht
Mit mir! Ich kam seit wenig Monden erst
3315 In dieses Amt! Ich kenne nicht die Sprache
Der Höfe und der Könige — In schlicht
Einfacher Sitte bin ich aufgewachsen;
Drum habe du Geduld mit deinem Knecht!
Laß dich das Wort nicht reun, das mich belehrt,
3320 Mich klar macht über meine Pflicht —

Er nähert sich ihr in flehender Stellung, sie kehrt ihm den Rücken zu, er steht in Verzweiflung, dann spricht er mit entschloßnem Ton.

Nimm dies Papier zurück! Nimm es zurück!
Es wird mir glühend Feuer in den Händen.
Nicht mich erwähle, dir in diesem furchtbaren
Geschäft zu dienen!

Elisabeth.

Thut, was Eures Amts ist!

Sie geht ab.

Zwölfter Auftritt.

Davison, gleich darauf Burleigh.

Davison.

3325 Sie geht! Sie läßt mich ratlos, zweifelnd stehn
Mit diesem fürchterlichen Blatt — Was thu' ich?
Soll ich's bewahren? Soll ich's übergeben?

Zu Burleigh, der hereintritt.

O, gut, gut, daß Ihr kommt, Mylord! Ihr seid's,
Der mich in dieses Staatsamt eingeführt.
3330 Befreiet mich davon! Ich übernahm es,
Unkundig seiner Rechenschaft! Laßt mich
Zurückgehn in die Dunkelheit, wo Ihr
Mich fandet, ich gehöre nicht auf diesen Platz —

Burleigh.

Was ist Euch, Sir? Faßt Euch! Wo ist das Urteil?
3335 Die Königin ließ Euch rufen.

Davison.

Sie verließ mich
In heft'gem Zorn. O, ratet mir! Helft mir!
Reißt mich aus dieser Höllenangst des Zweifels!
Hier ist das Urteil — Es ist unterschrieben.

Burleigh hastig.

Ist es? O, gebt! Gebt her!

Davison.

Ich darf nicht.

Burleigh.

Was?

Davison.

3340 Sie hat mir ihren Willen noch nicht deutlich —

Burleigh.

Nicht deutlich! Sie hat unterschrieben. Gebt!

Davison.

Ich soll's vollziehen lassen — soll es nicht
Vollziehen lassen — Gott! Weiß ich, was ich soll?

Burleigh heftiger dringend.

Gleich, augenblicks sollt Ihr's vollziehen lassen.
3345 Gebt her! Ihr seid verloren, wenn Ihr säumt.

Davison.

Ich bin verloren, wenn ich's übereile.

Burleigh.

Ihr seid ein Thor! Ihr seid von Sinnen! Gebt!

Er entreißt ihm die Schrift und eilt damit ab.

Davison ihm nacheilend.

Was macht Ihr? Bleibt! Ihr stürzt mich in's Verderben!

Fünfter Aufzug.

Die Scene ist das Zimmer des ersten Aufzugs.

Erster Auftritt.

Hanna Kennedy in tiefe Trauer gekleidet, mit verweinten Augen und einem großen, aber stillen Schmerz, ist beschäftigt, Pakete und Briefe zu versiegeln. Oft unterbricht sie der Jammer in ihrem Geschäft, und man sieht sie dazwischen still beten. Paulet und Drury, gleichfalls in schwarzen Kleidern, treten ein, ihnen folgen viele Bediente, welche goldne und silberne Gefäße, Spiegel, Gemälde und andere Kostbarkeiten tragen und den Hintergrund des Zimmers damit anfüllen. Paulet überliefert der Amme ein Schmuckkästchen nebst einem Papier und bedeutet ihr durch Zeichen, daß es ein Verzeichnis der gebrachten Dinge enthalte. Beim Anblick dieser Reichtümer erneuert sich der Schmerz der Amme; sie versinkt in ein tiefes Trauern, indem jene sich still wieder entfernen. Melvil tritt ein.

Kennedy

schreit auf, sobald sie ihn gewahr wird.

Melvil! Ihr seid es! Euch erblick' ich wieder!

Melvil.

3350 Ja, treue Kennedy, wir sehn uns wieder!

Kennedy.

Nach langer, langer, schmerzenvoller Trennung!

Melvil.

Ein unglückselig, schmerzvoll Wiedersehn!

Kennedy.

O Gott! Ihr kommt —

Melvil.

Den letzten, ewigen
Abschied von meiner Königin zu nehmen.

Kennedy.

3355 Jetzt endlich, jetzt am Morgen ihres Todes,
Wird ihr die langentbehrte Gegenwart
Der Ihrigen vergönnt — O teurer Sir,
Ich will nicht fragen, wie es Euch erging,
Euch nicht die Leiden nennen, die wir litten,
3360 Seitdem man Euch von unsrer Seite riß.
Ach, dazu wird wohl einst die Stunde kommen!
O Melvil! Melvil! Mußten wir's erleben,
Den Anbruch dieses Tags zu sehn!

Melvil.

Laßt uns
Einander nicht erweichen! Weinen will ich,
3365 Solang' noch Leben in mir ist; nie soll
Ein Lächeln diese Wangen mehr erheitern,
Nie will ich dieses nächtliche Gewand
Mehr von mir legen! Ewig will ich trauern;
Doch heute will ich standhaft sein — Versprecht
3370 Auch Ihr mir, Euren Schmerz zu mäßigen —
Und wenn die andern alle der Verzweiflung
Sich trostlos überlassen, lasset uns
Mit männlich edler Fassung ihr vorangehn
Und ihr ein Stab sein auf dem Todesweg!

Kennedy.

3375 Melvil! Ihr seid im Irrtum, wenn Ihr glaubt,
Die Königin bedürfe unsers Beistands,

Um standhaft in den Tod zu gehn! Sie selber ist's,
Die uns das Beispiel edler Fassung giebt.
Seid ohne Furcht! Maria Stuart wird
3380 Als eine Königin und Heldin sterben.

Melvil.

Nahm sie die Todespost mit Fassung auf?
Man sagt, daß sie nicht vorbereitet war.

Kennedy.

Das war sie nicht. Ganz andre Schrecken waren's,
Die meine Lady ängstigten. Nicht vor dem Tod,
3385 Vor dem Befreier zitterte Maria.
— Freiheit war uns verheißen. Diese Nacht
Versprach uns Mortimer von hier wegzuführen,
Und zwischen Furcht und Hoffnung, zweifelhaft,
Ob sie dem kecken Jüngling ihre Ehre
3390 Und fürstliche Person vertrauen dürfe,
Erwartete die Königin den Morgen.
— Da wird ein Auflauf in dem Schloß, ein Pochen
Schreckt unser Ohr, und vieler Hämmer Schlag.
Wir glauben, die Befreier zu vernehmen,
3395 Die Hoffnung winkt, der süße Trieb des Lebens
Wacht unwillkürlich, allgewaltig auf —
Da öffnet sich die Thür — Sir Paulet ist's,
Der uns verkündigt — daß — die Zimmerer
Zu unsern Füßen das Gerüst aufschlagen!

Sie wendet sich ab, von heftigem Schmerz ergriffen.

Melvil.

3400 Gerechter Gott! O, sagt mir! wie ertrug
Maria diesen fürchterlichen Wechsel?

Kennedy

nach einer Pause, worin sie sich wieder etwas gefaßt hat.

Man löst sich nicht allmählich von dem Leben!
Mit Einem Mal, schnell, augenblicklich muß
Der Tausch geschehen zwischen Zeitlichem
3405 Und Ewigem, und Gott gewährte meiner Lady
In diesem Augenblick, der Erde Hoffnung
Zurück zu stoßen mit entschloßner Seele,
Und glaubenvoll den Himmel zu ergreifen.
Kein Merkmal bleicher Furcht, kein Wort der Klage
3410 Entehrte meine Königin — Dann erst,
Als sie Lord Lesters schändlichen Verrat
Vernahm, das unglückselige Geschick
Des werten Jünglings, der sich ihr geopfert,
Des alten Ritters tiefen Jammer sah,
3415 Dem seine letzte Hoffnung starb durch sie,
Da flossen ihre Thränen; nicht das eigne Schicksal,
Der fremde Jammer preßte sie ihr ab.

Melvil.

Wo ist sie jetzt? Könnt Ihr mich zu ihr bringen?

Kennedy.

Den Rest der Nacht durchwachte sie mit Beten,
3420 Nahm von den teuern Freunden schriftlich Abschied
Und schrieb ihr Testament mit eigner Hand.
Jetzt pflegt sie einen Augenblick der Ruh,
Der letzte Schlaf erquickt sie.

Melvil.

Wer ist bei ihr?

Kennedy.

Ihr Leibarzt Burgoyn und ihre Frauen.

Zweiter Auftritt.

Margareta Kurl zu den Vorigen.

Kennedy.

3425 Was bringt Ihr, Mistreß? Ist die Lady wach?

Kurl ihre Thränen trocknend.

Schon angekleidet — Sie verlangt nach Euch.

Kennedy.

Ich komme.

Zu Melvil, der sie begleiten will.

Folgt mir nicht, bis ich die Lady
Auf Euren Anblick vorbereitet!

Geht hinein.

Kurl.

Melvil!
Der alte Haushofmeister!

Melvil.

Ja, der bin ich!

Kurl.

3430 O, dieses Haus braucht keines Meisters mehr!
— Melvil! Ihr kommt von London. Wißt Ihr mir
Von meinem Manne nichts zu sagen?

Melvil.

Er wird auf freien Fuß gesetzt, sagt man,
Sobald —

Kurl.

Sobald die Königin nicht mehr ist!
3435 O der nichtswürdig schändliche Verräter!
Er ist der Mörder dieser teuren Lady;
Sein Zeugnis, sagt man, habe sie verurteilt.

Melvil.

So ist's.

Kurl.

O, seine Seele sei verflucht
Bis in die Hölle! Er hat falsch gezeugt —

Melvil.

3440 Mylady Kurl! Bedenket Eure Reden!

Kurl.

Beschwören will ich's vor Gerichtes Schranken,
Ich will es ihm ins Antlitz wiederholen,
Die ganze Welt will ich damit erfüllen.
Sie stirbt unschuldig,—

Melvil.

O, das gebe Gott!

Dritter Auftritt.

Burgoyn zu den Vorigen. Hernach Hanna Kennedy.

Burgoyn erblickt Melvil.

3445 O Melvil!

Melvil ihn umarmend.

Burgoyn!

Burgoyn zu Margareta Kurl.

Besorget einen Becher
Mit Wein für unsre Lady! Machet hurtig!

Kurl geht ab.

Melvil.

Wie? Ist der Königin nicht wohl?

Burgoyn.

Sie fühlt sich stark, sie täuscht ihr Heldenmut,
Und keiner Speise glaubt sie zu bedürfen;
3450 Doch ihrer wartet noch ein schwerer Kampf,
Und ihre Feinde sollen sich nicht rühmen,
Daß Furcht des Todes ihre Wangen bleichte,
Wenn die Natur aus Schwachheit unterliegt.

Melvil zur Amme, die hereintritt.

Will sie mich sehn?

Kennedy.

Gleich wird sie selbst hier sein.
3455 — Ihr scheint Euch mit Verwundrung umzusehn,
Und Eure Blicke fragen mich: Was soll
Das Prachtgerät in diesem Ort des Todes?
— O Sir! Wir litten Mangel, da wir lebten,
Erst mit dem Tode kommt der Überfluß zurück.

Vierter Auftritt.

Vorige. Zwei andre Kammerfrauen der Maria, gleichfalls in Trauerkleidern. Sie brechen bei Melvils Anblick in laute Thränen aus.

Melvil.

3460 Was für ein Anblick! Welch ein Wiedersehn!
Gertrude! Rosamund!

Zweite Kammerfrau.

Sie hat uns von sich
Geschickt! Sie will zum letztenmal allein
Mit Gott sich unterhalten!

Es kommen noch zwei weibliche Bediente, wie die vorigen in Trauer, die mit stummen Gebärden ihren Jammer ausdrücken.

Fünfter Auftritt.

Margareta Kurl zu den Vorigen. Sie trägt einen goldnen Becher mit Wein, und setzt ihn auf den Tisch, indem sie sich bleich und zitternd an einen Stuhl hält.

Melvil.

Was ist Euch, Mistreß? Was entsetzt Euch so?

Kurl.

3465 O Gott!

Burgoyn.

Was habt Ihr?

Kurl.

Was mußt' ich erblicken!

Melvil.

Kommt zu Euch! Sagt uns, was es ist!

Kurl.

Als ich
Mit diesem Becher Wein die große Treppe
Herauf stieg, die zur untern Halle führt,
Da that die Thür sich auf — ich sah hinein —
3470 Ich sah — o Gott! —

Melvil.

Was saht Ihr? Fasset Euch!

Kurl.

Schwarz überzogen waren alle Wände,
Ein groß Gerüst, mit schwarzem Tuch beschlagen,
Erhob sich von dem Boden, mitten drauf
Ein schwarzer Block, ein Kissen, und daneben
3475 Ein blankgeschliffnes Beil — Voll Menschen war
Der Saal, die um das Mordgerüst sich drängten
Und, heiße Blutgier in dem Blick, das Opfer
Erwarteten.

Die Kammerfrauen.

O Gott sei unsrer Lady gnädig!

Melvil.

Faßt euch! Sie kommt!

Sechster Auftritt.

Die Vorigen. Maria. Sie ist weiß und festlich gekleidet; am Halse trägt sie an einer Kette von kleinen Kugeln ein Agnus Dei, ein Rosenkranz hängt am Gürtel herab, sie hat ein Kruzifix in der Hand und ein Diadem in den Haaren, ihr großer schwarzer Schleier ist zurückgeschlagen. Bei ihrem Eintritt weichen die Anwesenden zu beiden Seiten zurück und drücken den heftigsten Schmerz aus. Melvil ist mit einer unwillkürlichen Bewegung auf die Kniee gesunken.

Maria

mit ruhiger Hoheit im ganzen Kreise herumsehend.

3480 Was klagt ihr? Warum weint ihr? Freuen solltet
Ihr euch mit mir, daß meiner Leiden Ziel

Nun endlich naht, daß meine Bande fallen,
Mein Kerker aufgeht, und die frohe Seele sich
Auf Engelsflügeln schwingt zur ew'gen Freiheit.
3485 Da, als ich in die Macht der stolzen Feindin
Gegeben war, Unwürdiges erduldend,
Was einer freien, großen Königin
Nicht ziemt, da war es Zeit, um mich zu weinen!
— Wohlthätig, heilend, nahet mir der Tod,
3490 Der ernste Freund! Mit seinen schwarzen Flügeln
Bedeckt er meine Schmach — Den Menschen adelt,
Den tiefgesunkenen, das letzte Schicksal.
Die Krone fühl' ich wieder auf dem Haupt,
Den würd'gen Stolz in meiner edeln Seele!

Indem sie einige Schritte weiter vortritt.

3495 Wie? Melvil hier? — Nicht also, edler Sir!
Steht auf! Ihr seid zu Eurer Königin
Triumph, zu ihrem Tode nicht gekommen.
Mir wird ein Glück zu teil, wie ich es nimmer
Gehoffet, daß mein Nachruhm doch nicht ganz
3500 In meiner Feinde Händen ist, daß doch
Ein Freund mir, ein Bekenner meines Glaubens,
Als Zeuge dasteht in der Todesstunde.
— Sagt, edler Ritter! Wie erging es Euch
In diesem feindlichen, unholden Lande,
3505 Seitdem man Euch von meiner Seite riß?
Die Sorg' um Euch hat oft mein Herz bekümmert.

Melvil.

Mich drückte sonst kein Mangel als der Schmerz
Um dich, und meine Ohnmacht, dir zu dienen!

Maria.

Wie steht's um Didier, meinen alten Kämmrer?

3510 Doch der Getreue schläft wohl lange schon
Den ew'gen Schlaf, denn er war hoch an Jahren.

Melvil.

Gott hat ihm diese Gnade nicht erzeigt,
Er lebt, um deine Jugend zu begraben.

Maria.

Daß mir vor meinem Tode noch das Glück
3515 Geworden wäre, ein geliebtes Haupt
Der teuern Blutsverwandten zu umfassen!
Doch ich soll sterben unter Fremdlingen,
Nur eure Thränen soll ich fließen sehn!
— Melvil, die letzten Wünsche für die Meinen
3520 Leg' ich in Eure treue Brust — Ich segne
Den allerchristlichsten König, meinen Schwager,
Und Frankreichs ganzes königliches Haus —
Ich segne meinen Öhm, den Kardinal,
Und Heinrich Guise, meinen edlen Vetter.
3525 Ich segne auch den Papst, den heiligen
Statthalter Christi, der mich wieder segnet,
Und den kathol'schen König, der sich edelmütig
Zu meinem Retter, meinem Rächer anbot —
Sie alle stehn in meinem Testament;
3530 Sie werden die Geschenke meiner Liebe,
Wie arm sie sind, darum gering nicht achten.

Sich zu ihren Dienern wendend.

Euch hab' ich meinem königlichen Bruder
Von Frankreich anempfohlen, er wird sorgen
Für euch, ein neues Vaterland euch geben.
3535 Und ist euch meine letzte Bitte wert,
Bleibt nicht in England, daß der Britte nicht
Sein stolzes Herz an eurem Unglück weide,

Nicht die im Staube seh', die mir gedient.
Bei diesem Bildnis des Gekreuzigten
3540 Gelobet mir, dies unglücksel'ge Land
Alsbald, wenn ich dahin bin, zu verlassen!

Melvil berührt das Kruzifix.

Ich schwöre dir's im Namen dieser aller.

Maria.

Was ich, die Arme, die Beraubte, noch besaß,
Worüber mir vergönnt ist frei zu schalten,
3545 Das hab' ich unter euch verteilt; man wird,
Ich hoff' es, meinen letzten Willen ehren.
Auch was ich auf dem Todeswege trage,
Gehöret euch — Vergönnet mir noch einmal
Der Erde Glanz auf meinem Weg zum Himmel!

Zu den Fräulein.

3550 Dir, meine Alix, Gertrud, Rosamund,
Bestimm' ich meine Perlen, meine Kleider,
Denn eure Jugend freut sich noch des Putzes.
Du, Margareta, hast das nächste Recht
An meine Großmut, denn ich lasse dich
3555 Zurück als die Unglücklichste von allen.
Daß ich des Gatten Schuld an dir nicht räche,
Wird mein Vermächtnis offenbaren — Dich,
O meine treue Hanna, reizet nicht
Der Wert des Goldes, nicht der Steine Pracht,
3560 Dir ist das höchste Kleinod mein Gedächtnis.
Nimm dieses Tuch! Ich hab's mit eigner Hand
Für dich gestickt in meines Kummers Stunden,
Und meine heißen Thränen eingewoben.
Mit diesem Tuch wirst du die Augen mir verbinden,

3565 Wenn es so weit ist — diesen letzten Dienst
Wünsch' ich von meiner Hanna zu empfangen.

Kennedy.

O Melvil! Ich ertrag' es nicht!

Maria.

Kommt alle!
Kommt und empfangt mein letztes Lebewohl!

Sie reicht ihre Hände hin; eins nach dem andern fällt ihr zu Füßen und küßt die dargebotne Hand unter heftigem Weinen.

Leb' wohl, Margreta — Alix, lebe wohl —
3570 Dank, Burgoyn, für Eure treuen Dienste —
Dein Mund brennt heiß, Gertrude — Ich bin viel
Gehasset worden, doch auch viel geliebt!
Ein edler Mann beglücke meine Gertrud,
Denn Liebe fordert dieses glüh'nde Herz —
3575 Bertha! Du hast das beßre Teil erwählt,
Die keusche Braut des Himmels willst du werden!
O, eile, dein Gelübde zu vollziehn!
Betrüglich sind die Güter dieser Erden,
Das lern' an deiner Königin! Nichts weiter!
3580 Lebt wohl! Lebt wohl! Lebt ewig wohl!

Sie wendet sich schnell von ihnen; alle, bis auf Melvil, entfernen sich.

Siebenter Auftritt.

Maria. Melvil.

Maria.

Ich habe alles Zeitliche berichtigt,
Und hoffe keines Menschen Schuldnerin
Aus dieser Welt zu scheiden — Eins nur ist's,

Melvil, was der beklemmten Seele noch
3585 Verwehrt, sich frei und freudig zu erheben.

Melvil.

Entdecke mir's! Erleichtre deine Brust,
Dem treuen Freund vertraue deine Sorgen!

Maria.

Ich stehe an dem Rand der Ewigkeit;
Bald soll ich treten vor den höchsten Richter,
3590 Und noch hab' ich den Heil'gen nicht versöhnt.
Versagt ist mir der Priester meiner Kirche.
Des Sakramentes heil'ge Himmelspeise
Verschmäh' ich aus den Händen falscher Priester.
Im Glauben meiner Kirche will ich sterben,
3595 Denn der allein ist's, welcher selig macht.

Melvil.

Beruhige dein Herz! Dem Himmel gilt
Der feurig fromme Wunsch statt des Vollbringens.
Tyrannenmacht kann nur die Hände fesseln,
Des Herzens Andacht hebt sich frei zu Gott;
3600 Das Wort ist tot, der Glaube macht lebendig.

Maria.

Ach, Melvil! Nicht allein genug ist sich
Das Herz, ein irdisch Pfand bedarf der Glaube,
Das hohe Himmlische sich zuzueignen.
Drum ward der Gott zum Menschen, und verschloß
3605 Die unsichtbaren himmlischen Geschenke
Geheimnisvoll in einen sichtbar'n Leib.
— Die Kirche ist's, die heilige, die hohe,
Die zu dem Himmel uns die Leiter baut;
Die allgemeine, die kathol'sche heißt sie,

3610 Denn nur der Glaube aller stärkt den Glauben;
Wo Tausende anbeten und verehren,
Da wird die Glut zur Flamme, und beflügelt
Schwingt sich der Geist in alle Himmel auf.
— Ach, die Beglückten, die das froh geteilte
3615 Gebet versammelt in dem Haus des Herrn!
Geschmückt ist der Altar, die Kerzen leuchten,
Die Glocke tönt, der Weihrauch ist gestreut,
Der Bischof steht im reinen Meßgewand,
Er faßt den Kelch, er segnet ihn, er kündet
3620 Das hohe Wunder der Verwandlung an,
Und niederstürzt dem gegenwärt'gen Gotte
Das gläubig überzeugte Volk — Ach! Ich
Allein bin ausgeschlossen, nicht zu mir
In meinen Kerker dringt der Himmelsegen.

Melvil.

3625 Er dringt zu dir! Er ist dir nah! Vertraue
Dem Allvermögenden — der dürre Stab
Kann Zweige treiben in des Glaubens Hand!
Und der die Quelle aus dem Felsen schlug,
Kann dir im Kerker den Altar bereiten,
3630 Kann diesen Kelch, die irdische Erquickung,
Dir schnell in eine himmlische verwandeln.

Er ergreift den Kelch, der auf dem Tische steht.

Maria.

Melvil! Versteh' ich Euch? Ja! Ich versteh' Euch!
Hier ist kein Priester, keine Kirche, kein
Hochwürdiges — Doch der Erlöser spricht:
3635 Wo zwei versammelt sind in meinem Namen,
Da bin ich gegenwärtig unter ihnen.
Was weiht den Priester ein zum Mund des Herrn?

Das reine Herz, der unbefleckte Wandel.
— So seid Ihr mir, auch ungeweiht, ein Priester,
3640 Ein Bote Gottes, der mir Frieden bringt.
— Euch will ich meine letzte Beichte thun,
Und Euer Mund soll mir das Heil verkünden.

Melvil.

Wenn dich das Herz so mächtig dazu treibt,
So wisse, Königin, daß dir zum Troste
3645 Gott auch ein Wunder wohl verrichten kann.
Hier sei kein Priester, sagst du, keine Kirche,
Kein Leib des Herrn? — Du irrest dich. Hier ist
Ein Priester, und ein Gott ist hier zugegen.

Er entblößt bei diesen Worten das Haupt, zugleich zeigt er ihr eine Hostie in einer goldenen Schale.

— Ich bin ein Priester; deine letzte Beichte
3650 Zu hören, dir auf deinem Todesweg
Den Frieden zu verkündigen, hab' ich
Die sieben Weih'n auf meinem Haupt empfangen,
Und diese Hostie überbring' ich dir
Vom heil'gen Vater, die er selbst geweihet.

Maria.

3655 O, so muß an der Schwelle selbst des Todes
Mir noch ein himmlisch Glück bereitet sein!
Wie ein Unsterblicher auf goldnen Wolken
Herniederfährt, wie den Apostel einst
Der Engel führte aus des Kerkers Banden,
3660 Ihn hält kein Riegel, keines Hüters Schwert,
Er schreitet mächtig durch verschloss'ne Pforten,
Und im Gefängnis steht er glänzend da,
So überrascht mich hier der Himmelsbote,
Da jeder ird'sche Retter mich getäuscht!

3665 — Und Ihr, mein Diener einst, seid jetzt der Diener
Des höchsten Gottes, und sein heil'ger Mund!
Wie Eure Kniee sonst vor mir sich beugten,
So lieg' ich jetzt im Staub vor Euch.

Sie sinkt vor ihm nieder.

Melvil

indem er das Zeichen des Kreuzes über sie macht.

Im Namen
Des Vaters und des Sohnes und des Geistes!
3670 Maria, Königin! Hast du dein Herz
Erforschet, schwörst du und gelobest du,
Wahrheit zu beichten vor dem Gott der Wahrheit?

Maria.

Mein Herz liegt offen da vor dir und ihm.

Melvil.

Sprich, welcher Sünde zeiht dich dein Gewissen,
3675 Seitdem du Gott zum letzten Mal versöhnt?

Maria.

Von neid'schem Hasse war mein Herz erfüllt,
Und Rachgedanken tobten in dem Busen.
Vergebung hofft' ich Sünderin von Gott,
Und konnte nicht der Gegnerin vergeben.

Melvil.

3680 Bereuest du die Schuld, und ist's dein ernster
Entschluß, versöhnt aus dieser Welt zu scheiden?

Maria.

So wahr ich hoffe, daß mir Gott vergebe.

Melvil.

Welch andrer Sünde klagt das Herz dich an?

Maria.

Ach, nicht durch Haß allein, durch sünd'ge Liebe
3685 Noch mehr hab' ich das höchste Gut beleidigt.
Das eitle Herz ward zu dem Mann gezogen,
Der treulos mich verlassen und betrogen!

Melvil.

Bereuest du die Schuld, und hat dein Herz
Vom eiteln Abgott sich zu Gott gewendet?

Maria.

3690 Es war der schwerste Kampf, den ich bestand,
Zerrissen ist das letzte ird'sche Band.

Melvil.

Welch andrer Schuld verklagt dich dein Gewissen?

Maria.

Ach, eine frühe Blutschuld, längst gebeichtet,
Sie kehrt zurück mit neuer Schreckenskraft
3695 Im Augenblick der letzten Rechenschaft,
Und wälzt sich schwarz mir vor des Himmels Pforten.
Den König, meinen Gatten, ließ ich morden,
Und dem Verführer schenkt' ich Herz und Hand!
Streng büßt' ich's ab mit allen Kirchenstrafen,
3700 Doch in der Seele will der Wurm nicht schlafen.

Melvil.

Verklagt das Herz dich keiner andern Sünde,
Die du noch nicht gebeichtet und gebüßt?

Maria.

Jetzt weißt du alles, was mein Herz belastet.

Melvil.

Denk an die Nähe des Allwissenden!
3705 Der Strafen denke, die die heil'ge Kirche

Der mangelhaften Beichte droht! Das ist
Die Sünde zu dem ew'gen Tod, denn das
Ist wider seinen heil'gen Geist gefrevelt.

Maria.

So schenke mir die ew'ge Gnade Sieg
3710 Im letzten Kampf, als ich dir wissend nichts verschwieg.

Melvil.

Wie? Deinem Gott verhehlst du das Verbrechen,
Um dessentwillen dich die Menschen strafen?
Du sagst mir nichts von deinem blut'gen Anteil
An Babingtons und Parrys Hochverrat?
3715 Den zeitlichen Tod stirbst du für diese That,
Willst du auch noch den ew'gen dafür sterben?

Maria.

Ich bin bereit, zur Ewigkeit zu gehn;
Noch eh sich der Minutenzeiger wendet,
Werd' ich vor meines Richters Throne stehn;
3720 Doch wiederhol' ich's: meine Beichte ist vollendet.

Melvil.

Erwäg' es wohl! Das Herz ist ein Betrüger.
Du hast vielleicht mit list'gem Doppelsinn
Das Wort vermieden, das dich schuldig macht,
Obgleich der Wille das Verbrechen teilte.
3725 Doch wisse, keine Gaukelkunst berückt
Das Flammenauge, das ins Innre blickt!

Maria.

Ich habe alle Fürsten aufgeboten,
Mich aus unwürd'gen Banden zu befrein;
Doch nie hab' ich durch Vorsatz oder That
3730 Das Leben meiner Feindin angetastet!

Melvil.

So hätten deine Schreiber falsch gezeugt?

Maria.

Wie ich gesagt, so ist's. Was jene zeugten,
Das richte Gott!

Melvil.

So steigst du, überzeugt
Von deiner Unschuld, auf das Blutgerüste?

Maria.

3735 Gott würdigt mich, durch diesen unverdienten Tod
Die frühe schwere Blutschuld abzubüßen.

Melvil macht den Segen über sie.

So gehe hin, und sterbend büße sie!
Sink, ein ergebnes Opfer, am Altare!
Blut kann versöhnen, was das Blut verbrach;
3740 Du fehltest nur aus weiblichem Gebrechen,
Dem sel'gen Geiste folgen nicht die Schwächen
Der Sterblichkeit in die Verklärung nach.
Ich aber künde dir, kraft der Gewalt,
Die mir verliehen ist, zu lösen und zu binden,
3745 Erlassung an von allen deinen Sünden!
Wie du geglaubet, so geschehe dir!

Er reicht ihr die Hostie.

Nimm hin den Leib, er ist für dich geopfert!

Er ergreift den Kelch, der auf dem Tische steht, konsekriert ihn mit stillem Gebet, dann reicht er ihr denselben. Sie zögert, ihn anzunehmen, und weist ihn mit der Hand zurück.

Nimm hin das Blut, es ist für dich vergossen!
Nimm hin! Der Papst erzeigt dir diese Gunst!
3750 Im Tode noch sollst du das höchste Recht
Der Könige, das priesterliche, üben!

Sie empfängt den Kelch.

Und wie du jetzt dich in dem ird'schen Leib
Geheimnisvoll mit deinem Gott verbunden,
So wirst du dort in seinem Freudenreich,
3755 Wo keine Schuld mehr sein wird und kein Weinen,
Ein schön verklärter Engel, dich
Auf ewig mit dem Göttlichen vereinen.

Er setzt den Kelch nieder. Auf ein Geräusch, das gehört wird, bedeckt er sich das Haupt und geht an die Thüre; Maria bleibt in stiller Andacht auf den Knien liegen.

Melvil zurückkommend.

Dir bleibt ein harter Kampf noch zu bestehn.
Fühlst du dich stark genug, um jede Regung
3760 Der Bitterkeit, des Hasses zu besiegen?

Maria.

Ich fürchte keinen Rückfall. Meinen Haß
Und meine Liebe hab' ich Gott geopfert.

Melvil.

Nun, so bereite dich, die Lords von Lester
Und Burleigh zu empfangen. Sie sind da.

Achter Auftritt.

Die Vorigen. Burleigh. Leicester und Paulet. Leicester bleibt ganz in der Entfernung stehen, ohne die Augen aufzuschlagen. Burleigh, der seine Fassung beobachtet, tritt zwischen ihn und die Königin.

Burleigh.

3765 Ich komme, Lady Stuart, Eure letzten
Befehle zu empfangen.

Maria.

Dank, Mylord!

Burleigh.

Es ist der Wille meiner Königin,
Daß Euch nichts Billiges verweigert werde.

Maria.

Mein Testament nennt meine letzten Wünsche.
3770 Ich hab's in Ritter Paulets Hand gelegt,
Und bitte, daß es treu vollzogen werde.

Paulet.

Verlaßt Euch drauf!

Maria.

Ich bitte, meine Diener ungekränkt
Nach Schottland zu entlassen oder Frankreich,
3775 Wohin sie selber wünschen und begehren.

Burleigh.

Es sei, wie Ihr es wünscht.

Maria.

Und weil mein Leichnam
Nicht in geweihter Erde ruhen soll,
So dulde man, daß dieser treue Diener
Mein Herz nach Frankreich bringe zu den Meinen.
3780 — Ach! Es war immer dort!

Burleigh.

Es soll geschehn.
Habt Ihr noch sonst —

Maria.

Der Königin von England
Bringt meinen schwesterlichen Gruß — Sagt ihr,

Daß ich ihr meinen Tod von ganzem Herzen
Vergebe, meine Heftigkeit von gestern
3785 Ihr reuevoll abbitte — Gott erhalte sie,
Und schenk' ihr eine glückliche Regierung!

Burleigh.

Sprecht! Habt Ihr noch nicht bessern Rat erwählt?
Verschmäht Ihr noch den Beistand des Dechanten?

Maria.

Ich bin mit meinem Gott versöhnt — Sir Paulet!
3790 Ich hab' Euch schuldlos vieles Weh bereitet,
Des Alters Stütze Euch geraubt — O, laßt
Mich hoffen, daß Ihr meiner nicht mit Haß
Gedenket —

Paulet giebt ihr die Hand.

Gott sei mit Euch! Gehet hin im Frieden!

Neunter Auftritt.

Die Vorigen. Hanna Kennedy und die andern Frauen der Königin dringen herein mit Zeichen des Entsetzens; ihnen folgt der Sherif, einen weißen Stab in der Hand, hinter demselben sieht man durch die offen bleibende Thüre gewaffnete Männer.

Maria.

Was ist dir, Hanna? — Ja, nun ist es Zeit!
3795 Hier kommt der Sherif, uns zum Tod zu führen.
Es muß geschieden sein! Lebt wohl! Lebt wohl!

Ihre Frauen hängen sich an sie mit heftigem Schmerz; zu Melvil.

Ihr, werter Sir, und meine treue Hanna,

Sollt mich auf diesem letzten Gang begleiten.
Mylord, versagt mir diese Wohlthat nicht!

Burleigh.

3800 Ich habe dazu keine Vollmacht.

Maria.

Wie?
Die kleine Bitte könntet Ihr mir weigern?
Habt Achtung gegen mein Geschlecht! Wer soll
Den letzten Dienst mir leisten! Nimmermehr
Kann es der Wille meiner Schwester sein,
3805 Daß mein Geschlecht in mir beleidigt werde,
Der Männer rohe Hände mich berühren!

Burleigh.

Es darf kein Weib die Stufen des Gerüstes
Mit Euch besteigen — Ihr Geschrei und Jammern —

Maria.

Sie soll nicht jammern! Ich verbürge mich
3810 Für die gefaßte Seele meiner Hanna!
Seid gütig, Lord! O, trennt mich nicht im Sterben
Von meiner treuen Pflegerin und Amme!
Sie trug auf ihren Armen mich ins Leben,
Sie leite mich mit sanfter Hand zum Tod.

Paulet zu Burleigh.

3815 Laßt es geschehn!

Burleigh.

Es sei!

Maria.

Nun hab' ich nichts mehr
Auf dieser Welt —

Sie nimmt das Kruzifix und küßt es.

Mein Heiland! Mein Erlöser!
Wie du am Kreuz die Arme ausgespannt,
So breite sie jetzt aus, mich zu empfangen!

Sie wendet sich zu gehen; in diesem Augenblick begegnet ihr Auge dem Grafen Leicester, der bei ihrem Aufbruch unwillkürlich aufgefahren und nach ihr hingesehen. — Bei diesem Anblick zittert Maria, die Kniee versagen ihr, sie ist im Begriff hinzusinken; da ergreift sie Graf Leicester und empfängt sie in seinen Armen. Sie sieht ihn eine Zeitlang ernst und schweigend an, er kann ihren Blick nicht aushalten, endlich spricht sie.

Ihr haltet Wort, Graf Lester — Ihr verspracht
3820 Mir Euren Arm, aus diesem Kerker mich
Zu führen, und Ihr leihet mir ihn jetzt!

Er steht wie vernichtet. Sie fährt mit sanfter Stimme fort.

Ja, Lester, und nicht bloß
Die Freiheit wollt' ich Eurer Hand verdanken.
Ihr solltet mir die Freiheit teuer machen;
3825 An Eurer Hand, beglückt durch Eure Liebe,
Wollt' ich des neuen Lebens mich erfreun.
Jetzt, da ich auf dem Weg bin, von der Welt
Zu scheiden, und ein sel'ger Geist zu werden,
Den keine ird'sche Neigung mehr versucht,
3830 Jetzt, Lester, darf ich ohne Schamerröten
Euch die besiegte Schwachheit eingestehn —
Lebt wohl, und wenn Ihr könnt, so lebt beglückt!
Ihr durftet werben um zwei Königinnen;
Ein zärtlich liebend Herz habt Ihr verschmäht,
3835 Verraten, um ein stolzes zu gewinnen.
Kniet zu den Füßen der Elisabeth!
Mög' Euer Lohn nicht Eure Strafe werden!
Lebt wohl! — Jetzt hab' ich nichts mehr auf der Erden!

Sie geht ab, der Sherif voraus, Melvil und die Amme ihr zur Seite. Burleigh und Paulet folgen, die übrigen sehen ihr jammernd nach, bis sie verschwunden ist; dann entfernen sie sich durch die zwei andern Thüren.

Zehnter Auftritt.

Leicester, allein zurückbleibend.

Ich lebe noch! Ich trag' es, noch zu leben!
3840 Stürzt dieses Dach nicht sein Gewicht auf mich?
Thut sich kein Schlund auf, das elendeste
Der Wesen zu verschlingen? Was hab' ich
Verloren! Welche Perle warf ich hin!
Welch Glück der Himmel hab' ich weggeschleudert!
3845 — Sie geht dahin, ein schon verklärter Geist,
Und mir bleibt die Verzweiflung der Verdammten
— Wo ist mein Vorsatz hin, mit dem ich kam,
Des Herzens Stimme fühllos zu ersticken?
Ihr fallend Haupt zu sehn mit unbewegten Blicken?
3850 Weckt mir ihr Anblick die erstorbne Scham?
Muß sie im Tod mit Liebesbanden mich umstricken?
— Verworfener, dir steht es nicht mehr an,
In zartem Mitleid weibisch hinzuschmelzen;
Der Liebe Glück liegt nicht auf deiner Bahn;
3855 Mit einem eh'rnen Harnisch angethan
Sei deine Brust! Die Stirne sei ein Felsen!
Willst du den Preis der Schandthat nicht verlieren,
Dreist mußt du sie behaupten und vollführen!
Verstumme, Mitleid! Augen, werdet Stein!
3860 Ich seh' sie fallen, ich will Zeuge sein.

Er geht mit entschloss'nem Schritt der Thüre zu, durch welche Maria gegangen, bleibt aber auf der Mitte des Weges stehen.

Umsonst! Umsonst! Mich faßt der Hölle Grauen,
Ich kann, ich kann das Schreckliche nicht schauen,
Kann sie nicht sterben sehen — Horch! Was war das?

Sie sind schon unten — Unter meinen Füßen
3865 Bereitet sich das fürchterliche Werk.
Ich höre Stimmen — Fort! Hinweg! Hinweg!
Aus diesem Haus des Schreckens und des Todes!

Er will durch eine andre Thür entfliehen, findet sie aber verschlossen, und fährt zurück.

Wie? Fesselt mich ein Gott an diesen Boden?
Muß ich anhören, was mir anzuschauen graut?
3870 Die Stimme des Dechanten — Er ermahnet sie —
— Sie unterbricht ihn — Horch! — Laut betet sie —
Mit fester Stimme — Es wird still — Ganz still!
Nur Schluchzen hör' ich, und die Weiber weinen —
Sie wird entkleidet — Horch! Der Schemel wird
3875 Gerückt — Sie kniet aufs Kissen — legt das Haupt —

Nachdem er die letzten Worte mit steigender Angst gesprochen und eine Weile inne gehalten, sieht man ihn plötzlich mit einer zuckenden Bewegung zusammenfahren und ohnmächtig niedersinken; zugleich erschallt von unten herauf ein dumpfes Getöse von Stimmen, welches lange forthallt.

Elfter Auftritt.

Das zweite Zimmer des vierten Aufzugs.

Elisabeth

tritt aus einer Seitenthüre, ihr Gang und ihre Gebärden drücken die heftigste Unruhe aus.

Noch niemand hier — Noch keine Botschaft — Will es
Nicht Abend werden? Steht die Sonne fest
In ihrem himmlischen Lauf? Ich soll noch länger
Auf dieser Folter der Erwartung liegen.

3880 — Ist es geschehen? Ist es nicht? — Mir graut
Vor beidem, und ich wage nicht zu fragen!
Graf Lester zeigt sich nicht, auch Burleigh nicht,
Die ich ernannt, das Urteil zu vollstrecken.
Sind sie von London abgereist — dann ist's
3885 Geschehn, der Pfeil ist abgedrückt, er fliegt,
Er trifft, er hat getroffen; gält's mein Reich,
Ich kann ihn nicht mehr halten — Wer ist da?

Zwölfter Auftritt.

Elisabeth. Ein Page.

Elisabeth.

Du kommst allein zurück — Wo sind die Lords?

Page.

Mylord von Lester und der Großschatzmeister —

Elisabeth
in der höchsten Spannung

3890 Wo sind sie?

Page.

Sie sind nicht in London.

Elisabeth.

Nicht?

— Wo sind sie denn?

Page.

Das wußte niemand mir zu sagen.
Vor Tagesanbruch hätten beide Lords

Eilfertig und geheimnisvoll die Stadt
Verlassen.

Elisabeth lebhaft ausbrechend.

Ich bin Königin von England!

Auf- und niedergehend in der höchsten Bewegung.

3895 Geh! Rufe mir — nein, bleibe — Sie ist tot!
Jetzt endlich hab' ich Raum auf dieser Erde.
— Was zittr' ich? Was ergreift mich diese Angst?
Das Grab deckt meine Furcht, und wer darf sagen,
Ich hab's gethan! Es soll an Thränen mir
3900 Nicht fehlen, die Gefallne zu beweinen!

Zum Pagen.

Stehst du noch hier? — Mein Schreiber Davison
Soll augenblicklich sich hierher verfügen.
Schickt nach dem Grafen Shrewsbury — Da ist
Er selbst!

Page geht ab.

Dreizehnter Auftritt.

Elisabeth. Graf Shrewsbury.

Elisabeth.

3905 Willkommen, edler Lord! Was bringt Ihr?
Nichts Kleines kann es sein, was Euren Schritt
So spät hierher führt.

Shrewsbury.

Große Königin,
Mein sorgenvolles Herz, um deinen Ruhm
Bekümmert, trieb mich heute nach dem Tower,
3910 Wo Kurl und Nau, die Schreiber der Maria,
Gefangen sitzen; denn noch einmal wollt' ich
Die Wahrheit ihres Zeugnisses erproben.
Bestürzt, verlegen weigert sich der Leutnant
Des Turms, mir die Gefangenen zu zeigen;
3915 Durch Drohung nur verschafft' ich mir den Eintritt.
— Gott! Welcher Anblick zeigte mir sich da!
Das Haar verwildert, mit des Wahnsinns Blicken,
Wie ein von Furien Gequälter, lag
Der Schotte Kurl auf seinem Lager — Kaum
3920 Erkennt mich der Unglückliche, so stürzt er
Zu meinen Füßen — schreiend, meine Knie
Umklammernd mit Verzweiflung, wie ein Wurm
Vor mir gekrümmt — fleht er mich an, beschwört mich,
Ihm seiner Königin Schicksal zu verkünden;
3925 Denn ein Gerücht, daß sie zum Tod verurteilt sei,
War in des Towers Klüfte eingedrungen.
Als ich ihm das bejahet nach der Wahrheit,
Hinzugefügt, daß es sein Zeugnis sei,
Wodurch sie sterbe, sprang er wütend auf,
3930 Fiel seinen Mitgefangnen an, riß ihn
Zu Boden, mit des Wahnsinns Riesenkraft,
Ihn zu erwürgen strebend. Kaum entrissen wir
Den Unglücksel'gen seines Grimmes Händen.
Nun kehrt' er gegen sich die Wut, zerschlug
3935 Mit grimm'gen Fäusten sich die Brust, verfluchte sich
Und den Gefährten allen Höllengeistern.

Er habe falsch gezeugt, die Unglücksbriefe
An Babington, die er als echt beschworen,
Sie seien falsch, er habe andre Worte
3940 Geschrieben, als die Königin diktiert,
Der Böswicht Nau hab' ihn dazu verleitet.
Drauf rannt' er an das Fenster, riß es auf
Mit wütender Gewalt, schrie in die Gassen
Hinab, daß alles Volk zusammenlief,
3945 Er sei der Schreiber der Maria, sei
Der Böswicht, der sie fälschlich angeklagt;
Er sei verflucht, er sei ein falscher Zeuge!

Elisabeth.

Ihr sagtet selbst, daß er von Sinnen war.
Die Worte eines Rasenden, Verrückten,
3950 Beweisen nichts.

Shrewsbury.

Doch dieser Wahnsinn selbst
Beweiset desto mehr! O Königin!
Laß dich beschwören, übereile nichts,
Befiehl, daß man von neuem untersuche!

Elisabeth.

Ich will es thun — weil Ihr es wünschet, Graf,
3955 Nicht weil ich glauben kann, daß meine Peers
In dieser Sache übereilt gerichtet.
Euch zur Beruhigung erneure man
Die Untersuchung — Gut, daß es noch Zeit ist!
An unsrer königlichen Ehre soll
3960 Auch nicht der Schatten eines Zweifels haften.

Vierzehnter Auftritt.

Davison zu den Vorigen.

Elisabeth.

Das Urteil, Sir, das ich in Eure Hand
Gelegt — Wo ist's?

Davison im höchsten Erstaunen.

Das Urteil?

Elisabeth.

Das ich gestern
Euch in Verwahrung gab —

Davison.

Mir in Verwahrung?

Elisabeth.

Das Volk bestürmte mich, zu unterzeichnen,
3965 Ich mußt' ihm seinen Willen thun, ich that's,
Gezwungen that ich's, und in Eure Hände
Legt' ich die Schrift, ich wollte Zeit gewinnen;
Ihr wißt, was ich Euch sagte — Nun! Gebt her!

Shrewsbury.

Gebt, werter Sir, die Sachen liegen anders,
3970 Die Untersuchung muß erneuert werden.

Davison.

Erneuert? — Ewige Barmherzigkeit!

Elisabeth.

Bedenkt Euch nicht so lang'. Wo ist die Schrift?

Davison in Verzweiflung.

Ich bin gestürzt, ich bin ein Mann des Todes!

Elisabeth hastig einfallend.

Ich will nicht hoffen, Sir —

Davison.

Ich bin verloren!

3975 Ich hab' sie nicht mehr.

Elisabeth.

Wie? Was?

Shrewsbury.

Gott im Himmel!

Davison.

Sie ist in Burleighs Händen — schon seit gestern.

Elisabeth.

Unglücklicher! So habt Ihr mir gehorcht?
Befahl ich Euch nicht streng, sie zu verwahren?

Davison.

Das hast du nicht befohlen, Königin.

Elisabeth.

3980 Willst du mich Lügen strafen, Elender?
Wann hieß ich dir die Schrift an Burleigh geben?

Davison.

Nicht in bestimmten, klaren Worten — aber —

Elisabeth.

Nichtswürdiger! Du wagst es, meine Worte
Zu deuten? Deinen eignen blut'gen Sinn
3985 Hinein zu legen? — Wehe dir, wenn Unglück

Aus dieser eigenmächt'gen That erfolgt!
Mit deinem Leben sollst du mir's bezahlen.
— Graf Shrewsbury, Ihr sehet, wie mein Name
Gemißbraucht wird.

Shrewsbury.

Ich sehe — O mein Gott!

Elisabeth.

3990 Was sagt Ihr?

Shrewsbury.

Wenn der Squire sich dieser That
Vermessen hat auf eigene Gefahr,
Und ohne deine Wissenschaft gehandelt,
So muß er vor den Richterstuhl der Peers
Gefordert werden, weil er deinen Namen
3995 Dem Abscheu aller Zeiten preisgegeben.

Letzter Auftritt.

Die Vorigen. Burleigh, zuletzt Kent.

Burleigh

beugt ein Knie vor der Königin.

Lang' lebe meine königliche Frau,
Und mögen alle Feinde dieser Insel
Wie diese Stuart enden!

Shrewsbury verhüllt sein Gesicht, Davison ringt verzweiflungsvoll die Hände.

Elisabeth.

Redet, Lord!

Habt Ihr den tödlichen Befehl von mir
4000 Empfangen?

Burleigh.

Nein, Gebieterin! Ich empfing ihn
Von Davison.

Elisabeth.

Hat Davison ihn Euch
In meinem Namen übergeben?

Burleigh.

Nein!
Das hat er nicht —

Elisabeth.

Und Ihr vollstrecktet ihn,
Rasch, ohne meinen Willen erst zu wissen?
4005 Das Urteil war gerecht, die Welt kann uns
Nicht tadeln; aber Euch gebührte nicht,
Der Milde unsres Herzens vorzugreifen —
Drum seid verbannt von unserm Angesicht!

Zu Davison.

Ein strengeres Gericht erwartet Euch,
4010 Der seine Vollmacht frevelnd überschritten,
Ein heilig anvertrautes Pfand veruntreut.
Man führ' ihn nach dem Tower! Es ist mein Wille,
Daß man auf Leib und Leben ihn verklage.
— Mein edler Talbot! Euch allein hab' ich
4015 Gerecht erfunden unter meinen Räten;
Ihr sollt fortan mein Führer sein, mein Freund —

Shrewsbury.

Verbanne deine treusten Freunde nicht,
Wirf sie nicht ins Gefängnis, die für dich

Gehandelt haben, die jetzt für dich schweigen!
4020 — Mir aber, große Königin, erlaube,
Daß ich das Siegel, das du mir zwölf Jahre
Vertraut, zurück in deine Hände gebe.

Elisabeth betroffen.

Nein, Shrewsbury! Ihr werdet mich jetzt nicht
Verlassen, jetzt —

Shrewsbury.

Verzeih, ich bin zu alt,
4025 Und diese grade Hand, sie ist zu starr,
Um deine neuen Thaten zu versiegeln.

Elisabeth.

Verlassen wollte mich der Mann, der mir
Das Leben rettete?

Shrewsbury.

Ich habe wenig
Gethan — Ich habe deinen edlern Teil
4030 Nicht retten können. Lebe, herrsche glücklich!
Die Gegnerin ist tot. Du hast von nun an
Nichts mehr zu fürchten, brauchst nichts mehr zu achten!

Geht ab.

Elisabeth

zum Grafen Kent, der hereintritt.

Graf Lester komme her!

Kent.

Der Lord läßt sich
Entschuldigen, er ist zu Schiff nach Frankreich.

Sie bezwingt sich und steht mit ruhiger Fassung da. Der Vorhang fällt.

NOTES.

NOTES.

The action of the play is supposed to take place on the last three days of Mary's life, the first and fifth acts occupying respectively the first and third days. The date is accordingly Feb. 6–8, 1587. The scene is laid alternately at London and at Fotheringhay, but changes from one to the other in a way that argues close proximity instead of a distance of some fifty miles. The castle of Fotheringhay, which was razed by James I., stood on a slight eminence, overlooking the river Nen, 27 m. N. E. of Northampton. Mary was taken there in Sept., 1586, and her trial and execution occurred there.

ACT I.

Sir Amyas Paulet was a strict and incorruptible Puritan nobleman, to whom the charge of Mary was intrusted in April, 1585. Sir Drugeon, or, as Robertson writes, Sir Drue Drury, was his assistant.

1. **Sir.** The words Sir and Lady, as titles, are of frequent occurrence. They retain their English pronunciation. — **Dreistigkeit** may be translated *presumption.*

3. Schiller represents Mary as having long sought an opportunity of communicating with Leicester (cf. 675), and in the hope of bribing the gardener for this purpose, the trinket had probably just been thrown from the window.

4. **hat bestochen werden sollen,** *was to have been bribed.* On the form sollen for gesollt and cases of similar usage, in which after a de-

---

B. with a reference signifies Brandt's German Grammar, J., Joynes-Meissner's, and W., Whitney's.

† After a line number refers to the following stage direction.

pendent infinitive the past participle is assimilated to the infinitive form, cf. B. 108, 1–2, J. 264–5, W. 251, 4 *a*, and 240, 1 *c*.

7 †. **sich über . . . machend.** *Going to work at the desk.*

17. **Die überliefr' ich.** He means, of course, to Elizabeth.

17 †. **geheimen Ressort,** *secret compartment.* The noun retains its French pronunciation. It means primarily 'a spring,' and in a derived sense, 'a drawer or compartment opened by a spring.'

19. **Durchzogen . . . Frankreich,** *set with the lilies of France*, i. e. the jewels were arranged in the form of the *fleur de lis*, the royal emblem of France.

20. **Legt's zu dem übrigen,** referring to Mary's money and valuables which Paulet had seized Sept. 9, 1586. Previously, upon the discovery of the Babington plot, cf. l. 70, note, her papers had been seized.

22. **besitzt,** *owns anything.* The use of the verb without an object is unusual.

29. **zu seiner Zeit,** *at the proper time.*

30. **Wer sieht . . . an,** *who can tell from these bare walls.*

32. **Die Himmeldecke.** After Mary's sentence, Paulet removed her cloth of state, and she was no longer treated with the former ceremony.

33. **den zärtlich weichgewöhnten Fuß.** *Her delicate foot used to soft carpets* will perhaps give the idea of the original.

37. **speiste,** here *served.* — **Sterlyn** is the French form of Sterling. — **Gatten** refers to Darnley, as **Buhlen,** in the following line, does to Bothwell.

38. **Da,** *while,* denoting the purely temporal relation. Cf. B. 330, 1.

39. **Sogar . . . mangelt.** *Even the trifling necessity of a mirror is lacking.* Notdurft denotes the barest necessity in contrast to superfluity.

47–48. Mary was only six days old when, upon the death of her father, James V., she was proclaimed queen of Scotland. In her sixth year she was betrothed to the Dauphin and sent to France, where she was brought up at the luxurious court of Catherine de Medici.

49. **Freuden** is an old form of the genitive singular. Cf. B. 434, 1, J. 106, note, W. 95.

53. **In großes Unglück . . . sich finden,** *to be reconciled to great misfortune.* Cf. Die Piccolomini, l. 190:

> Und (die Menschen) finden sich in ein verhaßtes Müssen
> Weit besser, als in eine bittre Wahl.

56. **in sich gehen,** *examine itself.*

57. **büßt sich,** *is expiated.* On the idiomatic use of the reflexive form cf. B. 272, J. 274, 2, W. 281.

66. **Bürgerkrieges,** referring to the revolt of the northern nobles headed by the Earls of Northumberland and Westmoreland in 1569. Their object was to restore the Catholic worship and to secure the recognition of Mary's succession. Norfolk's plot was connected with this movement.

70. **Parry,** a member of the House of Commons who plotted to assassinate Elizabeth. His plot was betrayed and he was executed early in 1585. **Babington** was one of the leaders in a conspiracy formed in 1586 to murder Elizabeth and to free Mary. It was on charge of complicity in this plot that Mary was brought to trial.

73. **Norfolk.** Thomas Howard, fourth Duke of Norfolk, was one of the most powerful and trusted of Elizabeth's nobles. He proposed to marry Mary and was implicated in a Catholic conspiracy. He was convicted of treason and beheaded in 1572.

78. **Um ihrentwillen.** The form was originally **um ihren willen,** then ihrentwillen, with inorganic t, and lastly the common form **ihretwillen.** Cf. B. 87.

84. **Helena,** wife of Menelaus and the most beautiful of women, whose abduction by Paris was the cause of the Trojan war. The religious and political conflicts caused by Mary's presence in England, as well as her beauty, suggest the comparison.

85. **hätte.** Note the force of the pluperfect subjunctive as an emphatic denial. Cf. B. 284, 3, J. 467, *e*, W. 333, 7.

87. **Da.** The temporal particle belongs also with **kam,** which may be shown by supplying *and* before **Als.** In her agitation Kennedy uses a succession of relative clauses, and does not bring the period to a logical conclusion.

94. **Bittres** is treated as a noun in apposition with **was.** Cf. B. 181, W. 129, 5.

95–97. **vor . . . Leben,** *is summoned before the bar of justice and insultingly accused of capital crime.* Note the tautological formal phrase Leib und Leben, in which Leib still retains its original meaning, 'life.'

98. **Mörderin,** referring to the murder of Darnley, a crime in which

Mary was implicated, though there is some doubt about the extent of her guilt. Cf. ll. 272, note, and 327, note.

100. **geschändet.** Here and often the auxiliary is omitted. Cf. B. 346, J. 350, 4, W. 439, 3 *a*.

101. **Verschworen,** *engaged in conspiracy.* Cf. W. 357. Its position is emphatic.

102. Referring to Elizabeth's predecessor on the throne, who ruled from 1553 till 1558. In calling her Spanish, the poet thinks of her as the daughter of Catherine of Arragon and the wife of Philip II. Her reign was made odious by her bitter persecution of the Protestants.

103. **Engelland.** Schiller uses this form occasionally, for the sake of meter. Cf. ll. 521, 820 and 958.

104. **Franzmann,** perhaps slightly contemptuous instead of Franzose. The word has now become colloquial, but does not seem to have been so regarded by Goethe and Schiller. Supply *it*, referring to England, after **verraten.**

105. **Edinburger Vertrag.** The treaty of Edinburgh was negotiated in 1560, and its most important article provided that in future Mary should not assume the arms or title of queen of England. She refused to ratify it then, and again in 1566, because it might be so construed as to prejudice her right of succession. This was before her imprisonment, and that its subsequent ratification was demanded, or would have purchased her freedom, is the poet's invention.

114. **unheilspinnend,** *plotting mischief.* The metaphor, in which Mary is compared with a spider, is lost in translation.

117. **hegte.** Cf. note on l. 85. The usage is common.

118. Here and throughout the drama Schiller represents Mary's imprisonment as much more severe than it was. Under Paulet's charge and for a few months after Norfolk's conspiracy, she was closely watched. In general, while her escape was guarded against, she was allowed all the pleasures of English country life.

124. **Anverwandten** refers to Paulet's nephew, Mortimer. Cf. Scene 3 of this act.

131. **das mir geworden ist,** *that has been assigned to me.*

134. **Nachts.** Adverbial genitive. Cf. B. 429, 1.

142. **Den Christus.** The noun is declined as in Latin, or, as here, is uninflected. Its use instead of das Crucifix is unusual. As a translation Breul suggests *Christ's image.*

147. **dein.** Bellermann calls attention to the fact that Kennedy betrays her agitation in this scene by the use of the pronouns du and dein. Elsewhere she addresses the queen with Ihr. Cf. B. 230–31.

155. **uns . . . erniedrigen,** *treat us basely, not debase us,* is suggested by Breul.

157. **lernen.** Cf. l. 4, note.

161. **Brief.** Mary's last letter to Elizabeth was written Dec. 19, 1586. Its purport was essentially as given by Schiller, except that no request for an interview was made. Mary had, however, often expressed such a desire.

166. **zu thun,** *to be done.* Cf. B. 291, 1, J. 475, 2, W. 343, III. *b.*

171. **Gericht,** referring to the special court, appointed for Mary's trial. Cf. l. 217, note.

172. **meines gleichen,** *my equals.* On this form cf. B. 87. Heyne explains the forms of this sort as developed, perhaps, from such a combination, as „daß deines Gleichen keiner unter den Königen ist," 1 Kings 3, 13.

173. **Zu denen . . . kann,** *in whom I can place no confidence.*

183. Mary's chaplain, du Preau, was not allowed to see her for nearly a month before her execution. Cf. l. 3591, note.

184. **die,** *she who.* The omission of the antecedent is irregular, but occurs several times in the drama. Cf. ll. 316 and 1608.

187. **Dechant des Orts,** i. e. Dr. Fletcher, the Dean of Peterborough. He was present at Mary's execution, but she refused to listen to him.

203–4. When Babington's plot was discovered, Mary's secretaries were arrested and the number of her servants greatly reduced.

207. **nicht . . . entbehren,** *are not suffering and in want.*

210. **fürchtend** for fürchtendes. Similar examples of the omission of the ending occur in ll. 218, 221, 277, and often. Cf. B. 212, J. 449, 2 *b*, W. 126.

216. **Monat.** The Commission appointed for Mary's trial sat at Fotheringhay, Oct. 14 and 15, 1586, and pronounced sentence at Westminster, Oct. 25. The sentence was published Dec. 6, and at the same time was communicated to her. The time, therefore, had been longer than a month.

217. For Mary's trial Elizabeth appointed a Commission, chosen

from the most eminent nobles, with whom the privy council and five judges were associated. Rapin gives the list of names. The number seems to have been forty-two, and Schiller so speaks of it in ll. 578 and 697. Robertson, however, mentions the number as forty, and others as forty-six.

241. **diese** refers to Richter. (Düntzer.)

244. **Hattons Eifer.** Mary at first refused to recognize the jurisdiction of the court. Elizabeth's vice-chamberlain and favorite, Sir Christopher Hatton, urged that by her refusal she deprived herself of the only opportunity of showing her innocence. By this argument, though still under protest, she was induced to appear.

246. **wagen darf zu thun,** *may venture to do.* On the force of darf cf. B. 267, 3, W. 253, 1.

250 †. The character of Mortimer is Schiller's invention, though Bellermann thinks that various features of the delineation were suggested by the career of Babington.

251. **Oheim** is used instead of Onkel, chiefly in higher diction. Contracted forms, **Ohm,** ll. 776 and 2333, and **Öhm,** l. 3523, occur.

261. **dem.** Note the emphatic use of the demonstrative instead of a personal pronoun. Cf. B. 244, J. 457, 4 *a*, W. 166, 2 *b*.

269. **Wart Ihr doch.** A verb placed for emphasis at the beginning of a sentence is usually followed by doch. Cf. B. 343, *e*, W. 431, *g*.

272. **König Darnley.** Henry Stewart, Lord Darnley, was Mary's second husband, to whom she was married in 1565, and whom she gave the title of King. Her love was alienated by his conduct, and Feb. 9, 1567, he was murdered. Bothwell was accused of the crime and Mary of having instigated it. She never acknowledged her guilt, but her subsequent course makes it strongly probable.

274. **Friede.** This form as accusative singular is unusual now. The word belonged originally to the strong declension. Cf. l. 372 for another instance of this form, and l. 3651 for the usual one.

278. **Der Jahrstag.** This is not, historically, correct. The anniversary of Darnley's murder was Feb. 9, the day after Mary's death, and this scene is supposed to occur Feb. 6.

284. **Löseschlüssel,** *key of absolution.*

285. **hat vergeben.** The singular verb shows that the two subjects Kirche and Himmel constitute but one idea in the speaker's mind.

289. **Messedieners,** *ministrant's.* It is the office of the ministrant to assist the priest in the celebration of the mass.

290. **Hochwürdiges.** An ecclesiastical term, *Host*, i. e. the consecrated wafer believed to be the body of Christ, which in Mass is offered as a sacrifice.

293. **Todesnetz.** Referring to the fact that at Mary's order Darnley was lodged in the solitary house, Kirk of Field, where she visited him, and where he was murdered.

295. **zarten Alters.** For the construction cf. B. 180, 5, W. 220, 2.

318. **Euch,** ethical dative. Cf. B. 192, J. 439, W. 222, III.

319. David Rizzio, son of a Tuscan musician, originally gained a place in Mary's household by his skill in music. He was afterward appointed secretary of French dispatches, and in this position became her chief adviser. His influence aroused the hatred of the nobility, and the queen's confidence provoked Darnley's jealousy. A plot was formed in which Darnley participated, and Rizzio was murdered in Mary's presence.

327. **Bothwell.** James Hepburn, Earl of Bothwell, was one of the most powerful and turbulent of the Scottish nobles. In the matter of Rizzio's murder he was Mary's partisan and defender, and urged her divorce from Darnley. When the latter was murdered he was accused of the crime, but after a hasty and unfair trial was acquitted. Several of the leading nobles proposed his marriage with the queen, and he carried her off to his castle of Dunbar, whether with or without her consent is disputed. He forced through a divorce from his wife and soon after married Mary. This step aroused popular resistance, and in the hostilities that followed he was defeated and fled to Denmark. Mary was deposed and imprisoned.

329. **Zaubertränke.** The idea of love aroused by a philter or magic potion is common in dramatic literature, and is based upon a superstition prevalent in the Middle Ages. Cf. Othello I., 2: 73, and Faust I., Die Hexenküche.

335. **wob.** Originally weben was a strong verb, and is still so used in poetry and exalted discourse.

346–49. Upon the opening of parliament it was customary for the noblest lords to carry the royal insignia before the sovereign. This honor Mary bestowed upon Bothwell, two days after his trial.

350. That Mary attempted to overawe her parliament by an armed force is not historical. Upon his trial for Darnley's murder, however, Bothwell had appeared before the court with so large a retinue of armed followers, that no one ventured to vote for his condemnation.

387. Charles of Guise, Archbishop of Rheims and Cardinal of Lorraine, was Mary's maternal uncle. She had been guided by his influence and that of his brother, the Duke of Guise, at the outset of her career. As the Cardinal died in 1574, Mortimer's letter implies, of course, an intentional anachronism.

397. **Doch der ich's danke,** *yet to which I owe it.* Cf. B. 190, J. 437, 2.

410. **In strengen Pflichten,** *amid austere duties,* characteristic of the Puritan conception of life. Translate **aufgesäugt** in the following line by *nursed.*

413. **Das feste Land,** *the Continent.*

418. **Kirchenfests.** Schiller probably refers to Easter. That supposition would at least, as regards time, accord with Mortimer's description of his return and his stay at Rheims. It is hardly probable, as Düntzer remarks, that the poet was thinking of the jubilee of 1575.

420. **Gottesbild,** referring to the wayside shrines common in Catholic countries.

428. **hoher Bildnergeist,** *a lofty spirit of art.*

436–7. **Gestalten . . . quoll,** *profuse from wall and ceiling streamed the wealth of form,* referring, of course, to the famous frescoes. A few lines further on the poet enumerates several favorite subjects of Italian religious art.

449. **sein Haus,** i. e. St. Peter's Cathedral.

451. **mein** is the older genitive singular of the first personal pronoun, and its use is now archaic and poetic. For the construction cf. B. 184, J. 434, *a*, W. 219, 5.

451–3. **Höret auf . . . auszubreiten.** English usage does not sanction quite the same figure. Say, *Cease to paint the bright hues of life before me.*

457. **Buch.** As Düntzer points out, **Buch** is here opposed to **Kranz** in the following line, and expresses figuratively the contrast between the bare and literal Puritan conception of worship and the imposing

ritual and sensuous enjoyment of art that the Roman Catholic church revealed to him.

461. **Landsmannschaften.** Literally, 'countrymen.' Say here *the merry crowds of Frenchmen.*

463. **Kardinal von Guise.** Schiller has used the title carelessly, for he refers evidently to Mary's uncle mentioned in l. 387. The Cardinal of Guise was another man. **Guise** is here dissyllabic.

469. The genitive case is here repeated for emphasis after the possessive **sein** in the preceding line. A similar case occurs l. 1710. On the usage cf. B. 242, 2, J. 455, *d.*

478. **in . . . leitet,** *leads about in error.* Note the force of the dative. In the preceding line *speculating* seems to approach most nearly the sense of **grübelnde.**

490. **Prediger des Berges,** i. e. Christ. The reference is to the Sermon on the Mount.

493. **Rheims.** In 1568 a Roman Catholic college for the education of English youth was opened by Dr. (afterward Cardinal) Allen at Douai. It was subsequently removed to Rheims, where it enjoyed the patronage of the Guise family. From this school Jesuit priests were sent to England.

496. **Morgan,** one of Mary's most devoted adherents, was the son of a Welsh gentleman, and not, as Schiller states, a Scotchman. For some time he was Shrewsbury's secretary, and used his position to betray to Mary what passed between his master and the court. Afterward he lived in Paris on an allowance that she made him, and managed her ciphers and her correspondence with the Pope, Allen, and the English Catholics. He was implicated in Parry's conspiracy.

497. **Leßley,** Bishop of Ross, was Mary's Ambassador at Elizabeth's court. He was a religious zealot, and did much to foment the discontent of the English Catholics. Upon the discovery of his complicity in Norfolk's plot he was arrested, and after several months' imprisonment, was ordered to leave England. For the sake of metre Schiller inflects the form **Rosse,** as if it were a German word.

503. **Fiel mir . . . in die Augen,** *caught my eye.*

518. **Stammbaum,** *pedigree.* Mary was the granddaughter of Margaret Tudor, the eldest sister of Henry VIII., and hence, after the legitimate descendants of that monarch, the next in succession to the English throne.

523–4. The Catholics, who denied the legality of Henry VIII.'s divorce from Catherine of Arragon, regarded the union with Anne Boleyn as adulterous and Elizabeth as illegitimate. After the execution of her mother, Henry VIII. himself declared Elizabeth a bastard, alleging that her mother's previous betrothal to the Earl of Northumberland had rendered his marriage illegal.

537. **Talbots.** During her imprisonment Mary was entrusted to the care of George Talbot, Earl of Shrewsbury, from 1568 till 1584. He faithfully performed the duties of his charge, but at the same time treated his prisoner with gentleness and the respect due her rank and station.

548. **zehen.** An old form of the numeral, used because the metre demands an extra syllable. Cf. l. 1781.

553. **des Glücklichen.** On the use of the genitive cf. B. 188, J. 435, *c*, W. 220, 5.

559. **sähe.** On the use of the subjunctive cf. B. 284, 5, J. 470, *a*, W. 332, 1.

580. Four days after the Commission pronounced sentence, Parliament met, confirmed the sentence and petitioned the queen to put it in immediate execution. Twelve days later she sent to both houses, desiring that they devise means to spare Mary's life. They again petitioned for her death, and Elizabeth, after returning an answer, prorogued the session.

591. **In ew'gem Kerker.** It was reported, in diplomatic circles, that instead of suffering the death penalty, Mary was to be brought to the Tower and kept as a Carmelite nun. Cf. Froude, 12: 308.

604. **aller Könige.** Die referring to **Majestät** must be supplied.

607. **Duc von Anjou,** son of Catherine de Medici and brother of the king of France. The proposed alliance was broken off at the end of 1581, and the duke died in 1584. Schiller commits the anachronism for poetic reasons. Cf. l. 1217 †, note.

613. **Der . . . mehr,** *more than one royal woman.* Mehr in the uninflected form with the partitive genitive is unusual, but compare Goethe, Ilmenau 1783:

„Ich seh' im Busch der kleinen Feuer mehr."

615–17. Anne Boleyn, the second wife of Henry VIII., was executed in 1536 on charge of unfaithfulness, and Catherine Howard, his fifth wife, suffered the same fate in 1542. Lady Jane Gray, who upon the death of Edward VI. was proclaimed queen, was executed after Mary's accession, on charge of treason.

630. **Kredenzt**, *presented.* The word is based upon the Italian credénza, which signifies 'belief,' and in a derived sense 'taste.' It originally referred to the custom of having food and drink tasted, to prove its harmlessness.

638. **Graf Aubespine** was the regularly accredited French ambassador at Elizabeth's court. Schiller follows Robertson in writing Aubespine for L'Aubespine. Shortly before Mary's execution a rumor became current that the French ambassador was engaged in a plot to assassinate Elizabeth. Cf. l. 2671, note.

644. **Tichburns.** Chidioc Tichbourne, as Robertson gives the name, was one of the conspirators in the Babington plot. He was executed with Babington in Sept., 1586. The heads of decapitated criminals were often displayed on London Bridge, but that it was done in this instance is Schiller's invention.

650. **Burleigh.** It was Walsingham whose spies had discovered the various plots, but as Schiller did not introduce him into the play, he represents it as Burleigh's work.

668. **Graf Lester.** In the list of characters Schiller wrote Leicester, but throughout the text he spells the name phonetically. The rôle is the poet's invention and finds no counterpart in the character of the historical Leicester.

692. Mary's sentence was announced to her by Lord Buckhurst, accompanied by secretary Beal. Schiller assigns the duty to Burleigh in order to introduce the substance of the argument at the trial.

701. **so viel vergeben**, *compromise so much.* Note the construction with the dative.

704. **seinesgleichen**, *his equals.* Cf. l. 172, note. The law to which reference is made was established by one of the provisions of Magna Charta.

706. **Peers** is the English word and retains its pronunciation as such.

724. **Kenn' ich sie doch kaum.** Cf. l. 269, note.

731. **stünd'.** This is an old and obsolescent form, but is still occasionally heard in South Germany. It occurs again in l. 1039. Cf. B. 129.

732. **Themis**, the mythological goddess of justice. She is represented as a majestic woman, her eyes blindfolded, and holding in one hand a balance, in the other a sword.

737–8. **Sind . . . Verworfene**, *Are they, pray, outcasts picked up from the common rabble.*

740–1. **sich zum . . . willig dingen lassen**, *are willingly hired as.*

751. **Primas.** The reference is to John Whitgift, Archbishop of Canterbury.

752. **Talbot.** The Chancellor at this time was Thomas Bromley. Though the three men specially mentioned here were members of the Commission, they were none of them present at the trial at Fotheringhay, and Talbot was also absent when sentence was pronounced at Westminster.

753. **Howard.** Lord Howard of Effingham was Lord High Admiral. He is famous for his victory over the Spanish Armada.

758. **Wär's.** Cf. l. 559, note.

775. **Serail's**, *seraglio.* The word is pronounced as in French.

778. **Gemeinen**, *Commons.*

782. Not only Elizabeth, cf. ll. 523–4, note, but also her half-sister Mary, who preceded her on the throne, had been declared illegitimate.

786. **viermal ändern.** In the form of the play upon which Mellish based his translation, the facts seem to have been stated specifically:—

> "renounce the Pope
> With Henry, yet retain the old belief;
> Reform themselves with Edward; hear the mass
> Again with Mary; with Elizabeth
> Who governs now, reform themselves again."

801. **Protestanten.** As Froude points out (cf. vol. 12: 276), several members of the Commission appointed for Mary's trial had shown themselves favorable to her cause, and were Catholics in their sympathies.

806. **Herkömmlich**, *customary.* Schiller took his idea here, as Düntzer remarks, from the account of the trial of the Bishop of Ross. (Rapin 2: 100.) The custom seems to have prevailed only on the border.

835. **ew'ge Tage**, *for ever.*

836. **Richmond.** Henry of Richmond, who ascended the throne as Henry VII. in 1485, belonged to the House of Lancaster. By his marriage with Elizabeth, eldest daughter of Edward IV., he united the claims of the House of York with his own, and thereby ended the War of the Roses.

843. Not only the context, but the use of the subjunctive denotes emphatic denial. Cf. l. 85, note.

848. **dem Gesetz verfallen,** *have incurred the penalty of the law.*

849. The statute here mentioned, of which Schiller gives the substance, was enacted in 1585, after the discovery of Parry's plot.

850. **erhübe** is an old form for which **erhöbe** is now generally used. It occurs again in l. 3022. Cf. B. 129 and 132.

863. Of this act Elizabeth wrote in an address to parliament, "So far was it from being made to entrap her, that it was rather intended to forewarn and terrify her from attempting anything against it." Cf. Rapin, vol. 2, 129.

874. At the close of 1585 Walsingham, with the aid of a certain Gifford, a man trusted by the Catholic party, but whom he had found means to bribe, devised a plan by which all Mary's correspondence passed through his hands. Both letters to her and her replies were deciphered and copied by his secretary, and afterward resealed and forwarded. In this way the Babington conspiracy was detected, but upon her trial Mary denied all knowledge of Babington, and claimed that the copy of her reply to his letter was forged.

886. **aus Eurem Munde.** Mary was accustomed to dictate in French to Nau, whose notes as well as his finished draft she afterward examined. It was then ciphered, or if the letter was to be in English, Curle first translated it, and Mary listened to his version. The testimony of the two secretaries is historical, and so is Mary's exception to their evidence on the ground that it involved perjury to her. The subsequent retraction, however, cf. l. 3939 ff., is the poet's invention.

909. A resolution to this effect was passed by the parliament of the 13th of Elizabeth.

913. **jetzo** is an archaic form for **jetzt**.

915. **Das . . . Rechtens,** *That is lawful with us.* The phrase belongs to legal parlance. For the genitive cf. B. 180, 5, J. 435, *b*, W. 220, 2.

919. **umgehen.** The infinitive is used absolutely. Other examples occur l. 1447 and l. 2136. Cf. J. 474, *f*, W. 347, 1.

925–6. Mary did not deny that she had thrown herself upon the support of the Catholic Powers. Complicity in a conspiracy against Elizabeth's life could alone deprive her of the right of succession, or make her amenable to the law, and that she strenuously denied.

929. **Mendoza.** Don Bernando de Mendoza was the Spanish minister at Elizabeth's court from 1578 till 1584. He advised Philip II. to invade England, and corresponded with Mary. His house was a rendezvous for the disaffected Catholics, and he was privy to the Jesuit plans and conspiracy.

946. **Zwangsrecht,** here, *right of self-defense.*

950. **Was irgend nur,** *whatsoever.*

959. **Nicht . . . Euch,** *Do not appeal to the awful right of force.*

961. **sie.** Düntzer remarks the indefinite half contemptuous use of the pronoun referring to Elizabeth.

971. **richten,** in the sense of hinrichten, *put to death.*

978. **Urtelspruch.** As before remarked, cf. l. 692, note, the preceding scene is not historical, but Mary did receive her sentence calmly, exclaiming, "After so many sufferings death comes to me as a welcome deliverer. I am proud to think that my life is deemed of importance to the Catholic religion, and,as a martyr for it, I am now willing to die."—Camden, quoted by Robertson, vol. 2, 134.

991–2. **Zu groß . . . Gewalt,** *Too great is her control over their minds and the power of her womanly tears.* Macht and Gewalt are often used in nearly the same sense, but the latter adds to the idea of ability or strength (cf. mögen) the notion of compulsion (cf. walten).

994. **Käm' es dazu . . . auszusprechen,** *if it came to uttering* On the use of the infinitive cf. B. 291, 2, J. 477, 1 *a*, W. 346, 2.

997. **Alle Welt.** Usually all denotes 'the whole as composed of units,' but is sometimes, as here, used where ganz, 'the whole as a unit,' might be expected.

999. **festliches Gepräng,** *solemn pomp.*

1003. **gestorben wäre.** For the force of the subjunctive cf. B. 284, 2, J. 468, *b*, W. 331, 2.

1031. There is no doubt that Elizabeth did desire Mary's assassination. After signing the death-warrant she instructed Davison to write to Paulet and Drury, and sound their willingness to undertake her murder.

1038. **steht nicht zu ändern,** *is not to be changed.* Stehen, as a neuter verb, takes the infinitive in a passive sense. Cf. B. 291, W. 343, III., 1 *b.*

1054. **Schergen=amt,** *jailor's task.* The word is used in a somewhat contemptuous sense.

1059–60. **Man . . . verscheiden.** *The rumor spreads, she is failing, she is reported growing more and more infirm, finally passing quietly away.* Contrast the euphemistic language of Burleigh's hints with Paulet's bluntness.

1066. **Götter.** Both Schiller and Goethe often use the plural when the singular would seem more natural, Schiller doing so even when a biblical allusion is suggested. Cf. Jungfrau, V., 4, „ohne Götter fällt kein Haar vom Haupt des Menschen." In this connection the *dii penates* of Roman mythology may have been suggested to the poet's mind, and in general the usage must be attributed to classical influence. Cf. Bellermann, vol. 2, 219.

ACT II.

1080. The reference is probably to some one of the splendid pageants in honor of the French embassy that was sent to England in 1581, to arrange a marriage treaty. As Boxberger notes, the similarity between this scene, and the first one in Shakespeare's Henry VIII., has been pointed out as more than accidental.

1085. **berennt.** This form as the past participle of **berennen** is now obsolete. Cf. B. 455.

1093. **Wohlriechend köstliche Essenzen,** *fragrant delicious perfumes.*

1104. **Monsieur** was the customary title of the eldest brother of the King of France. The word retains its French pronunciation. In the matter of the treaty Schiller is thinking of the articles drafted in 1581, in which the provisions mentioned were agreed to. Cf. Rapin, vol. 2, 113.

1120. **so prächt'ge Götterfeste,** *fêtes of such surpassing splendor.* In the following line **die königliche Mutter** refers, of course, to Catharine de Medici. Cf. l. 48. Her court of St. Germain was the most luxurious and splendid in Europe.

1122. **Ein gesittet fröhlich Volk,** *a law-abiding happy people.*

1129. **schimmerlos,** *unostentatious.*

1145. **Graf Bellievre.** Schiller follows Robertson in writing the name so instead of 'de Bellièvre.' He was a special envoy sent by the King of France to protest against Mary's execution.

1147. **Hochzeitsfackel,** *nuptial torch.* The torch was one of the symbols of Hymen, the god of marriage.

1160. Schiller has taken this from Elizabeth's reply to the address of the Commons, Feb. 4, 1559, respecting her marriage. Cf. Rapin, vol. 2, 53.

1163. **wo ich dahin sein werde,** *when I shall be gone.* The German phrase, like the English, is a euphemism to express the idea of death.

1169. **Es** refers to **Volk** as its antecedent, as does **ihm** in the same line. The English idiom requires the pronoun in the plural, *They show, etc.*

1175. Henry VIII. suppressed the smaller monasteries in 1536, and in 1539 the larger ones. Further confiscations of Church property also occurred under Edward VI.

1181. **die sollte.** On the use of the demonstrative instead of the personal pronoun cf. J. 457, 4 *a*, W. 166, 2 *b*.

1190. **auf Erden,** dative singular. Cf. l. 49, note, for a similar form of the genitive and grammatical reference. Das Lied von der Glocke begins with the words, „Fest gemauert in der Erden."

1192–3. Froude characterizes the prince as a dishonest and cowardly adventurer. He was small, brown and deeply pock-marked, and had a hoarse croaking voice. Elizabeth nicknamed him *grenouille,* 'frog,' and he signed himself so in his letters to her.

1199. Note the appositive construction of the infinitive phrase. Cf. l. 994, note.

1212. The incident is historical, cf. Froude, vol. 11, 413. It seems probable, however, that Schiller had in mind another occasion, when Elizabeth placed a ring on the duke's finger. Cf. Düntzer, 81.

1217. **meiner Fürstin.** Fürst is used as a title of high rank, as Fürst Bismarck, and in poetic language in the sense of Oberster, Gebieter, Vornehmster. Cf. l. 467 and Jungfrau, III., 10, „Der letzte von den Fürsten unseres Heers." Usually, however, as here, it is bestowed only upon an actual ruler, and its use in this case shows de Bellièvre's expectation that Elizabeth will conclude the marriage-treaty and become his sovereign.

1217†. As already noted, cf. l. 607, note, the marriage negotiations belong to an earlier date. Schiller's purpose was to show in Leicester's jealousy the cause that prompts his action in the play. Cf. ll. 1794 ff.

1220. meines Ordens. The order of the Garter, instituted by Edward III., probably in 1344, is the highest British order of knighthood. The garter of dark blue velvet and gold is worn on the left leg, below the knee, and bears the motto: *Honny soit qui mal y pense* (Evil to him who evil thinks). A broad blue ribbon over the left shoulder with a pendant figure of St. George and the dragon is also part of the insignia.

1257. Licht der Wahrheit, referring to the Protestant reformation in England. Cf. l. 1424 for a similar expression.

1266. lothringischen Brüdern. The Lorraine brothers were Mary's cousins, the three sons of Francis of Guise, but Schiller refers especially to two of them, Henry, Duke of Guise, and Louis, Archbishop of Rheims and Cardinal of Guise. They were nephews of the Cardinal of Lorraine mentioned in l. 387, and were distinguished as most zealous Catholics and implacable enemies of Queen Elizabeth. They instigated or abetted various plots against her.

1267. unversöhnten, instead of unversöhnlichen, *implacable.*

1273. Dort wird der Königsmord gelehrt. Cardinal Allen, who was at the head of the Jesuit College, wrote a book maintaining the thesis that the murder of an excommunicated prince was not only lawful, but a meritorious action.

1277. der dritte Mörder. The poet evidently has in mind the conspiracies of Throgmorton in 1583, Parry in 1585, and Babington in 1586. In none of these was the queen's life actually attempted.

1281. Ate, the goddess of discord, was the daughter of Jupiter, whom, in a moment of anger, he hurled from heaven to earth with an oath that she should never return to Olympus. Since then she hovers over the heads of mortals, everywhere sowing dissensions, broils and ruin.

1290–91. Schiller here confuses the princes of Lorraine, mentioned in l. 1266, with their father, the Duke of Guise, and his brother, the Cardinal of Lorraine. It was at the instigation of the latter that Mary and the Dauphin quartered the arms of England. In l. 2333 the allusion is correctly made.

1301 †. **Talbot.** It is perhaps, as Düntzer remarks, an oversight that in this, and in the following scene, the rôle is indicated by the family name Talbot. Elsewhere only the title Shrewsbury is used to designate the rôle, and this is the case throughout with Burleigh and Leicester, though, as with Talbot, their family names, Cecil and Dudley, occasionally occur in the text.

1303. **mir.** On this use of the dative cf. B. 192, J. 439, W. 222, III.

1345. **Herrscherzügel,** *reins of government.*

1352. **Zu ihrem Vorteil sprechend,** *pleading in her behalf.* Cf. B. 294, 3, J. 480, 1 *b*, W. 357.

1363. **Nicht . . . Wort,** *I do not defend her guilt.* On the use of the dative cf. B. 190, 6, J. 437, 4, W. 222, I., *d.*

1365. **ehlichte.** The usual form is ehelichte.

1371. **Dem Mutvollstärksten,** *Of the boldest and strongest.* On the use of the dative cf. J. 439, *b*, W. 222, III., *a.*

1379–80. Elizabeth's Protestant sympathies caused Mary Tudor to regard her probable succession to the throne with jealousy, and when Sir Thomas Wyatt undertook to raise an insurrection in order to prevent Mary's marriage with Philip II., Elizabeth was accused of complicity in the plot and lodged in the Tower. Part of the queen's council favored her execution and the Spanish ambassador warmly urged it, but Mary refused to listen to such proposals. Elizabeth was however, forced to conform to the Catholic faith, and was sent to Woodstock, where she was detained for some time.

1382. **der gnäd'ge Vater.** Talbot here refers to God, and regards the stern experiences of Elizabeth's youth as divinely ordered, for the development of her character. The words are sometimes explained as referring to Henry VIII., but the antithesis beginning six lines below, as well as the fact that Elizabeth was sent to the Tower and to Woodstock by Mary, argue against that idea.

1395–97. Talbot is not diplomatic; he offends Elizabeth's personal vanity and her sensitiveness regarding her birth.

1421. Elizabeth's first Parliament passed an act to recognize the queen's title as settled by an act of Parliament in 1544. That act established the succession of Edward, Mary and Elizabeth, and empowered the king to make further disposition by his will. This he did, and passing over the line of his elder sister Margaret of Scotland, he named, as next in succession after Elizabeth, the descendants of his younger sister Mary, by her marriage with the Duke of Suffolk.

1432. **Jugendkraft.** Elizabeth was in her 54th, and Mary in her 45th year. Schiller represents them both as much younger, and says expressly, in a letter to Iffland: "In the play Mary is perhaps twenty-five, and Elizabeth at most thirty years old."

1449. **Nicht.** On the redundant use of nicht in a dependent clause after a verb of "forbidding" cf. B. 309, 1, 2.

1453. **wie,** denotes action antecedent to the main clause. Cf. B. 330, 2. Translate *let it fall quickly*, *as soon as*, etc.

1470. **den großen Weg,** the usual phrase to describe the foreign travel that completed the education of the wealthy English youth.

1476. **ränkespinnenden,** *intriguing.*

1480. **In . . . mich,** *I insinuated myself into their confidence.* To show the force of the indirect question introduced by ob, supply *to see if.*

1489. Walsingham had been sent to Paris in 1581, but was at this time in England. Cf. l. 650, note.

1490. **Bulle.** The Bull of Deposition here alluded to was published by Pius V., in 1570. It had been secretly issued the preceding year.

1496. **Man . . . schuld, daß . . . besucht,** *they charged you with having visited*, etc.

1509–10. **Mit . . . soll,** *With which the queen's compassionate heart shall not be troubled.* On the use of man with an active verb instead of the passive voice cf. B. 272, J. 274, 1, W. 281. For the force of soll cf. B. 267, 5, W. 257, 1.

1527. Bellermann cites here the familiar English proverb, "King's face makes grace."

1531. **ältsten Thron,** i. e. the throne of France. The French monarchy was founded by Clovis, upon whom, after his conversion A. D. 496, the pope bestowed the title of "the most Christian King." The title became hereditary, and was borne by all French monarchs.

1573. **Eurer.** On this form of the genitive cf. B. 82, J. 182, *a*, W. 152, 1.

1606. **Thaten doppelter Gestalt,** i. e. deeds capable of a twofold interpretation or of opposite interpretations. The last two lines of the speech are somewhat obscure; the meaning, according to Bellermann, is, "Only the step that is acknowledged is bad; if one preserve the appearance of virtue, and do not himself, by imprudent admission, forfeit it, then he has never lost it." Cf. also Düntzer, 149.

1615. Cf. l. 1031, note.

1631. **zärtesten.** This adjective is generally compared without Umlaut. Cf. B. 74.

1636. **Ruchlose Fertigkeit,** *a ruffian's readiness.*

1657. **den Lord.** Mortimer thinks, of course, of Leicester, to whom he has promised to deliver Mary's letter.

1669. **Ich wünschte,** *I wish.* The literal translation of the tense, 'I could wish,' lacks the direct and positive force that common usage gives to the original. Cf. Eng. "I should say so," as an emphatic assertion.

1685. **dich verwerfe.** Leicester's entrance cuts short the sentence. As Düntzer suggests, Paulet was about to add jeder Redliche, or something similar.

1699. Leicester and Mortimer had exchanged words while Elizabeth was reading Mary's letter. Cf. stage direction after l. 1507.

1710. On the use of the genitive cf. l. 469, note.

1736. **Muß dem so sein,** *That must be so.* On the impersonal use of sein with the dative cf. J. 437, 5 *b*, W. 222, II., 1 *f*.

1741. **mit wenigem,** *briefly.*

1759. **die Maria.** On the use of the definite article cf. B. 147, 1, J. 416, W. 66, 4 *c*.

1762. In 1564, during the negotiations concerning Mary's marriage, Elizabeth proposed for her an alliance with Leicester. Mary resented the proposal, and it is probable that Elizabeth never seriously intended it. Cf. Robertson, vol. 1, 249.

1789. **Argusblick.** Argus was a mythological monster to whom Ovid attributes a hundred eyes, of which only two ever slept at the same time.

1790. **ins Verhör genommen,** *taken to task.*

1795. **teuren.** 'Dear,' in the sense of costly, is the primary meaning, but here, referring to Leicester's long continued efforts to win Elizabeth, perhaps *tedious* will be a suitable rendering.

1815. mein Verschulden. Mary's misfortunes followed her marriage with Darnley. Had Leicester been her husband, her career would have been different, and it is probably in this sense that he regards her downfall as his fault.

1830. Sonst, *otherwise.* Note the force of the word, intimating that what precedes is regarded conditionally. Cf. W. 332, 2 *e*.

1837. leidend, *passively.* On the adverbial use of the participle cf. B. 294, W. 356.

1863. Es . . . Gewalt, *Nothing can be done with violence.*

1866. will. Cf. B. 326, J. 459, 2 *b*, W. 181.

1868–79. Note the short sentences in this dialogue. Such an arrangement is called 'stichomythia' (talking in alternate lines), and is imitated from Greek tragedy.

1876. Norfolk . . . heimgeführt, *Norfolk has not wedded his betrothed.* Braut is not equivalent to the English 'bride,' but refers to the woman who is promised in marriage. Heimgeführt signifies especially 'the bringing into the new home.'

1920. Ob . . . gestürzt, *Although their leaders are overthrown.* Thomas Howard, Duke of Norfolk and head of the Howard family, was, as above remarked (l. 83, note), executed in 1572. Thomas Percy, Earl of Northumberland, who was implicated in Norfolk's treason, was also beheaded the same year. Note the separation of the conjunction ob=gleich into its two elements.

1928. It will be remembered that Elizabeth's visit to the Earl of Leicester in 1575 forms part of the plot of Sir Walter Scott's "Kenilworth."

1937. Schlüssel. The reference to the key, the symbol of a housewife, is contemptuous.

1938. jedes Mutes Federn abgespannt, *the springs of every man's courage relaxed.*

1962. The Duke of Anjou visited Elizabeth in August, 1579, and again in November, 1581.

1982. The use of **doch** here and in the following lines demands attention. *Surely* (doch) *I too . . . yet* (doch) *I preferred . . . and after all* (doch).

1996. Larve. In the sense of *face* the word is usually, as here, contemptuous.

2000. **Was** used instead of **warum**. Cf. B. 251, 4, J. 458, 2 *b*, W. 176, 3.

2010. **der sie . . . weicht,** *to whom she is inferior.*

2015. **machte.** The preterit indicative instead of the subjunctive gives the force of assurance or certainty. In the next line **hat** is used in the same way. Cf. B. 340, 3.

2020–21. **Da . . . Vermählung,** *Since she has always piqued herself upon, and been so proud of her French marriage.*

2034. **Bräutlichkeit,** *bridal loveliness.*

ACT III.

2075. **genießen.** On the use of this verb with the genitive cf. B. 184, J. 434, *a*, 2, W. 219, 5 and 6. The more common construction with the accusative occurs in ll. 719 and 2149.

2094–95. Poetic statement. The Scottish border is nearly two hundred miles from Fotheringhay.

2099. **Wer . . . wanderte,** *If one could but go with you.* The exclamation has the arrangement of a dependent clause, and the preterit subjunctive implies impossibility. Cf. W. 439, 4 *a.*

2106. **macht Euch schwärmen,** *fills your mind with fancies.*

2107. **den Nachen.** Mary perhaps thinks of her escape from the Castle of Lochlevin in 1567, for on that occasion she was rowed to the shore in a small boat.

2129. **reimen** has here the sense *reconcile.*

2130–31. These lines with l. 3386 afford the data for determining the time occupied by the drama.

2133. **die ew'ge Freiheit,** i. e. death.

2135. **mächtigen Rufes.** On the use of the genitive cf. B. 187, J. 435, *a*, W. 220, 1.

2138. **Noch mehr,** refers to the horns that are heard again. The Leipzig-Dresden Theater MS. has a stage direction to that effect.

2170–71. **Es ist . . . Mut —.** This is in reply to Paulet. The dash indicates her recognition of Shrewsbury.

2202. **mögen,** *are able.* Cf. B. 267, 3, 1, W. 255.

2215. **Es . . . begegnet,** *I have been harshly dealt with.* Cf. J. 437, 2 *c*, W. 222, II., 2.

2236. **Nun** as a causal conjunction is rare and archaic. Cf. B. 337, 1, J. 486, 2 *c*, W. 386, 4 *d*.

2241. **vergeht,** *languishes.*

2244. **geschmeidigt,** *softened.*

2250. **Schwester.** In their correspondence Mary and Elizabeth usually addressed each other as sister, and in the same formal sense brother is the customary form of address between kings. Cf. Steele, Spectator, No. 64 " . . . princes and sovereigns, who, in the language of all nations, are styled brothers to each other."

2270. **der Strandende,** *the cast-away.*

2292. **Ihr.** The dative with a verb of removal frequently answers to the objective with *from*. Cf. J. 440, W. 222, I., 3.

2301. **die Freunde.** Note the use of the definite article instead of the possessive pronoun. Cf. B. 154, J. 416, 5, W. 66, 3.

2313. **fachten . . . Atem zu,** *fanned.*

2323–24. Soon after she came into England, Mary repeatedly urged Elizabeth to grant her an interview.

2329. The allusion is evidently to Aesop's Fable of the Countryman, who warmed in his bosom the snake that afterward attacked his children.

2330. The sense requires that an adversative particle (sondern) be supplied between the contrasted objects of the imperative, **klagt an.**

2334. **Herrschwüt'ge,** *despotic.*

2347–8. **Ihr . . . überheben,** *You will not take such cruel pride in your power.*

2352. **Barthelemi.** Schiller follows the French form *Barthélemy.* The Massacre of St. Bartholomew began the night of August 23, 1572. The Duke of Guise took an active part in it, and the king afterward accused him of having ordered it without the royal sanction. That was, however, not true, for Catherine de Medici obtained the king's signature to the order. The inception and history of the plot, as well as the share of the Guises in instigating it, is a disputed question.

2360. **Sankt Peters Schlüssel,** i. e. papal dispensation.

2366. **Erbin.** Mary requested in 1561 that she might be declared next in succession. Elizabeth's reply to the effect that 'she would not run the risk of seeing her subjects adore the rising sun,' is alluded to in the next speech.

2370. **Freundschaft,** *kindred;* the older meaning of the word seems, as Breul suggests, to be the best translation.

2374. **Armida.** In Tasso's "Jerusalem Delivered," Armida is a beautiful sorceress who ensnares the hero in her nets.

2410. **Freier.** Elizabeth refers to the Duke of Norfolk. Cf. l. 73, note.

2422. **Die Macht.** Bellermann understands Mary to mean that her sense of irresponsibility as an absolute sovereign caused her to give free rein to her passions. He cites Wallenstein, Prolog, 117:

„Denn seine Macht ist's, die sein Herz verführt."

This seems more in harmony with Mary's character than the usual explanation, which refers Macht to the violence practiced by Bothwell.

2434. **Mäßigung,** *self-restraint.*

2441. **Basilisk.** A fabulous serpent whose breath, and whose glance even, was fatal.

2451. **König.** The masculine is used for greater emphasis. Cf. B. 167. Cf. l. 2169, vor Eurem Richter, and l. 2470, sie der Verbrecher.

2469. **Du.** In his passionate outburst Mortimer forgets himself and addresses Mary with Du, though he twice recollects himself, and uses Ihr.

2491. **was bedarf man sein,** *why is he needed?* Cf. l. 2000, note, and l. 451, note. On the use of was cf. W. 176, 3.

2503. **In heimlicher Kapelle.** Cf. ll. 640 and 2679.

2509. **zu der letzten Reise,** i. e. for death. Cf. l. 2133, note.

2537. Tyburn was, till 1783, the place of public executions in London.

2557. **dem Lebensgott der Freuden.** Poetical for dem Gott des Lebens und der Freuden.

2580. **seiner** refers to **Leben.** Düntzer.

2604. **Straßen** is dative singular. Cf. l. 1190, note.

2613. **Sauvage** or Savage was a leader in the Babington conspiracy, to whom, with five associates, Elizabeth's murder was entrusted, while Babington himself should free Mary. Savage was not a monk, and Okelly, as the name of one of the conspirators, is the poet's invention. The plot was discovered in time to prevent any attempt to carry it out.

2640. **wo nicht.** Cf. B. 340 and 340, 4, W. 386, 4 *f.*

ACT IV.

2641. **Ihro** is probably formed from analogy with **dero**, an old genitive plural form of the demonstrative **der**. It is used before titles. Cf. B. 86 and 440, 2, J. 455 *c*, W. 162.

2671. **Verbrechen.** Schiller here follows Rapin, who relates that, while Mary's sentence was pending, L'Aubespine hired two assassins to murder Elizabeth, and that, when accused before the Council, he was unable to make any further defense than to plead the privileges of ambassadors. Such a rumor was current at the time and served to arouse the fury of the people, but modern research has shown that it had no foundation in fact. Cf. Froude, vol. 12, 316–20.

2688. **Hotel** is sometimes used in the sense of *palace* or *mansion.*

2711. **Atlas** was, according to Homer, the keeper of the pillars that supported heaven. He is often represented as a man bearing a globe upon his shoulders. The irony of the comparison is evident.

2726. **Person,** *rôle.*

2743. **Unglückselige** refers here, as Düntzer notes, to one who brings misfortune to another. The use of **Unglücklicher** in l. 2761 is similar.

2757. The line is parenthetical, and is in apposition to the whole sentence.

2767. **Was unterfangt Ihr Euch,** *how do you dare.*

2785. **kommt ihm zuvor,** *anticipate him*, referring, of course, to Burleigh.

2819–20. These two lines are a prayer addressed to the Blessed Virgin. Düntzer is undeniably right, that both clearness and force would have been gained by writing **heil'ge Jungfrau.**

2870. **Die Königin verbiet',** *Tell him the queen forbids.* The verb upon which the indirect subjunctive depends is not expressed. Cf. J. 467, *a*, W. 333, 3 *d.*

2875. **eine abgefeimte Bübin,** *a crafty jade.*

2913. **zweier.** On the use of the inflected form cf. B. 226, J. 302, W. 199.

2952. **schwatzen,** *prate.* The contemptuous force of the word is emphasized by the contrast with **reden**, which Leicester applies to himself.

2962–63. **war . . . noch heute,** *would be this very day.* Cf. l. 2015, note. **Spürkunst** may be translated *shrewdness.*

2979. **Unterhandlung . . . pflog,** *negotiated.* Pflegen is usually a weak verb, but in exalted discourse, and when the idea of management or the carrying on of one's occupation is indicated, the strong form of the preterit is often used.

3014. **Engel.** Cf. Tell, I., 1:

„Mein Retter seid Ihr und mein Engel Tell."

3048–49. The execution of the death sentence was intrusted to the Earls of Kent and Shrewsbury, together with the sheriff of Northamptonshire.

3055. **Der Schrecken geht,** *the panic spreads.* Schiller here follows Rapin, who speaks of various rumors that were afloat at the time.

3068. This line suggests the familiar proverb, *Vox populi, vox Dei,* Des Volkes Stimme, Gottes Stimme.

3070. **Wenn ich . . . nun gehorcht,** *When I have hearkened.* Cf. B. 330, 2.

3084. **Hier gilt es,** *now is the time.*

3090. **Zu fällen,** *to be pronounced.* A legal term.

3104. **Dreimal.** Cf. l. 1277, note.

3145–50. In her reply to the Petition of Parliament urging Mary's execution, Elizabeth wrote, "If England might by my death obtain a more flourishing Estate and a better Prince, I would most gladly lay down my life. For, for your sakes it is, and for my People's, that I desire to live." Cf. Rapin, vol. 2, 129.

3176–77. The allusion is to Pope Innocent III., who put England under an interdict in 1208, and deposed King John in 1212.

3194. **Meinung,** as the context shows, is to be translated here by *public opinion.*

3205. **War,** *If I had been.* Cf. l. 2015, note.

3216–19. **Bannfluch** refers to the Bull of Deposition. Cf. l. 1490, note. The allusion to France is less definite, but the marriage-treaty is probably meant. As to Spain, diplomatic relations had ceased in 1584, but though Philip II. was preparing for war, the Armada did not sail till 1587.

3234–35. **Geliebten** evidently refers to Leicester, whose innocence Elizabeth still doubts. By **Bräut'gam** is meant the Duke of Anjou;

that the queen did not marry him was in no way due to Mary Stuart, but Schiller has chosen to represent it so. Cf. ll. 2683–85.

3248. **im echten Ehebett,** *in true wedlock.* (Breul.)

3248 †. Elizabeth signed the death-warrant at Greenwich, Feb. 1, 1587, and gave Davison directions concerning the place of execution. The next day she sent word to him, unless he had already had the warrant sealed, not to do so till he had seen her again. He hastened to her and told her it was already sealed. Though she said she had not changed her mind, she seemed displeased and suddenly left the room. Fearing that she might try to avoid the responsibility of the act, he took the warrant to Burleigh, and the following day it was laid before the members of the Council. They all agreed that the queen should be troubled no further and put the warrant in execution.

3258. **so kraftvoll überzeugend,** *with such strong assurance.*

3273. **steh'nden Fußes.** On the use of the genitive cf. l. 2135, note.

3306–7. **daß ich . . . will . . . haben,** dependent like the preceding clause, upon ich will, is logically incoherent, and shows Elizabeth's excitement.

3314. **Monden** is here poetical for Monaten. Davison had held the office of Secretary but a short time, but had been employed repeatedly in diplomatic services.

3324. **Eures Amts.** On the use of the genitive cf. J. 435, *b*, W. 220, 4.

ACT V.

3349. Sir Andrew Melvil was master of Mary's household. After her sentence was made known to her, he persisted in maintaining the customary ceremonial, and was, on that account, excluded from her presence. He was not allowed to see her till she descended the staircase on her way to the scaffold.

3366. **diese Wangen . . . erheitern,** say *gladden these features.*

3367. **nächtliche Gewand,** *gloomy garb,* referring to his mourning dress.

3398. Between two and three o'clock in the afternoon the Earls of Kent and Shrewsbury waited upon Mary, and notified her to prepare for death the following morning. The announcement was unexpected, but, according to Robertson, Mary heard it without emotion, and crossing herself replied: "That soul is not worthy the joys of heaven which repines, because the body must endure the stroke of the executioner; and though I did not expect that the queen of England would set the first example of violating the person of a sovereign prince, I willingly submit to that which Providence has decreed to be my lot."

3417. **preßte sie ihr ab,** *forced them from her.*

3433. **Auf freiem Fuß gesetzt.** A synonym for freigeben or freilassen.

3457. **Prachtgerät.** As Düntzer remarks, Schiller represents Mary's possessions as returned on the morning of her death, in order that the sight of former splendor may make her fate appear more pitiable. The incident is the poet's invention.

3472. **beschlagen,** *draped.*

3479 †. Mary's dress was black with a long white veil. Schiller makes it the reverse. The Agnus Dei is an oval of metal or wax, consecrated by the pope, and having upon one side the Lamb of God with the standard of the cross, and upon the reverse the figure of a saint. Its use was forbidden by the English law.

3509. Didier was one of the servants who were permitted to attend Mary to the scaffold.

3521. **Den allerchristlichsten König,** i. e. Henry III. of France. Cf. l. 1531, note.

3525. **Papst,** i. e. Sextus V., who became pope in 1585.

3527. **Kathol'schen König,** i. e. Philip II. of Spain. The title of Catholic was conferred upon the Spanish sovereigns, Ferdinand and Isabella, by Pope Alexander VI.

3575. **das beßre Theil erwählt,** referring to Luke x., 42.

3591. Mary was refused the attendance of her almoner and declined the services of the Dean of Peterborough. In preparing for death she spent some time in private devotion, and according to Brantôme made a general confession in writing, and celebrated the communion with a consecrated wafer, that had been sent to her years before by Pope Pius V.

3618. **im reinen Meßgewand,** *in spotless vestment.* The chasuble, or robe worn during the celebration of mass, is evidently intended.

3625. As remarked in the Introduction, Schiller was obliged to comply with Karl August's wishes and to change this scene so that he avoided the communion office. In doing this he represented Melvil as not yet consecrated to the priesthood, and as the cup of wine was not needed, the references to it in Scenes 3 and 5 were omitted. The remaining changes were as follows: — Instead of ll. 3625–31 Melvil says:

Er dringt zu dir, er ist dir nah, ihn schließt
Kein Tempel ein, kein Kerker schließt ihn aus.
Nicht in der Formel ist der Geist enthalten,
Den Ewigen begrenzt kein irdisch Haus.
Das sind nur Hüllen, nur die Scheingestalten
Der unsichtbaren Himmelskraft:
Es ist der Glaube, der den Gott erschafft.

Mary's reply remained unaltered, except that the word Beichte in l. 3641 was changed to Bekenntniß. For ll. 3643–72 was substituted,—

Melvil.

Wenn mich dein Herz dafür erklärt, so bin ich
Für dich ein Priester, diese Kerzen sind
Geweihet, und wir stehn an heil'ger Stätte,
Ein Sakrament ist jegliches Bekenntnis,
Das du der ewigen Wahrheit thust. Spricht doch
Im Beichtstuhl selbst der Mensch nur zu dem Menschen,
Es spricht der Sündige den Sünder frei;
Und eitel ist des Priesters Lösewort,
Wenn dich der Gott nicht löst in deinem Busen.
Doch kann es dich beruhigen, so schwör' ich dir,
Was ich jetzt noch nicht bin, ich will es werden.
Ich will die Weih'n empfangen, die mir fehlen.
Dem Himmel widm' ich künftig meine Tage;
Kein irdisches Geschäft soll diese Hände
Fortan entweihn, die dir den Segen gaben,
Und dieses Priesterrecht, das ich voraus
Mir nehme, wird der Papst bestätigen.
Das ist die Wohlthat unsrer heil'gen Kirche,
Daß sie ein sichtbar Oberhaupt verehrt,
Dem die Gewalt inwohnet, das Gemeine

> Zu heil'gen und den Mangel zu ergänzen;
> Drum wenn der Mangel nicht in deinem Herzen,
> Nicht in dem Priester ist er — diese Handlung
> Hat volle Kraft, sobald du daran glaubst.

Then followed Mary's confession, but the absolution and communion office, ll. 3738–57, were replaced by,—

> So gehe hin, und sterbend büße sie!
> Du fehltest nur aus weiblichem Gebrechen.
> B l u t kann versöhnen, was das B l u t verbrach,
> Dem sel'gen Geiste folgen nicht die Schwächen
> Der Sterblichkeit in die Verklärung nach.
> Sink' ein ergebnes Opfer am Altar!
> Gieb hin dem Staube, was vergänglich war,
> Die ird'sche Schönheit und die ird'sche Krone!
> Und als ein schöner Engel schwinge dich
> In seines Lichtes freudenreiche Zone,
> Wo keine Schuld mehr sein wird und kein Weinen,
> Gereinigt in den Schoß des ewig Reinen!

3626. **der dürre Stab.** Cf. Numbers 17: 8 and two lines below on Quelle, Exodus 17: 6.

3635–6. In these two lines Schiller has but slightly changed Mat. 18: 20, which in Luther's translation reads: „Denn wo Zwei oder Drei versammelt sind in meinem Namen, da bin ich mitten unter ihnen."

3648 †. By uncovering his head Melvil shows the tonsure, which is the sign of priesthood.

3652. **Die sieben Weih'n.** The priestly office implies the sevenfold consecration of the four minor orders, Porter, Lector, Exorcist, Acolyte, and of the three major orders, Subdeacon, Deacon and Priest.

3658. Cf. Acts 12: 7–11.

3685. **das höchste Gut,** *Supreme Goodness.* This designation of God is taken, according to Düntzer, from the usual penitential formula.

3696. **mir.** Cf. l. 1303, note.

3700. **Wurm,** *Worm,* i. e. 'remorse.' Cf. Shakespeare, Richard III., 1, 3, 222: "The worm of conscience still begnaw thy soul."

3707. Though the Catholic church teaches that incomplete confession is a mortal sin, it is not the unpardonable sin against the Holy Ghost.

3736. **abzubüßen.** As Düntzer points out, Mary speaks in accordance with the Catholic conception that sin, though confessed and forgiven, yet involves a punishment either in this world or in the world to come. She accepts her death, therefore, as the punishment for her youthful crime, which God graciously deems her worthy to suffer in this temporal life.

3739. **Blut . . . verbrach,** *Blood can expiate the deed of blood,* will perhaps best give the force of the original.

3751. The Catholic church permits the laity to partake only of the bread in the communion. This practice was formally sanctioned by the Council of Constance in 1414. Occasionally, however, communion in both kinds was allowed as a particular favor of the Holy See. This privilege was enjoyed by the kings of France, on the day of their coronation, and also when at the point of death.

3773. This was one of the requests made in a letter to Elizabeth, Dec. 19, 1586. In the same letter she also asked that her body might be buried in France.

3777. **geweihter Erde.** Mary was buried in Peterborough Cathedral, but soon after his accession to the throne, James I. had her remains removed to Westminster Abbey.

3785. Upon the scaffold Mary prayed that Elizabeth might enjoy a long life and a peaceable reign.

3800. The Earl of Kent at first refused to allow any of Mary's servants to witness her death, but as she urged her request and promised that they should make no disturbance, she was allowed to choose six of her own people to accompany her.

3816–18. At the close of her prayer upon the scaffold, Mary kissed the crucifix and exclaimed: "As thy arms, O Jesus, were extended on the cross; so with the outstretched arms of thy mercy receive me, and forgive my sins." Cf. Robertson, vol. 2, 142.

3866. **Ich höre Stimmen** seems to refer to the reading of the death-warrant. The details of the execution are reported according to Archenholz, except the moving of the block, which Schiller adds.

3926. **Klüfte,** here *the cells.*

3980. **mich Lügen strafen,** *give me the lie.* Cf. B. 199, 2.

4008. At the first meeting of the Council after Mary's death

Elizabeth ordered Burleigh out of her presence, and for two months he was forbidden to approach her.

4012. Davison was ordered to the Tower. A charge of treason could not be made out, but Elizabeth appointed a commission to try him, and he was sentenced to pay a fine of £10,000, and to suffer imprisonment during the queen's pleasure.

4020–22. Shrewsbury's resignation is a fiction, for, as pointed out, cf. l. 752, note, he was not Chancellor.

VOCABULARY

VOCABULARY

The Vocabulary is intended to contain all words except proper nouns and the names of the *dramatis personæ*. Regarding them the Notes furnish the necessary information, and in the matter of pronunciation, except a few French forms, the usage of the German stage inclines to treat them as German. All references are to line numbers; in the case of stage directions, to that of the preceding line followed by a plus sign.

The gender of all nouns is indicated, as also the genitive singular and nominative plural, when not regular, under the most general rules.

Verbs are marked as *tr.* (transitive), *intr.* (intransitive), and *reflex.* (reflexive), and the parts of strong verbs are indicated, when regular, by the vowel change, otherwise they are given in full. Those conjugated with sein are marked s. Separable verbs are indicated by the accent which is also given with the doubtful prefixes.

In all other matters the ordinary abbreviations are used, but parts of speech are not indicated unless it is necessary. With adjectives that are also employed as adverbs, only the adjective meaning is ordinarily given. As the thought in preparing the Vocabulary has been to adapt the edition to school use, many phrases and idioms have been translated. In such instances the line number is added, sometimes with a reference to the notes.

A

ab, *adv. and sep. pref.*, off, down, away.

Abbild, *n.*, –er, image.

ab'bitten (a, e), *tr.*, ask pardon for.

ab'büßen, *tr.*, expiate, atone for.

ab'drücken, *tr.*, shoot, let fly (an arrow).

ab'eilen, *intr.*, s., hasten away, hurry off.

Abend, *m.*, evening.

Abenteuer, *m.*, adventure.

Aberglaube, *m.*, –ens, –en, superstition.

abermals, again, once more.

ab'fassen, *tr.*, to write, compose, draw up.

ab'feuern, *tr.*, discharge, fire off.

abgefeimt, arrant, crafty.

ab'gehen, –ging, –gegangen, *intr.*, s., exit, exeunt; go off, depart.

Abgesandte, *m.*, –en, –en, ambassador.

Abgott, *m.*, ⁻er, idol.
abgöttisch, idolatrous.
Abgrund, *m.*, ⁻e, abyss, chasm.
ab'hören, *tr.*, try, examine, question (a witness).
Abkunft, *f.*, ⁻e, descent.
Ablaß, *m.*, –sses, ⁻sse, indulgence, absolution.
ab'nehmen (a, o), *tr.*, take off.
ab'pressen, *tr.*, wring from, extort.
ab'reisen, *intr.*, s., leave, depart.
Abscheu, *m.*, loathing, horror, deep aversion.
abscheulich, horrible, heinous, execrable.
Abscheulichkeit, *f.*, atrocity, enormity, horror.
Abschied, *m.*, farewell; — nehmen, take leave.
ab'schildern, *tr.*, depict, describe, portray.
ab'schlagen (u, a), *tr.*, beat off, repulse.
ab'schließen (o, o), *tr.*, close, conclude, settle.
ab'schwören (o *or* u, o), *tr.*, abjure, renounce.
Absicht, *f.*, purpose, design, intention.
ab'spannen, *tr.*, unbend, relax.
ab'sprechen (a, o), *tr.*, declare forfeit, condemn; die ihr das Haupt abspricht, which condemns her to death, 1451.
ab'thun, –that, –gethan, *tr.*, take off; arrange, settle.
ab'treten (a, e), *intr.*, s., withdraw, retire.
ab'weisen (ie, ie), *tr.*, refuse admittance, dismiss.
ab'wenden, –wandte, –gewandt (*also reg.*), *tr.*, avert; *reflex.*, turn away.
ab'wägen (o, o), *tr.*, weigh, balance, consider carefully.
ach, ah! alas!
Acht, *f.*, care, heed; sich in — nehmen, take care.
acht, eight.
achten, *tr.*, regard, respect, care for; nichts geachtet, set at nought, 1979.
Achtung, *f.*, respect, esteem.
Adel, *m.*, nobility, the nobles; — der Gestalt, stateliness of form, 2009.
adeln, *tr.*, ennoble, exalt, dignify.
Ader, *f.*, vein.
Affekt', *m.*, emotion, passion.
Afterkönigin, *f.*, –innen, pretended queen, pretender.
Agnus Dei (*Lat.*), Agnus Dei; *cf.* 3479 +, *note*.
Ahnen, *n.*, foreboding.
Ahnherr, *m.*, –n, –en, ancestor.
Ahnung, *f.*, presentiment, misgiving.
Akte, *f.*, act (of Parliament).
all, *adj. and indef. pron.*, all, everything, whole, entire; *of persons*, all, everybody.

allein, *indec. adj. and adv.,* alone, only; *conj.,* but.
allerchristlich, most Christian.
allerlei, all sorts *or* kinds.
allertreu, very faithful, most loyal.
allgemein, general, universal, common.
allgewaltig, all-powerful, mighty.
Allmacht, *f.,* Omnipotence, the Almighty.
allmächtig, omnipotent.
allmählich, gradual, by degrees.
allvermögend, all-efficient, all-powerful, omnipotent; *as noun,* Almighty God.
allwichtig, all-important.
allwissend, omniscient, all-knowing.
allzuheftig, too violent.
als, when, as, than.
alsbald, at once, forthwith.
also, so, thus, then.
alt, old, former, ancient.
Altar', *m.,* –e *and* ⁼e, altar.
altenglisch, old English.
Alter, *n.,* age, old age.
altern, *intr.,* grow old; vor der Zeit gealtert, prematurely aged, 2014.
Amen, amen, so be it.
Amme, *f.,* nurse, attendant.
Amt, *n.,* ⁼er, office, duty.
an, *prep. and sep. pref.,* at, by, in, near, to.
Anathem', *n.,* anathema, curse (involving excommunication).
an'befehlen (a, o), *tr.,* command, order, authorize.
an'beten, *tr.,* worship, adore.
Anbetung, *f.,* worship, adoration.
an'bieten (o, o), *tr.,* offer; *reflex.,* volunteer.
an'blasen (ie, a), *tr.,* blow, kindle.
Anblick, *m.,* sight, spectacle, sight of, glance.
an'bringen, –brachte, –gebracht, *tr.,* make use of, adapt.
Anbruch, *m.,* ⁼e, break, dawn.
Andacht, *f.,* devotion.
ander, other, else.
ändern, *tr.,* change.
anders, otherwise.
an'empfehlen (a, o), *tr.,* recommend (strongly).
an'erkennen, –erkannte, –erkannt, *tr.,* acknowledge, own, avow.
an'fallen (ie, a), *tr.,* attack, assail.
Anfang, *m.,* ⁼e, beginning.
an'fangen (i, a), *tr.,* begin, commence.
anfangs, at first, at the outset.
an'fechten (o, o), *tr.,* contest, controvert, dispute.
an'fesseln, *tr.,* chain fast, fetter.
an'flehen, *tr.,* implore, beseech, entreat.

an'füllen, *tr. and reflex.,* fill up; *intr.,* be filled.

angebetet, adored.

Angedenken, *n.,* memory, remembrance, token.

angefangen, begun; partly written, 2779.

angefochten, contested.

an'gehen, –ging, –gegangen, *tr.,* concern.

Angeklagte, *m. or f. (dec. as adj.),* the accused, defendant.

Angesicht, *n.,* –er, face, presence.

angestammt, hereditary, ancestral.

an'greifen (i, i), *tr.,* attack, charge upon.

Angst, *f.,* ⸚e, anguish, anxiety, dread, apprehension.

ängsten, *see* ängstigen.

Angstgedränge, *n.,* dilemma, perplexity.

ängstigen, *tr.,* alarm, strike with fear, frighten.

an'heften, *tr.,* fasten to.

an'hören, *tr.,* listen to, hear, give ear to.

an'klagen, *tr.,* accuse, arraign, indict.

an'kleiden, *tr.,* dress.

an'kommen (a, o), *intr.,* s., arrive.

Ankömmling, *m.,* arrival, new comer.

an'künden, *tr.,* announce, declare, proclaim, inform of.

an'kündigen, *see* ankünden.

an'legen, *tr.,* lay on; draw up (a boat), 2107.

anmaßlich, presumptuous, assuming.

Anmut, *f.,* sweetness, charm, grace.

an'nehmen (a, o), *tr.,* assume.

an'raten (ie, a), *tr.,* recommend, suggest, advise.

an'reden, *tr.,* address, speak to.

an'rufen (ie, u), *tr.,* appeal to, invoke, call upon.

an'sagen, *tr.,* announce, speak out, say on.

an'schauen, *tr.,* look at, see, gaze at (admiringly).

Anschlag, *m.,* ⸚e, plan, projet, design.

an'sehen (a, e), look at; einem etwas —, perceive something in one; man sieht's ihr nicht an, she does not look it, 2013.

Ansehen, *n.,* authority, high standing, appearance.

an'sinnen (a, o), *tr.,* suggest to, expect of.

Anspruch, *m.,* ⸚e, claim, title.

anspruchslos, unostentatious, unpretending.

Anstalt, *f.,* preparation; — machen, make arrangements, 1889.

Anstand, *m.,* propriety; — nehmen, hesitate, 1900.

an'stehen, –stand, –gestanden,

intr. with dat., become, befit.

an'tasten, *tr.*, touch, hurt, harm.

Anteil, *m.*, share, part, portion.

an'thun, –that, –gethan, *tr.*, put on, inflict; angethan sein, be clad.

Antlitz, *n.*, face; ins — sagen, say to your face, 262.

Antrag, *m.*, ⁼e, offer, proposal.

an'tragen (u, a), *intr. with* auf, move, make a motion.

an'treten (a, e), *tr.*, begin, enter upon.

antworten, *tr. and intr.*, answer, reply.

an'vertrauen, *tr.*, entrust to, trust, confide.

Anverwandte, *m.*, *dec. as adj.*, relative, kinsman, 124.

Anwalt, *m.*, advocate, defender.

an'wandeln, *tr. impers.*, befall, come over; what is the matter with, 1694.

anwesend, present.

an'zeigen, *tr.*, inform, point out.

an'zünden, *tr.*, kindle, light.

Apostel, *m.*, apostle.

arg, bad, wicked.

arglos, guileless, unsuspecting.

Argwohn, *m.*, suspicion.

Argusblick, *m.*, Argus glance, vigilance.

Arm, *m.*, arm.

arm, poor.

Arsenal', *n.*, arsenal.

Arti'kel, *m.*, article.

Arzt, *m.*, ⁼e, physician.

Atem, *m.*, breath.

atmen, *intr.*, breathe; alles Atmende, all living things, 2531.

auch, also, too, even; wie . . . auch, however.

auf, *prep.*, upon, on, to, toward, at; *sep. pref. and adv.*, up, upward.

auf'bieten (o, o), *tr.*, call up; alles biet' ich auf, use every effort, 1907.

auf'brechen (a, o), *tr.*, break open.

auf'bringen, –brachte, –gebracht, *tr.*, provoke, irritate, exasperate.

Aufbruch, *m.*, ⁼e, movement, departure, setting out.

auf'dringen (a, u), *tr.*, force upon, press on, intrude.

auf'erlegen, *tr.*, impose (something) on, enjoin (one) to.

auf'erstehen, –erstand, –erstanden, *intr.*, s., arise.

auf'erziehen, –erzog, –erzogen, *tr.*, rear, train up.

auf'fahren (u, a), *intr.*, s., start.

auf'fangen (i, a), *tr.*, intercept.

auf'fordern, *tr.*, challenge; das Schloß aufforderte,

summoned the castle to surrender, 1090.

auf'führen, *tr.*, lead up; represent, 1082.

auf'geben (a, e), *tr.*, give up, lay down, resign; die Aufgegebene, the helpless woman, 1356.

aufgebracht, excited, angry.

auf'gehen, –ging, –gegangen, *intr.*, s., rise; open (as a door).

auf'greifen (i, i), *tr.*, pick up.

auf'hören, *intr.*, cease, leave off.

auf'jagen, *tr.*, start, rouse.

auf'laden (u, a), *tr.*, load upon, burden with.

Auflauf, *m.*, ¨e, tumult, mob, rabble, uproar.

auf'lösen, *tr.*, dissolve, annul, cancel.

aufmerksam, attentive, heedful.

Aufmerksamkeit, *f.*, attention, courtesy.

auf'nehmen (a, o), *tr.*, receive.

auf'regen, *tr.*, arouse, alarm, excite.

auf'reiben (ie, ie), *tr.*, consume, exhaust, waste away (of disease).

auf'reißen (i, i), *tr.*, tear open, fling *or* burst open.

auf'rufen (ie, u), *tr.*, call up, summon.

auf'rühren, *tr.*, stir up, excite.

auf'säugen, *tr.*, suckle, rear (a child).

auf'schlagen (u, a), *tr.*, put up, raise, erect.

auf'schließen (o, o), *tr.*, open, disclose.

auf'schreien (ie, ie), *intr.*, cry out, scream.

Aufschub, *m.*, ¨e, delay, putting off.

auf'schwingen (a, u), *tr.*, swing up; *reflex.*, soar.

auf'setzen, *tr.*, put down (in writing), draw up, compose.

Aufsicht, *f.*, care, custody.

auf'springen (a, u), *intr.*, s., spring open, spring or jump up.

auf'stecken, *tr.*, set up.

auf'stehen, –stand, –gestanden, *intr.*, s., stand up, arise.

auf'steigen (ie, ie), *intr.*, s., rise, ascend.

auf'suchen, *tr.*, seek out.

auf'thun, –that, –gethan, *tr.*, open; *reflex.*, be opened.

Auftrag, *m.*, ¨e, charge, errand, commission.

auf'treten (a, e), *intr.*, s., step out, appear, enter.

Auf'tritt, *m.*, scene, appearance.

auf'wachen, *intr.*, s., awake.

auf'wachsen (u, a), *intr.*, s., grow up.

auf'zeigen, *tr.*, show, produce.

auf'ziehen, –zog, –gezogen, *tr.*, raise, draw up.

Aufzug, *m.*, ⁿe, act (in a drama).
Auge, *n.*, –es, –en, eye.
Augenblick, *m.*, moment.
augenblicklich, momentary; *as adv.*, instantly.
augenblicks, *see* augenblick=lich.
aus, *prep.*, out of, of, by, from, through; *adv. and sep. pref.*, out, over, past.
aus'beugen, *intr.*, evade.
aus'brechen (a, o), *intr.*, s., break out, exclaim, burst (into tears).
aus'breiten, *tr.*, extend, stretch out; spread (a rumor).
aus'deuten, *tr.*, interpret, explain.
Ausdruck, *m.*, ⁿe, expression, language, phrase.
ausdrücken, *tr.*, express.
ausdrücklich, explicit, positive.
auseinander, asunder, apart.
aus'fertigen, *tr.*, dispatch, draw up, execute.
Ausflucht, *f.*, ⁿe, evasion, subterfuge.
aus'forschen, *tr.*, search, sound, draw (one) out.
aus'führen, *tr.*, carry out, execute, perform.
aus'gehen, –ging, –gegangen, *intr.*, s., go out, go forth.
aus'halten (ie, a), *tr.*, endure, bear, hold out.
Ausland, *n.*, ⁿer, foreign land.
aus'lernen, *tr.*, learn thoroughly, master.
aus'lesen, *tr.*, select, pick out.
aus'löschen, *tr.*, extinguish, efface, blot out.
aus'machen, *tr.*, make, compose, constitute.
aus'nehmen (a, o), *tr.*, except.
aus'rufen (ie, u), *tr.*, proclaim.
aus'säen, *tr.*, sow, disseminate (false news).
aus'sagen, *tr.*, say, utter, state, declare.
aus'schließen (o, o), *tr.*, exclude.
aus'sehen (a, e), *intr.*, look, appear.
außen, out, without, abroad.
aus'senden, –sandte, –gesandt (*or reg.*), *tr.*, send out.
außer, without, out of, except; — sich, beside one's self, 2105.
außerordentlich, unusual, extraordinary.
äußerst, extreme, utmost.
aus'setzen, *tr.*, expose.
Aussicht, *f.*, outlook, prospect.
aus'sinnen (a, o), *tr.*, think out, plan, frame (some excuse).
aus'spannen, *tr.*, extend, spread.
aus'sprechen (a, o), *tr.*, pronounce, express.
aus'strecken, *tr.*, stretch forth, put out.

aus'teilen, *tr.*, give out, issue.

aus'trinken (a, u), *tr.*, drink up, drain.

aus'üben, *tr.*, exercise, practice.

aus'wirken, *tr.*, effect, procure, obtain.

Auswurf, *m.*, ″e, outcast, scum (of the people).

aus'zeichnen, *tr.*, mark out, distinguish.

Axt, *f.*, ″e, ax.

B

Bahn, *f.*, –en, road, path, career.

bahnen, *tr.*, smooth the way, remove obstacles, pave.

bald, soon.

Band, *n.*, –e, bond; *pl.* ″er, ribbon, band.

bändigen, *tr.*, restrain, check, subdue, control.

Bannfluch, *m.*, ″e, anathema, (papal) ban, excommunication.

Barmherzigkeit, *f.*, mercy, compassion.

Barthelemi, *for French* Barthélemy; *cf.* 2352, *note.*

Basilisk, *m.*, –en, –en, basilisk, cockatrice.

Bastard, *m.*, –e, bastard.

Bastardkönigin, *f.*, –innen, bastard queen.

Bastardname, *m.*, –ens, –en, bastard's name.

Bastardtochter, *f.*, ″, bastard *or* illegitimate daughter.

bauen, *tr.*, build.

Baum, *m.*, ″e, tree.

be=, *insep. pref. never accented, Eng.* be-.

beängstigen, *tr.*, frighten, cause anxiety.

Becher, *m.*, goblet, cup.

bedacht, discreet, prudent, deliberate.

bedecken, *tr.*, cover.

bedenken, –dachte, –dacht, *tr.*, consider, weigh, remember; *reflex.*, hesitate, bethink one's self, reflect.

bedenklich, hesitating, irresolute, doubtful.

bedeuten, *tr.*, mean, signify, denote.

bedeutend, grave, important, significant.

Bedeutung, *f.*, meaning, significance.

bedeutungsvoll, ominous, significant, meaning.

bedienen, *tr.*, serve.

Bediente, *m.* (*dec. as adj.*), servant.

bedrängen, *tr.*, oppress, harass, distress.

bedrohen, *tr.*, threaten, menace.

bedürfen, –durfte, –durft, *intr.* (*gen.*), need, require.

Befehl, *m.*, command, order.

befehlen (a, o), *tr.*, bid, order, command.

befinden (a, u), *reflex.*, do *or* be (well, etc.).
beflecken, *tr.*, spot, smirch, tarnish.
befleckt, polluted, defiled.
befleißen (i, i), *reflex.*, apply one's self, endeavor, strive.
beflügelt, winged.
befolgen, *tr.*, follow, obey.
befördern, *tr.*, forward.
befragen, *tr.*, ask, question, examine.
befreien, *tr.*, free, liberate, release, exempt.
Befreier, *m.*, liberator, deliverer.
Befreiung, *f.*, liberation, release.
befreundet, friendly, allied.
befürchten, *tr.*, apprehend, fear.
begeben (a, e), *reflex.*, betake one's self; *with gen.*, renounce, waive, forego.
begegnen, *intr.*, s., meet, befall; use, treat, 2215.
Begegnung, *f.*, meeting.
begehen, –ging, –gangen, *tr.*, do, commit.
begehren, *tr.*, desire eagerly, covet, demand.
Begierde, *f.*, desire.
beginnen (a, o), *tr. and intr.*, begin.
Beginnen, *n.*, action, beginning.
beglaubigen, *tr.*, attest, accredit.
begleiten, *tr.*, accompany, escort.
Begleiter, *m.*, companion.
Begleitung, *f.*, attendance.
beglücken, *tr.*, make happy.
beglückt, happy, blessed, favored.
begnadigen, *tr.*, pardon.
begnügen, *reflex.*, be contented, be satisfied with.
begraben (u, a), *tr.*, bury.
begreifen (i, i), *tr.*, understand, comprehend.
begreiflich, conceivable, comprehensible.
Begriff, *m.*, idea, notion; **im** — sein, to be about, on the point of.
begrüßen, *tr.*, greet, salute.
behalten (ie, a), *tr.*, keep, retain.
behandeln, *tr.*, treat, deal with.
behaupten, *tr.*, maintain, assert, affirm.
Beherrscher, *m.*, ruler, sovereign.
Beherrscherin, *f.*, –innen, ruler, queen, sovereign.
Beherrschung, *f.*, control.
beherzt, bold, manful, valorous.
bei, *prep., adv., and sep. pref.*, by, with, at, near, among, in, at the house of, on, upon.
Beichte, *f.*, confession.
beichten, *tr.*, confess.
beide, both.

Beifall, *m.*, approval, assent, applause.

Beil, *n.*, ax.

Beisein, *n.*, presence.

Beispiel, *n.*, example, pattern.

Beistand, *m.*, ¨e, assistance, support, helper.

bei'stimmen, *intr.*, agree, assent to, concur in.

bei'wohnen, *intr.*, be present at, attend.

bejahen, *tr.*, affirm, assert, answer affirmatively.

bejammern, *tr.*, bewail, lament.

bekannt, known.

bekennen, –kannte, –kannt, *tr.*, confess, admit, acknowledge.

Bekenner, *m.*, confessor; follower, 3501.

Bekenntnis, *n.*, –sses, –sse, avowal, acknowledgment, confession, admission.

beklagen, *tr.*, pity, deplore, commiserate.

Beklagte, *m. and f.* (*dec. as adj.*), accused, defendant.

bekleiden, *tr.*, clothe, invest; hold (office *or* rank), 2945.

beklemmt, afflicted, oppressed.

bekränzen, *tr.*, wreathe, festoon with garlands.

bekrönen, *tr.*, crown.

bekümmern, *tr.*, trouble, concern.

beladen (u, a), *tr.*, load, burden.

belasten, *tr.*, burden.

belegen, *tr.*, lay upon, impose.

belehren, *tr.*, instruct, advise.

beleidigen, *tr.*, offend, insult, outrage, affront.

Beleidigung, *f.*, offence, insult, injury.

belohnen, *tr.*, reward, requite.

bemerken, *tr.*, note, remark, observe.

bemühen, *tr.*, trouble, inconvenience; *reflex.*, trouble one's self, strive.

Bemühen, *n.*, endeavor, effort.

beneiden, *tr.*, envy.

beobachten, *tr.*, watch, observe.

berauben, *tr.*, plunder, strip, rob.

Beredsamkeit, *f.*, eloquence.

beredt, eloquent.

bereichern, *tr.*, enrich.

bereisen, *tr.*, travel over, make a tour of.

bereit, ready, prepared.

bereiten, *tr. and intr.*, get ready, prepare, cause; *reflex.*, prepare.

bereits, already.

bereuen, *tr.*, repent, regret, be sorry for.

berennen, –rannte, –rannt, –rennt, 1085, *tr.*, assault, invest.

Berg, *m.*, mountain.

bergen (a, o), *tr.*, hide, conceal.

Bergeslast, *f.*, –en, mountain's weight.
bergicht, hilly.
Bericht, *m.*, account, report; — erstatten, inform, 2999.
berichtigen, *tr.*, correct, rectify, set right.
berücken, *tr.*, impose upon, deceive, cheat.
berufen (ie, u), *tr.*, call, summon; *reflex.*, appeal to, 959, 2893.
beruhigen, *tr.*, quiet, calm; *reflex.*, be reassured, calm one's self.
Beruhigung, *f.*, comfort, ease of mind, appeasing.
berühmen, *reflex. with gen.*, boast of.
berühren, *tr.*, touch.
besänftigen, *tr.*, quiet, calm, soothe; *reflex.*, be soothed.
beschäftigen, *tr.*, busy, occupy, engage, employ.
Beschämung, *f.*, confusion, mortification.
beschauen, *tr.*, look at, view, contemplate.
Beschauung, *f.*, contemplation.
Bescheidenheit, *f.*, modesty, discretion.
beschlagen (u, a), *tr.*, cover, drape.
beschleunigen, *tr.*, quicken, hasten, expedite.
beschließen (o, o), conclude, decide, resolve upon.
beschuldigen, *tr.*, charge with, accuse of (*with gen.*).
beschützen, *tr.*, defend, protect, guard.
beschwatzen, *tr.*, talk over, persuade.
beschwören (o *or* u, o), *tr.*, confirm by oath, swear to; adjure, implore, entreat.
beseelen, *tr.*, animate, inspire.
beseligen, *tr.*, bless.
besessen, possessed.
besetzen, *tr.*, beset, occupy.
besiegeln, *tr.*, seal, ratify, attest by seal.
besiegen, *tr.*, vanquish, subdue, overcome.
Besitz, *m.*, possession, tenure.
besitzen, –saß, –sessen, *tr.*, possess.
besonnen, thoughtful, prudent, circumspect; plötzlich —, with sudden resolution, 2793 +.
besorgen, *tr.*, provide, procure, get.
Besorgnis, *f.*, –sse, fear, misgiving, apprehension.
besser, *comp. of* gut, better.
bessern, *tr.*, improve, reform, amend.
Besserung, *f.*, improvement, amendment.
best, *superl. of* gut, best.
bestätigen, *tr.*, confirm, corroborate, verify.
bestechen (a, o), *tr.*, bribe, corrupt.
Bestechung, *f.*, bribery, corruption.

bestehen, –stand, –standen, *intr.*, s., exist; — aus *or* in, consist of; — auf, insist upon; *tr.*, undergo.

besteigen (ie, ie), *tr.*, ascend, mount.

bestellen, *tr.*, appoint, order, arrange.

bestimmen, *tr.*, determine, intend for, destine.

bestimmt, destined, intended.

bestürmen, *tr.*, assail, storm, importune.

bestürzt, surprised, startled, dismayed.

Bestürzung, *f.*, consternation, confusion.

besuchen, *tr.*, visit.

betäuben, *tr.*, deafen, stun, amaze, confound.

betäubt, stunned.

beten, *intr.*, pray.

bethören, *tr.*, befool, infatuate, delude.

betrachten, *tr.*, look at, examine.

Betrachtung, *f.*, reflection, meditation.

betragen (u, a), *reflex.*, behave, conduct one's self.

betreten, surprised, confused, embarrassed.

betroffen, amazed, perplexed.

betrügen (o, o), *tr.*, deceive, dupe, impose upon.

Betrüger, *m.*, impostor, deceiver.

betrüglich, deceitful, illusory.

Bett (*older form* Bette), ***n.***, –es, –en, bed.

betten, *intr.*, make the bed; auf ihrem Sarge mir zu —, to fall upon her coffin, 2641.

Bettler, *m.*, beggar.

beugen, *tr. and reflex.*, bend, bow; *intr.*, be bowed *or* depressed.

bewachen, *tr.*, guard, watch.

bewaffnen, *tr.*, arm; mit Bewaffneten, with soldiers, 2794 +.

bewahren, *tr.*, keep, guard.

bewähren, *tr.*, prove, test, verify.

Bewahrung, *f.*, keeping, custody.

bewandert, versed, intimately acquainted with (in).

bewegen, *tr. and intr.*, move, touch; *reflex.*, be moved.

Bewegung, *f.*, movement, agitation, emotion.

bewehren, *tr.*, arm.

beweinen, *tr.*, weep for, bewail.

Beweis, *m.*, proof, evidence.

beweisen, *tr.*, prove, demonstrate.

bewilligen, *tr.*, grant, consent to, allow.

bewußt (*with gen.*), conscious, aware of.

bezahlen, *tr.*, pay.

bezeigen, *tr.*, show, manifest.

bezeugen, *tr.*, witness, attest.

bezwingen (a, u), *tr.*, control, master, overcome; *reflex.*, control one's self.

Bibel, *f.*, bible.

Biedermann, *m.*, ¨er, worthy *or* true-hearted man, upright man.

bieten (o, o), *tr.*, bid, offer, tender.

Bild, *n.*, ¨er, image, picture, effigy.

bilden, *tr.*, form, mould, shape.

Bildnergeist, *m.*, ¨er, spirit of art.

Bildnis, *n.*, –sses, –sse, portrait, picture.

billig, fair, just, proper, reasonable.

billigen, *tr.*, approve of, allow.

binden (a, u), *tr.*, bind.

bis, *adv.*, *prep.*, *and conj.*, till, until, to, as far as; — auf, except.

Bischof, *m.*, ¨e, bishop.

Bischofsitz, *m.*, (episcopal) see.

Bitte, *f.*, request, petition, demand.

Blatt, *n.*, ¨er, leaf, sheet of paper; warrant, 3278.

bitten (a, e), *tr.*, beg, request, ask; *intr.*, pray, intercede.

Bittende, *f.* (*dec. as adj.*), suppliant.

bitter, bitter.

Bitterkeit, *f.*, bitterness.

blankgeschliffen, gleaming, brightly ground.

blau, blue.

bleiben (ie, ie), *intr.*, s., stay, remain; bei der Sache —, stick to the point, 928.

bleich, pale, pallid.

bleichen, *tr.*, blanch, make pale.

blenden, *tr.*, dazzle, blind.

blendend, dazzling, radiant.

Blendwerk, *n.*, –e, delusion.

Blick, *m.*, look, glance.

blicken, *intr.*, look.

blind, blind.

Blitz, *m.*, lightning, bolt, flash.

blitzen, *tr.*, blast; mich zu Boden —, fell me as a thunderbolt, 3240; *intr.*, lighten.

Block, *m.*, ¨e, block.

Blödigkeit, *f.*, purblindness; shyness, diffidence.

bloß, *adj. and adv.*, bare, naked, mere; merely, only, simply.

Blöße, *f.*, weakness, weak side.

bloß'stellen, *tr.*, expose.

blühen, *intr.*, bloom, flourish; blühend, lovely, beautiful.

Blumenstrauß, *m.*, ¨e, nosegay.

Blut, *n.*, blood.

Blutbefehl, *m.*, fatal command.

Blüte, *f.*, bloom, prime (of life).

bluten, *intr.*, bleed.

Blutentwurf, *m.*, ″e, bloody design.
Blutgerüst, *n.*, scaffold (for execution).
Blutgier, *f.*, bloody-mindedness.
blutig, bloody, cruel.
Blutschuld, *f.*, capital crime, blood-guiltiness.
blutsverwandt, allied by blood, kindred.
Blutsverwandte, *m. and f.* (*dec. as adj.*), kinsman, kinswoman.
Blutsverwandtschaft, *f.*, consanguinity, blood-relationship.
Blutthat, *f.*, murder.
Boden, *m.*, – *and* ″, floor, ground.
borgen, *tr.*, borrow.
böse, bad, evil, wicked, angry.
Bösewicht, *m.*, villain, miscreant, reprobate.
Bosheit, *f.*, wickedness.
Böswicht, *see* Bösewicht.
Bote, *m.*, –n, –n, messenger.
Botschaft, *f.*, message, news.
Botschafter, *m.*, ambassador.
Brauch, *m.*, ″e, usage, custom.
brauchen, *tr.*, need, want, require.
Braut, *m.*, ″e, betrothed, affianced bride.
Brautgemach, *n.*, ″er, bridal chamber.
Brautgeschmeide, *n.*, –es, –, bridal jewel.
Bräutigam, *m.*, betrothed, affianced husband.
bräutlich, bridal.
Bräutlichkeit, *f.*, bridal loveliness.
Brautwerbung, *f.*, matchmaking, suit.
brav, good, honest, excellent.
Brecheisen, *n.*, crowbar.
brechen (a, o), *tr.*, break, violate.
brennen, brannte, gebrannt, *intr. and tr.*, burn.
Brett, *n.*, –er, plank.
Brief, *m.*, letter.
bringen, brachte, gebracht, *tr.*, bring.
Britannien, *n.*, Britain.
britannisch, British.
Britte, *m.*, –n, –n, Briton.
Brücke, *f.*, bridge.
Bruder, *m.*, ″, brother.
Bruderkuß, *m.*, –sses, ″sse, fraternal kiss.
brüderlich, brotherly.
Brust, *f.*, ″e, breast.
Bube, *m.*, –n, –n, villain, knave, varlet.
Bübin, *f.*, –innen, jade.
Buch, *n.*, ″er, book.
buchstäblich, *adj. and adv.*, literal; to the letter, literally.
Buhle, *m.*, –n, –n, lover, paramour.
buhlen, *intr.*, woo, coquet.
Buhlerin, *f.*, –innen, mistress.

Buhlernetz, *n.*, amorous snare.
Bühne, *f.*, stage.
Bulle, *f.*, edict, (papal) bull.
Bund, *m.*, "e, alliance, league.
Bündnis, *n.*, –ſſes, –ſſe, alliance, league.
Bürgerin, *f.*, –innen, female citizen, citizeness.
Bürgerkrieg, *m.*, civil war.
bürgerlich, civil.
Bürgerweib, *n.*, "er, burgher woman, woman of the common people.
Buſen, *m.*, bosom.
Buße, *f.*, penance.
büßen, *tr.*, atone for, expiate; *reflex.*, do penance, be atoned for, 57.

C

Charak'ter, *m.*, –te're, character; dignity *or* position, 2668.
Chriſtenheit, *f.*, Christendom.
Chriſtus, *m.* (*indec. or as in Latin*), Christ; crucifix *or* Christ's image, 142.
Committee, *f.*, Commission.

D

da, *adv. and conj.*, there, here, then; when, while, since, as.
dabei, therewith, thereby, at that, near by, so.
Dach, *n.*, "er, roof.
dadurch, thereby, by it, through it *or* that.
dahin, *adv. and sep. pref.*, thither, there, away; — ſein, be gone (= dead), 1163.
dahin'geben (a, e), *tr.*, abandon.
dahin'kommen, –kam, –gekommen, *intr.*, ſ., come along.
damals, then, at that time.
Dame, *f.*, lady.
damit, *adv. and conj.*, therewith, with *or* by it *or* that *or* them; so that, in order that.
daneben, beside it *or* that *or* [them.
Dank, *m.*, thanks.
Dankbarkeit, *f.*, gratitude.
danken, *tr. and intr.*, thank.
dann, then.
daran, thereat, to it.
darauf, thereon, thereupon, afterwards, then, on *or* upon it.
daraus, thence, from this, out of it.
dar'bieten (o, o), *tr.*, present, tender, proffer.
darein, therein, in that.
darin, therein, in it *or* that.
darnach, thereafter, after it.
dar'ſtellen, *tr.*, exhibit; *reflex.*, ſtellt ſich verſammelt dar, is shown united, 1133.
dar'thun, –that, –gethan, *tr.*, verify, demonstrate, prove.

darüber, about it *or* that, on account of that, concerning it *or* that.

darum, about it *or* that, for it, on that account, therefore.

darunter, among it *or* that *or* them; of these, 1704.

daß, that, so that.

da'stehen, –stand, –gestanden, *intr.,* stand there.

davon, *adv. and sep. pref.,* thereof, of it *or* that, from it *or* that.

davon'tragen (u, a), *tr.,* carry off, get, obtain.

davor, before that, from it *or* that.

dazu, thereto, to it *or* that, besides.

dazwischen, between them, at intervals.

dazwisch'enkommen, –kam, –gekommen, *intr.,* s., come between, intervene.

Dechant', *m.,* –en, –en, dean.

Decke, *f.,* ceiling.

decken, *tr.,* cover.

Degen, *m.,* sword.

dein, –e, –, thy, thine, your.

demütig, humble, submissive.

demütigen, *tr.,* humble, humiliate.

denken, dachte, gedacht, *intr.,* think; denkt . . . auf, considers, has in view, 2045; denk' an, think of, 3704; *tr.,* remember, think of, 3705.

Denkmal, *n.,* ¨er *and* –e, monument.

denn, *conj. and adv.,* for, then; than, but.

dennoch, yet, nevertheless.

der (**die, das**), *def. art., dem. and rel. pron.,* the, that, who, which.

dereinst, one day, in future.

derselbe (**dieselbe, dasselbe**), the same; *often substituted for third personal pronoun.*

desto, the, so much the (*with comparatives*).

deuten, *tr.,* interpret, explain.

deutlich, plain, distinct, explicit.

Diadem', *n.,* diadem.

dicht, dense, close.

dienen, *intr. with dat.,* serve.

Diener, *m.,* servant.

Dienerin, *f.,* –innen, (woman) servant, maid-servant.

Dienst, *m.,* service.

Dienstbarkeit, *f.,* servitude, bondage.

dienstfertig, officious, kind, obliging.

dieser (**diese, dieses**), this, this one, the latter.

diktieren, *tr.,* dictate.

Ding, *n.,* thing.

dingen (a *or* u, u, *also weak*), *tr.,* hire; wird . . . sich . . . — lassen, can be hired, 626.

doch, yet, still; indeed, really, surely; nevertheless *or* after all, 1985.

Dokument', *n.*, document.
Dolch, *m.*, dagger, poignard.
Donner, *m.*, thunder.
Donnerstreich, *m.*, thunderbolt.
Doppelsinn, *m.*, ambiguity, double meaning.
doppelt, double.
dornenvoll, thorny, difficult.
dort, there, yonder.
drängen, *tr.*, press, urge; *intr.*, jostle, 2227; *reflex.*, hasten to (an), crowd about (um).
drauf, *see* darauf.
draus, *see* daraus.
draußen, out there, abroad, [outside.
drei, three.
Dreifaltigkeit, *f.*, Trinity.
dreimal, three times, thrice.
Dreistigkeit, *f.*, boldness, audacity.
dringen (a, u), *intr.*, s., press, penetrate to (auf), urge; heftig dringend, with eager urgency, 581; auf den Grund —, fathom the matter, 1613; *tr.*, urge, force; *see* drängen.
Dringen, *n.*, urgency, importunity.
dringend, pressing, urgent.
drinnen, within, in there.
dritt, third.
drohen, *intr. and tr.*, threaten; *pres. part.*, threatening, impending, menacingly.
Drohung, *f.*, threat, menace.
drücken, *tr.*, press, annoy.
drum, *see* darum.
du, *pl.* ihr, thou, you.
Duc (*Fr.*), *m.*, Duke.
dulden, *tr.*, bear patiently, abide, endure.
dumpf, dull, gloomy.
Dunkelheit, *f.*, darkness, gloom.
dünken, deuchte, gedeucht, *intr. with dat.*, seem; *reflex.*, fancy, imagine one's self; *imp.*, mich dünkt, methinks.
durch, *prep.*, *adv.*, *sep. and insep. pref.*, through, by.
durchboh'ren, *tr.*, stab, run through.
durch'feilen, *tr.*, file through.
durch'gehen, –ging, –gegangen, *intr.*, s., pass (a bill), be approved.
durchlau'fen (ie, au), *tr.*, run through, read hastily.
durch'reißen (i, i, *also insep.*), *tr. and intr.*, s., tear, rend.
durchschau'en, *tr.*, see through.
durchschnei'den (i, i), *tr.*, cut through; sever, 2556.
durchstech'en (a, o), *tr.*, run through, stab.
durchsu'chen, *tr.*, search thoroughly.
durchwach'en, *tr.*, pass waking; keep vigil, 3419.
durchzieh'en, –zog, –gezogen, *tr.*, travel through, traverse.
durchzogen, intertwined; — mit den Lilien, set with the lilies, 19.

dürfen, durfte, gedurft, *intr. and modal aux.,* may, be permitted; wagen darf, dare venture, 246; darf nicht, must not, 1027.
dürftig, scanty, meager.
dürr, dry, withered, leafless.
dürsten, *tr.,* thirst, long for.
durstig, thirsty, eager.

E

eben, *adj. and adv.,* even, plain, level; just, just now.
ebenso, likewise.
echt, genuine, lawful.
edel, noble, generous.
Edelfrau, *f.,* lady, noble woman.
Edelfräulein, *n.,* noble maid; maid of honor, 1127.
edelherzig, noble-hearted.
Edelmut, *m.,* generosity, noble-mindedness.
edelmütig, noble, generous.
eh(e), before, ere; sooner *or* rather, 2202.
Ehe, *f.,* marriage.
Ehebett, *n.,* –es, –en, marriage bed; wedlock, 3248.
ehebrecherisch, adulterous.
Ehebündnis, *n.,* –sses, –sse, marriage, matrimonial engagement.
ehelichen, *tr.,* marry.
eh(e)mals, formerly.
eher, sooner, rather.
ehern, brazen, stern.
Ehrbarkeit, *f.,* modesty, chastity.
Ehre, *f.,* honor.
ehren, *tr.,* honor, respect, revere.
Ehrenmantel, *m.,* ", garb *or* cloak of honor.
ehrerbietig, deferential, respectful.
ehrfurchtsvoll, respectful.
Ehrgeiz, *m.,* ambition.
Ehrsucht, *f.,* immoderate *or* morbid ambition.
Eid, *m.,* oath.
Eifer, *m.,* zeal, fervor.
Eiferer, *m.,* zealot.
Eifersucht, *f.,* jealousy, envy.
eigen, own, proper, peculiar.
eigenmächtig, arbitrary, despotic.
Eigensinn, *m.,* caprice.
Eigenthum, *n.,* "er, property.
Eiland, *n.,* island.
Eile, *f.,* haste.
eilen, *intr.,* s. *or* h., make haste, hasten.
eilfertig, hasty, precipitate.
ein, *indef. art. and num.,* a, an, one; welch —, what a; was für (—), what kind of; *as sep. pref.,* in, into.
einander, *indec.,* one another, each other.
ein'dringen (a, u), *intr.,* s., press in, penetrate.
einfach, simple, plain.
ein'fallen (ie, a), *intr.,* s., fall

in, interrupt, come to mind, occur to.

ein'führen, *tr.,* usher in, introduce; induct (into office), 3329.

eingemauert, immured.

ein'gestehen, –gestand, –gestanden, *tr.,* confess, avow, acknowledge.

einig, one, united, some, any; *in pl.,* a few.

ein'lassen (ie, a), *tr.,* let in, admit.

ein'mal, once, one time; auf —, all at once, 455; *with accent on ultima,* once upon a time, even, just.

ein'nehmen (a, o), *tr.,* take in.

Einsamkeit, *f.,* solitude, loneliness.

ein'schlagen (u, a), *tr.,* take (a course), adopt (a policy).

ein'schließen (o, o), *tr.,* shut in, confine.

ein'schreiben (ie, ie), *tr.,* inscribe, enroll.

ein'sehen (a, e), *tr.,* perceive.

einst, some day, some time.

einstimmig, unanimous, as one man.

ein'stürmen, *intr.,* s., rush in.

ein'treten (a, e), *intr.,* s., enter, come in.

Eintritt, *m.,* entrance, admission.

Einverständnis, *n.,* –sses, –sse, agreement, complicity.

ein'verstehen, –verstand, –verstanden, *reflex.,* agree; einverstanden sein, be agreed.

ein'weben (o, o, *also weak*), *tr.,* weave into.

ein'weihen, *tr.,* consecrate, ordain.

ein'willigen, *intr.,* consent to.

einzeln, individual.

einzig, alone, single.

Eisengitter, *n.,* iron grating.

Eisenzange, *f.,* iron pincers, forceps.

Eisesblick, *m.,* cold *or* unconcerned glance.

eitel, vain, needless, empty.

Eitelkeit, *f.,* vanity.

Elend, *n.,* wretchedness, misery.

elend, miserable; exiled, 453.

emp=, *unaccented insep. pref., see* ent=.

empfangen (i, a), *tr.,* receive.

empfinden (a, u), *tr.,* feel, experience.

empören, *tr.,* agitate, shock (the feelings), be revolting to.

empor'steigen (ie, ie), rise.

Empörung, *f.,* revolt, rebellion.

Ende, *n.,* –s, –n, end.

enden, *tr.,* end, finish; *intr. and reflex.,* cease, end.

endigen, *see* enden.

endlich, at last, finally.

eng, narrow, tight, restricted.

Engel, *m.,* angel.

Engelsflügel, *m.*, angel's wings, angelic pinions.

englisch, English.

Enkeltochter, *f.*, ″, granddaughter; descendant, 3124.

ent=, *unaccented insep. pref., generally denoting privation, separation, etc.*

entbehren, *tr.*, be deprived of, dispense with; *intr.*, be in want, 207.

entblößen, *tr.*, strip, uncover, lay bare.

entdecken, *tr.*, discover, reveal, disclose.

entehren, *tr.*, dishonor, disgrace, degrade.

enterben, *tr.*, disinherit.

entfernen, *tr.*, remove, turn away; *reflex.*, withdraw, leave.

Entfernung, *f.*, distance; in einiger —, at a short distance.

entfesseln, *tr.*, unfetter, release.

entfliehen (o, o), *intr.*, s., escape.

entführen, *tr.*, carry off, abduct.

entgegen, *prep.* (*after dat.*) *and sep. pref.*, toward, against, to meet.

entge'geneilen, *intr.*, s., hasten to meet.

entge'genschreiten (i, i), *intr.*, s., advance toward.

entge'gensteigen (ie, ie), *intr.*, s., rise before, loom up.

entge'genstellen, *tr.*, contrast.

entge'gentreiben (ie, ie), *tr.*, drive, impel toward.

entgehen, entging, entgangen, *intr.*, s., escape, avoid.

enthalten (ie, a), *tr.*, contain.

enthaupten, *tr.*, behead.

entkleiden, *tr.*, disrobe.

entkräften, *tr.*, weaken, invalidate.

entladen (u, a), *tr.*, unburden, ease; *reflex.*, get rid of, relieve of.

entlarven, *tr.*, unmask.

entlassen (ie, a), *tr.*, release, let go.

entledigen, *tr.*, relieve, clear (the conscience).

entlehnen, *tr.*, borrow.

entraten, *generally only in inf. with acc. or gen.*, dispense with, do without, 206.

entreißen (i, i), *tr.*, snatch away, tear from.

entsagen, *intr. with dat.*, renounce, disclaim.

entscheiden (ie, ie), *tr. and intr.*, decide, determine.

Entscheidung, *f.*, decision, crisis.

entscheidungsvoll, decisive, critical.

entschlossen, determined, resolute, firm.

Entschluß, *m.*, –sses, ″sse, resolve, determination.

entschuldigen, *tr.*, excuse, justify; läßt sich —, presents his excuses, 4033.

Entschuldigung, *f.*, apology, excuse, plea.

entsetzen, *tr.*, remove, depose, frighten; *reflex.*, be shocked, shudder.

Entsetzen, *n.*, amazement, horror.

entsetzlich, shocking, terrible.

entsteigen (ie, ie), *intr.*, s., rise from, come forth from.

entthronen, *tr.*, dethrone, depose.

entwaffnen, *tr.*, disarm.

entweihen, *tr.*, profane, desecrate.

entwerfen (a, o), *tr.*, design, project, plan.

Entwurf, *m.*, ¨e, scheme, plan.

entziehen, entzog, entzogen, *tr.*, deprive, withdraw; *reflex.*, be exempted, 735.

entzücken, *tr.*, entrance, enrapture, charm.

Entzücken, *n.*, delight, ecstasy.

entzünden, *tr.*, set on fire, kindle, inflame.

entzweien, *tr.*, sever; alienate from (mit), 2874.

er, *pers. pron., pl.* sie, he, it.

Erbarmen, *n.*, pity, mercy.

erben, *tr.*, inherit.

Erbin, *f.*, –innen, heiress, successor.

erbitten (a, e), *tr.*, entreat; laß dich —, be moved by entreaty, 2239.

erblicken, *tr.*, catch sight of, see.

Erde, *f.*, earth; *cf.* 1190, *note.*

Erdengröße, *f.*, earthly greatness.

Erdenrund, *n.*, globe, face of the earth.

erdreisten, *reflex.*, make bold, dare, presume.

erdulden, *tr.*, endure, bear, suffer.

ereifern, *reflex.*, grow angry, fly into a passion.

erfahren (u, a), *tr.*, learn, experience.

erfassen, *tr.*, seize, lay hold of, grasp.

erfechten (o, o), *tr.*, get by fighting; win, 2714.

erfinden (a, u), *tr.*, devise, fabricate, invent.

Erfinder, *m.*, contriver, designer.

erflehen, *tr.*, entreat, obtain by entreaties.

Erfolg, *m.*, success, issue, result.

erfolgen, *intr.*, s., result from (aus).

erforschen, *tr.*, investigate, examine, test, detect.

erfreuen, *tr.*, delight, gladen, cheer; *reflex.*, rejoice, be glad.

erfüllen, *tr.*, fill, fulfill.

Erfüllung, *f.*, fulfillment.

ergeben (a, e), *tr.*, give up; *reflex.*, surrender, submit, be resigned.

Ergebung, *f.*, resignation.

ergehen, erging, ergangen, *reflex.*, stroll, walk; *intr.*, f., go, fare.

ergießen (o, o), *reflex.*, pour forth, break (into tears).

ergreifen (i, i), *tr.*, seize, take, move.

erhaben, noble, exalted, illustrious; weit —, raised far above (über), 745.

erhalten (ie, a), *tr.*, receive; preserve, keep.

erharren, *tr.*, expect, await (patiently).

erhärten, *tr.*, confirm, verify.

erheben (o *or* u, o), *tr.*, lift, raise, exalt; *reflex.*, rise, arise.

erheitern, *tr.*, brighten, gladden.

erhitzen, *tr.*, inflame, heat, fire.

erhöhen, *tr.*, raise, elevate, exalt.

erholen, *reflex.*, recover.

erhören, *tr.*, hear, grant; nie erhört, unheard of, 221.

erinnern, *tr.*, remind; *reflex.*, recall, remember.

Erinnerung, *f.*, recollection.

erkaufen, *tr.*, buy, bribe.

erkäuflich, corrupt, venal.

erkennen, erkannte, erkannt, *tr.*, recognize, acknowledge, admit; es ist erkannt, it is decided, 846.

erklären, *tr.*, make clear, set forth, explain; erklärt, avowed, 1733.

erkühnen, *reflex.*, dare, presume, have the boldness.

Erkühnen, *n.*, audacity, presumption.

erlangen, *tr.*, acquire, come by.

Erlassung, *f.*, dispensation, remission.

erlauben, *tr.*, allow, permit.

Erlaubnis, *f.*, permission.

erleben, *tr.*, live to see, experience.

erleichtern, *tr.*, ease, relieve, lighten.

erleiden, erlitt, erlitten, *tr.*, suffer, endure, bear.

erlesen (a, e), *tr.*, choose, pick *or* select.

erleuchten, *tr.*, illuminate, enlighten.

erlöschen (o, o, *sometimes weak*), *intr.*, f., go out, be extinguished.

Erlöser, *m.*, Redeemer, Savior; liberator.

ermahnen, *tr.*, admonish, warn, exhort.

ermorden, *tr.*, murder.

ernennen, ernannte, ernannt, *tr.*, nominate, appoint.

erneuen, *tr.*, renew; *reflex.*, be revived *or* renewed.

erniedrigen, *tr.*, humiliate, debase, 156.

Erniedrigung, *f.*, humiliation.

Ernst, *m.*, earnestness, seriousness.

ernst, earnest, stern.

ernsthaft, serious, grave, solemn.

ernstlich, earnest.

erobern, *tr.*, conquer, gain by conquest.

eröffnen, *tr.*, open.

erproben, *tr.*, try, test.

erquicken, *tr.*, refresh.

Erquickung, *f.*, refreshment, comfort.

erregen, *tr.*, arouse, stir up, move.

erreichen, *tr.*, reach, attain, gain.

erretten, *tr.*, save, rescue.

Erretter, *m.*, deliverer, rescuer.

Errettung, *f.*, deliverance, rescue.

errichten, *tr.*, erect, set up, institute.

erröten, *intr.*, s., blush.

erschaffen (u, a), *tr.*, create.

erschallen, *intr.*, s., sound, resound, ring with (von).

erscheinen (ie, ie), *intr.*, s., appear.

erschrecken (a, o), *intr.*, be frightened; *tr.* (*as weak vb.*), frighten, alarm.

erschüttern, *tr.*, shake, convulse.

ersehnen, *tr.*, long *or* yearn for.

ersinnen (a, o), devise, contrive, invent.

ersparen, *tr.*, spare, save from.

erst, *adj. and adv.*, first; only, not until.

erstatten, *tr.*, give (an account); — Bericht, inform, 2999.

erstaunen, *intr.*, s., be astonished *or* amazed.

Erstaunen, *n.*, astonishment, surprise, amazement; in — setzen, surprise, 242.

erstehen, erstand, erstanden, *intr.*, s., arise.

ersteigen (ie, ie), *tr.*, ascend, scale.

ersticken, *tr.*, choke, smother, stifle.

erstorben, extinguished, benumbed.

erteilen, *tr.*, grant, impart, give.

ertragen (u, a), *tr.*, bear, endure, support, tolerate.

erwägen, *tr.*, consider, ponder.

erwählen, *tr.*, choose, select.

erwarten, *tr.*, wait for, await, expect.

Erwartung, *f.*, expectation, suspense.

erwehren, *reflex.*, defend one's self.

erweichen, *tr.*, soften, weaken.

erweisen (ie, ie), show, render, do for (one).

erweitern, *tr.*, extend, widen.

erwerben (a, o), *tr.*, gain, acquire, earn.

Erwiderung, *f.*, response, reply.

erwürgen, *tr.,* choke, strangle, kill.
Erzbischof, *m.,* ⁼e, archbishop.
erzeigen, *tr.,* show, render.
erzeugen, *tr.,* beget; *reflex.,* be bred, 1279.
erzittern, *intr.,* s., tremble.
erzürnt, exasperated, angered, incensed.
es, *pl.* sie, it; *expletive,* there, *or untranslatable.*
Essenz', *f.,* essence.
etwa, perhaps, nearly, about.
euer, your, yours.
Euro'pa, *n.,* Europe.
ewig, perpetual, eternal; ewiges Gefängnis, life-long imprisonment, 1912; auf —, forever.
Ewigkeit, *f.,* eternity.
Exem'pel, *n.,* example.

F

Fach, *n.,* ⁼er, drawer.
fachen, *tr.,* fan.
Fackel, *f.,* torch, flame.
Fall, *m.,* ⁼e, fall, case, contingency, event; ruin *or* downfall, 2801.
fallen (ie, a), *intr.,* s., fall; fiel mir ... in die Augen, caught my eye, 503.
fällen, *tr.,* fell; *as legal term,* Urteil —, pronounce sentence, 576.
Fallstrick, *m.,* snare.
falsch, false.
fälschlich, falsely.
falschverstanden, wrongly understood, mistaken.
fangen (i, a), *tr.,* seize, capture, take.
Farbe, *f.,* color.
fassen, *tr.,* seize, understand, state, comprehend; *reflex.,* compose *or* collect one's self.
Fassung, *f.,* composure, self-possession.
Fasten, *n.,* fasting.
Faust, *f.,* ⁼e, fist.
Feder, *f.,* spring; pen, feather.
Federstrich, *m.,* stroke of the pen.
Federzug, *m.,* ⁼e, stroke of the pen.
Fehde, *f.,* feud.
fehlen, *intr.,* fail, be missing; an Büchern fehlt's, books are lacking, 42; err, commit a fault.
fehl'gehen, –ging, –gegangen, *intr.,* s., go wrong, miss.
feiern, *tr.,* keep (a day), celebrate.
feig(e), cowardly.
feil, venal; mercenary, hireling.
fein, fine, delicate, shrewd.
Feind, *m.,* enemy.
Feindin, *f.,* –innen, enemy, foe.
feindlich, hostile, inimical.
Feld, *n.,* –er, field; behält das —, succeed, 2345.

Feldstück, *n.*, field-piece, light piece of ordnance.
Fels, *m.*, –en, –en, rock, cliff.
Felsenklippe, *f.*, cliff, rocky height.
Fenster, *n.*, window.
fern(e), far, distant, remote; von ferne, from afar.
Ferse, *f.*, heel; an meine Fersen hängen, dog my steps, 2772.
Fertigkeit, *f.*, readiness.
Fessel, *f.*, fetter.
fessellos, unfettered.
fesseln, *tr.*, fetter, bind.
fest, fast, fixed, firm; das feste Land, the Continent, 413.
Feste, *f.*, stronghold, fortress.
fest'halten (ie, a), *intr.*, hold fast, be firm.
festlich, festive, solemn; splendidly, 3479+.
Festlichkeit, *f.*, festivity.
Festung, *f.*, fortress.
Feuer, *n.*, fire.
feurig, fiery, ardent, passionate.
Fieberwahn, *m.*, fevered delusion, delirium.
finden (a, u), *tr.*, find; *reflex.*, be found, be; be reconciled, 53.
Finger, *m.*, finger.
finster, dark, gloomy, sad, stern.
Fischer, *m.*, fisherman.
fixieren, *tr.*, fix; fixiert ihn mit ernstem Blick, looks at him intently and sternly, 1663.
Flamme, *f.*, flame.
Flammenauge, *n.*, –es, –en, flaming eye.
Flattersinn, *m.*, fickle mind, frivolity.
flechten (o, o), braid; involve, 2768.
Flecken, *m.*, blemish, stain, taint.
flehen, *intr.*, entreat, pray, beseech.
Flehen, *n.*, entreaty, supplication.
Flehenswort, *n.*, –e, entreaty, supplication.
fleißig, diligent, industrious.
fliegen (o, o), *intr.*, s., *also* h., fly.
fliehen (o, o), *intr.*, s., flee, escape; *tr.*, shun, flee from, 1029.
fließen (o, o), *intr.*, s., flow.
Flitter, *m.*, spangle, tinsel, adornment.
Flor, *m.*, ⁻e, crape, gauze, veil.
Flotte, *f.*, fleet.
Fluch, *m.*, ⁻e, curse.
fluchenswert, execrable.
Fluchgeschick, *n.*, accursed fate, evil destiny.
Flucht, *f.*, flight.
fluchvoll, curse-laden.
Flügel, *m.*, wing, pinion.
Flügelschnelligkeit, *f.*, winged speed.

flugs, immediately, instantly, speedily.

Folge, *f.*, consequence, result.

folgen, *intr.*, ſ., follow.

Folter, *f.*, rack, torture.

fordern, *tr.*, demand, ask; summon, 96.

fördern, *tr.*, further, promote, dispatch.

Form, *f.*, form.

Förmlichkeit, *f.*, formality.

forschen, *intr.*, search, inquire; forschend mit den Augen gemessen, inspected with a keen glance, 1571 +.

fort, *adv. and sep. pref.*, away, forth, gone.

fortan, henceforth.

fort'fahren (u, a), *intr.*, ſ., continue, go on.

fort'führen, *tr.*, carry away, go on with.

fort'hallen, *intr.*, continue to resound.

Frage, *f.*, question; die -- thu' ich Euch, that question I ask you, 1698.

fragen, *tr.*, ask, question.

Franke, *m.*, –n, –n, Frenchman.

Frankreich, *n.*, France.

Franzmann, *m.*, Frenchman; *cf.* 104, *note.*

Franzose, *m.*, –n, –n, Frenchman.

französisch, French.

Frau, *f.*, woman, lady, wife.

Frauengunst, *f.*, woman's favor.

Frauenkrone, *f.*, crown of womanhood.

Frauenreich, *n.*, woman's rule, female sway.

Fräulein, *n.*, young woman, damsel.

frech, shameless, insolent.

frei, free, voluntary.

Freibrief, *m.*, license, permit, charter.

Freier, *m.*, suitor.

Freiheit, *f.*, freedom, liberty, privilege.

freilich, to be sure, indeed, of course.

Freimut, *m.*, frankness, candor.

fremd, alien, foreign, strange, of another.

Fremde, *m.*, –n, –n, stranger.

Fremdling, *m.*, stranger, foreigner.

Fremdlingin, *f.*, –innen, female stranger, foreign woman.

Freude, *f.*, joy; *cf.* 49, *note.*

Freudenchor, *m.*, ⸗e, chorus of joy.

Freudenpost, *f.*, glad tidings.

Freudenreich, *n.*, realm of joy, happy realm.

Freudenseite, *f.*, joyous *or* happy side.

freudig, glad, joyous.

freudlos, joyless.

freuen, *tr. and impers.*, afford joy, delight; *reflex.*, rejoice, enjoy, delight in.

Freund, *m.*, friend.

Freundesbrust, *f.*, bosom of a friend.

Freundespflicht, *f.*, duty of a friend, friendly obligation.

Freundin, *f.*, =innen, (female) friend.

freundlich, friendly, kind, kindly.

Freundschaft, *f.*, friendship, kindred, friends.

Frevel, *m.*, crime, offence, outrage.

freveln, *intr.*, commit crime; gefrevelt wider, is a sin against, 3708.

Freveln, *n.*, commission of crime.

Friede(n), *m.*, –ns, peace.

Friedensinsel, *f.*, peaceful island.

Friedenssitz, *m.*, peaceful seat, abode of peace.

friedlich, peaceful.

frisch, fresh, vivid, ready.

frischblutend, bleeding anew, gory.

Frist, *f.*, time, delay.

froh, glad, joyful, happy.

fröhlich, joyous, gladsome, gay.

fromm, brave, honest, pious, simple.

Frucht, *f.*, ″e, fruit.

früh, early.

fügen, *tr.*, add, join; dispense, ordain.

Fügung, *f.*, contingency, dispensation (of Providence).

fühlen, *tr. and intr.*, feel.

fühllos, unfeeling, cold.

führen, *tr.*, lead, escort, bring, wield, deal (a blow), use (language), wage.

Führer, *m.*, guide, leader.

Fülle, *f.*, fulness, abundance, wealth.

füllen, *tr.*, fill; *reflex.*, be filled.

für, for; — sich, aside; was —, what kind *or* sort.

Furcht, *f.*, fear, dread.

furchtbar, terrible, fearful.

fürchten, *tr.*, fear, dread.

fürchterlich, fearful, terrible, frightful.

furchtlos, fearless.

Fu'rie, *f.*, fury; curse, 3230.

Fürst, *m.*, –en, –en, prince.

Fürstenfurcht, *f.*, dread of princes.

Fürstentochter, *f.*, ″, princess.

Fürstin, *f.*, princess; sovereign, 1217.

fürstlich, princely, like a prince.

fürwahr, in truth, indeed, verily.

Fürwort, *n.*, ″er, intercession.

Fuß, *m.*, ″e, foot; man tritt uns ganz mit Füßen, we are utterly trodden under foot, 144; stehenden Fußes, immediately *or* without delay, 3273; auf freien — gesetzt, released, 3433.

G

galant', gallant, polite.
Gang, *m.*, ⸗e, walk, course.
ganz, whole, entire; einer — Verlorenen wert, worthy of a thorough reprobate, 358.
gar, quite, altogether; — nicht, not at all.
Garn, *n.*, net, trap, snare.
Garten, *m.*, ⸗, garden.
Gärtner, *m.*, gardener.
Gasse, *f.*, street, road.
Gast, *m.*, ⸗e, guest.
gastfreundlich, hospitable.
Gastrecht, *n.*, right of (demanding) hospitality.
Gatte, *m.*, –n, –n, husband.
Gaukelkunst, *f.*, ⸗e, jugglery, trickery.
Gaukelspiel, *n.*, jugglery.
Gaukler, *m.*, juggler, trickster.
Gauklerin, *f.*, –innen, (female) trickster, juggler; impostor, 2449.
geängstigt, anxious.
Gebärde, *f.*, gesture; features, 2241 +.
gebären (a, o), *tr.*, bear, give birth to; geboren, born.
geben (a, e), *tr.*, give; es giebt, there is *or* are.
Gebet, *n.*, prayer.
gebeugt, downcast, depressed.
gebieten (o, o), *tr.*, command, control; *intr.*, subdue.
Gebieter, *m.*, master, lord.
Gebieterin, *f.*, –innen, mistress, sovereign.
gebieterisch, imperious, dictatorial, haughty.
Gebirge, *n.*, –s, –, (chain of) mountains.
geboren, *see* gebären.
Gebot, *n.*, command.
gebrauchen, *tr.*, use, employ.
Gebrechen, *n.*, fault, infirmity, frailty.
gebrechlich, frail.
Gebühr, *f.*, duty, due; nach —, properly, fittingly.
gebühren, *intr.*, belong to, befit; gebührend, fitting.
Geburt, *f.*, birth.
Gedächtnis, *n.*, –sses, –sse, memory.
Gedanke, *m.*, –ns, –n, thought.
gedankenlos, thoughtless.
gedenken, gedachte, gedacht, *intr.*, mention, be mindful of, remember.
gediegen, stirling, able, superior.
Geduld, *f.*, patience; habe — mit, bear with, 3318.
Gefahr, *f.*, danger.
gefährlich, perilous, hazardous.
Gefährte, *m.*, –n, –n, comrade, associate.
gefallen (ie, a), *intr.*, *usually impers.*, please.
gefällig, courteous, obliging.
Gefallne, *f.* (*dec. as adj.*), the fallen, 3900.
gefangen, caught, imprisoned.

Gefangene, *m. and f.* (*dec. as adj.*), prisoner, captive.

Gefängnis, *n.*, –sses, –sse, prison.

Gefängnisnacht, *f.*, prison's gloom.

Gefäß, *n.*, –es, –e, vessel.

gefaßt, prepared for (auf), composed.

geflügelt, winged; swiftly, 3271.

Gefolge, *n.*, –s, –, retinue, train.

Gefühl, *n.*, feeling, sentiment.

gefühllos, unfeeling.

gegen, against, toward; — dich, compared to you, 2528.

Gegend, *f.*, region, country, scene.

gegenüber, opposite, face to face with.

gegenü'berstehen, –stand, –gestanden, *intr. with dat.*, stand before, face.

gegenü'berstellen, *tr.*, confront (with).

Gegenwart, *f.*, presence.

gegenwärtig, present.

Gegner, *m.*, opponent, enemy.

Gegnerin, *f.*, –innen, (female) foe, adversary, rival.

gehaben, gehatte, gehabt, *reflex.*, fare *or* be; *only in idiom* gehabt Euch wohl, fare well, 1627.

gehässig, odious, hateful.

geheim, secret, private.

Geheimnis, *n.*, –sses, –sse, secret, mystery.

geheimnisreich, mysterious.

geheimnisvoll, mysterious.

gehen, ging, gegangen, *intr.*, s., go; in sich —, examine itself, 56.

Gehilfe, *m.*, –n, –n, helper, assistant.

Gehör, *n.*, hearing, audience.

gehorchen, *intr. with dat.*, obey.

gehören, *intr. with dat.*, belong.

Gehorsam, *m.*, obedience.

Geist, *m.*, –er, spirit, mind, intellect, intelligence; Holy Ghost, 3669.

Geiz, *m.*, avarice.

geizen, *intr.*, aspire after (nach), covet.

gekrönt, crowned, royal.

gelangen, *intr.*, s., arrive at, reach, get, obtain.

Gelassenheit, *f.*, calmness.

gelegen, conveniently, opportunely.

gelehrt, learned.

geleiten, *tr.*, escort, accompany; Gott geleite Eure Flucht, God speed your flight, 2639.

Geliebte, *m. and f.* (*dec. as adj.*), beloved, lover, loved one.

gelingen (a, u), *impers.*, *intr.*, s., *with dat.*, succeed.

geloben, *tr.*, promise, pledge, vow.

gelten (a, o), *intr.*, be a question of, be at stake, be worth.

Gelübde, *n.*, –s, –, vow.

Gemahl, *m.*, spouse, husband.

Gemälde, *n.*, –s, –, painting.

gemein, common; *pl.* die Gemeinen, the Commons, 580, *etc.*

Gemüt, *n.*, –er, mind, feelings, disposition, soul.

genießen (o, o), *tr.*, *also intr. with gen.*, enjoy.

genug, *adv.*, *indec. adj.*, *and noun,* enough.

Genüge, *f.*, sufficiency; — thun, content, satisfy.

Genügen, *n.*, satisfaction.

genug'thun, –that, –gethan, *tr.*, satisfy.

Genuß, *m.*, –sses, "sse, enjoyment, pleasure, use.

Gepränge, *n.*, –s, pomp.

gepriesen, praised, lauded.

gequält, tormented.

gerade, *adj. and adv.*, straight, upright. plain, unswerving, just, exactly.

geraten (ie, a), *intr.*, s., get; in Wut —, break out in frenzy, 3004.

Geräusch, *n.*, noise, din, stir.

gerecht, just.

Gerechtigkeit, *f.*, justice.

gereichen, *intr.*, tend *or* serve to (zu).

gereift, matured.

gereizt, vexed, exasperated, provoked.

Gericht, *n.*, court (of law), sentence; vor ein . . . — gestellt, summoned before a court, 221.

gerichtlich, judicial, legal, according to law.

Gerichtshof, *m.*, "e, court of justice.

gering, petty, trifling.

Gerücht, *n.*, rumor, report.

gerührt, moved, touched.

gerüstet, equipped.

Gesandte, *m.* (*dec. like adj.*), ambassador, envoy.

Geschäft, *n.*, business, occupation, affair.

geschäftig, active, officious.

geschehen (a, e), *intr.*, s., happen, occur.

Geschenk, *n.*, gift, present.

Geschichte, *f.*, history; annals, 772.

Geschick, *n.*, fate, destiny.

Geschlecht, *n.*, –er, sex, generation, race.

Geschmack, *m.*, *pl.*, *if used,* "e, taste.

Geschmeide, *n.*, –s, –, jewels.

geschmeidigt, made pliable *or* tractable, softened.

Geschöpf, *n.*, creature.

Geschrei, *n.*, –s, outcry, lamentations.

Geschütz, *n.*, –es, –e, cannon, artillery.

geschwind, speedy, swift, prompt.

Geschworene, *m.* (*dec. as adj.*), juryman, juror.

Gesellschaft, *f.*, company, society; die — Jesu, Society of Jesus, Order of Jesuits, 494.

Gesetz, *n.*, law.

gesetzt, granted, conceded (that).

Gesicht, *n.*, -er, face.

gesinnt, disposed, minded.

gesittet, orderly; law-abiding, 1122.

gespannt, fixed, intent.

Gespenst, *n.*, -er, spectre, phantom.

Gespräch, *n.*, conversation, talk.

Gestalt, *f.*, form; beauty, 1397; aspect, 1768.

Geständnis, *n.*, -sses, -sse, confession, avowal.

gestehen, gestand, gestanden, *tr.*, confess, acknowledge.

gestern, yesterday.

Gesträuch, *n.*, shrubbery, foliage.

gestürzt, undone.

geteilt, shared, common.

Getöse, *n.*, -s, -e, din, noise, clamor.

getreu, loyal, faithful, trusty.

getrost, confident, of good cheer.

Getümmel, *n.*, tumult.

gewagt, risky, hazardous.

gewahr, aware; — werden, notice.

Gewähr, *f.*, surety, guarantee.

gewähren, *tr.*, grant, afford; *intr. with dat.*, be a guarantee, 2357.

Gewahrsam, *f.*, custody, keeping.

Gewalt, *f.*, power, force, violence.

gewaltig, strong, violent.

gewaltsam, violent, by force.

Gewaltthat, *f.*, outrage, violence.

Gewand, *n.*, "er, robe, garb.

gewärtig, expecting.

Gewehr, *n.*, weapon.

geweiht, consecrated.

Gewicht, *n.*, weight, importance, consequence.

gewinnen (a, o), *tr.*, win, gain, get.

gewiß, certain, sure.

Gewissen, *n.*, conscience.

gewissenhaft, scrupulous, conscientious.

gewißlich, certainly, surely.

gewöhnen, *tr.*, accustom; *reflex.*, grow accustomed, get used to.

gezeugt, begotten.

geziemen, *intr.*, *impers. with dat., and reflex.*, befit, become, be seemly *or* appropriate; geziemend, fitting, appropriate.

Gezücht, *n.*, breed, brood.

gezwungen, constrained, forced.

giftig, poisonous, venomous.

gigantisch, gigantic.

Glanz, *m.*, splendor, brilliancy.

glänzen, *intr.*, shine, glitter.

glanzvoll, brilliant.
glatt, smooth, slippery.
Glaube, *m.*, –ns, –n, belief, faith.
glauben, *tr. and intr. with dat.*, believe, trust.
Glaubenslehre, *f.*, dogma, doctrine.
Glaubensveränderung, *f.*, change of creed.
Glaubensverwandte, *m. and f.* (*dec. as adj.*), fellow-believer.
glaubensvoll, devout.
gläubig, believing (easily), devout, faithful.
gleich, *adj. and adv.*, like, equal, same, direct; equally, immediately.
gleichfalls, likewise.
Gleichmut, *m.*, serenity, equanimity.
gleißen (i, i), *also weak*), glitter; play hypocrite, affect; gleißend, hypocritically, 2428.
gleisnerisch, hypocritical.
Glied, *n.*, –er, limb, member.
Glocke, *f.*, bell; die — Eurer Thaten, the herald of your own deeds, 2953.
Glorie, *f.*, halo, glory.
glorwürdig, illustrious.
Glück, *n.*, fortune, prosperity, happiness.
glücklich, fortunate, happy.
Glückwunsch, *m.*, ¨e, congratulation.

glühen, *intr.*, glow; glühend, ardent; red hot, 2538.
Glut, *f.*, flame, glow, ardor.
Gnade, *f.*, grace, mercy, favor.
gnadenvoll, gracious.
Gnadenweg, *m.*, way of grace, path of mercy.
gnädig, gracious, merciful.
gnug, *see* genug.
Gold, *n.*, gold.
golden, golden, gold.
gönnen, *tr.*, not to grudge, grant, allow.
Gott, *m.*, ¨er, God, god.
Götterfest, *n.*, fête for the gods; *cf.* 1120, *note.*
Götterhalle, *f.*, divine abode, hall of the gods.
Götterhand, *f.*, ¨e, divine hand.
Gottesbild, *n.*, –er, shrine, sacred image.
Gottesdienst, *m.*, worship, devotion, divine service.
Gottheit, *f.*, deity, divinity.
Göttin, *f.*, –innen, goddess.
göttlich, divine.
Götze, *m.*, –n, –n, idol.
Götzendienst, *m.*, idolatry.
Grab, *n.*, ¨er, grave.
Gräbernacht, *f.*, sepulchral gloom.
Grabesrand, *m.*, ¨er, verge of the grave.
Grabstein, *m.*, gravestone, tomb.
Graf, *m.*, –en, –en, count, earl.

Graffschaft, *f.*, county, shire.
Gram, *m.*, grief, sorrow.
gräßlich, ghastly, horrible, frightful.
grau, gray, aged, dim, hoary.
grauen, *intr.*, *impers.*, dread, fear.
Grauen, *n.*, horror.
grausam, cruel, ruthless.
Grausen, *n.*, dread, dismay.
greifen (i, i), *tr.* (*and intr. with* nach), seize, grasp at.
greis, old, hoary, aged.
Greis, *m.*, old man.
Grenze, *f.*, boundary, border, frontier.
Greuelthat, *f.*, cruel deed.
Grille, *f.*, whim, caprice.
grillenhaft, whimsical, capricious.
Grimm, *m.*, fury, rage, wrath.
grimmig, furious, wrathful, fierce.
grob, rude, ill-bred, insolent, homely.
Groll, *m.*, grudge, resentment.
groß, great, large.
Größe, *f.*, greatness.
Großmut, *f.*, generosity, great-mindedness.
großmütig, magnanimous, generous.
großmutsvoll, magnanimous.
Großohm, *m.*, granduncle.
Großschatzmeister, *m.*, lord high treasurer.
grübeln, *intr.*, speculate, be hypercritical.
Gruft, *f.*, ⁼e, tomb.
Gruftgewölbe, *n.*, *pl.* – *or* –r, vaulted tomb, sepulchre.
grün, green.
Grund, *m.*, ⁼e, ground, reason; ihr dringet auf den —, you fathom the matter, 1613.
gründen, *tr.*, establish, found.
Gruß, *m.*, ⁼e, greeting.
grüßen, *tr.*, greet.
Gunst, *f.*, favor.
günstig, favorable, gracious.
Günstling, *m.*, favorite.
Gürtel, *m.*, girdle, belt.
gut, good, well.
Gut, *n.*, ⁼er, estate, goods, possessions.
gütig, gracious, indulgent.

H

ha, ha! ah!
Haar, *n.*, hair.
haben, hatte, gehabt, *tr.*, have, possess; *past aux.*, have; was habt Ihr? what ails you? 3465.
Haft, *f.*, custody.
haften, *intr.*, cling to, be attached; haftet für, answer for, guarantee, 2691.
Hain, *m.*, grove, forest.
halb, half.
Hälfte, *f.*, half.
Halle, *f.*, hall.
Hals, *m.*, ⁼e, neck, throat.

halten (ie, a), *tr.*, hold, support; die Meinung hält es mit, public opinion sides with, 1015; Ihr haltet Wort, you keep your promise, 3819.

Hammer, *m.*, ¨, hammer.

Hand, *f.*, ¨e, hand; es liegt in guter —, it is well cared for, 28; bietet die Hände, offers aid, 639.

Handel, *m.*, ¨, business, affair, matter.

handeln, *intr.*, act; an mir gehandelt, treated me, 2295.

hangen (i, a), *intr.*, hang.

hängen, *tr.*, hang; *reflex.*, hang one's self; attach one's self to, 2771.

Harnisch, *m.*, armor.

harren, *intr.*, wait, hope, wait patiently.

hart, hard, harsh.

Härte, *f.*, hardness.

Haß, *m.*, –sses, hatred.

hassen, *tr.*, hate.

hastig, hasty.

häufen, *tr.*, pile, heap.

Haupt, *n.*, ¨er, head; in meinem —, in me, *or* in my person, 2682; ein geliebtes —, a beloved one, 3515.

Haus, *n.*, ¨er, house.

Hausbediente, *m.* (*dec. as adj.*), household servant.

Haushofmeister, *m.*, steward, master of the household.

heben (o *or* u, o), *tr.*, lift; *reflex.*, rise.

Heer, *n.*, army.

heftig, impatient, passionate, angry.

heftigdringend, with eager urgency, pressing, importunate.

Heftigkeit, *f.*, violence, anger, ardor.

hegen, *tr.*, cherish, harbor, entertain.

Heide, *f.*, heath.

Heil, *n.*, –es, welfare, redemption, salvation, happiness.

Heiland, *m.*, –s, Savior, Redeemer.

heilend, healing.

heilig, holy, sacred.

Heilige, *m. and f.* (*dec. as adj.*), Saint, the Holy One.

heiligen, *tr.*, hallow, consecrate, sanction.

Heimat, *f.*, home, native land.

heimführen, *tr.*, bring home (a bride).

heimlich, secret, private.

heischen, *tr.*, desire, demand, require.

heiß, hot, ardent.

Heißgeliebte, *f.* (*dec. as adj.*), ardently loved one.

heißen (ie, ei), *tr.*, call, name; *intr.*, be called, be, mean.

heiter, glad, merry, joyous, serene.

Held, *m.*, –en, –en, hero.

Heldengeist, *m.*, –er, heroic spirit.

Heldenmut, *m.*, heroism.

Heldentugend, *f.*, heroic virtue.

Heldin, *f.*, -innen, heroine.

Helfer, *m.*, helper, ally.

hell, bright, clear.

hemmen, *tr.*, hinder, check.

Henker, *m.*, headsman, executioner.

Henkerbeil, *n.*, headsman's ax.

Henkerblock, *m.*, ⸚e, executioner's block.

her, *adv. and sep. pref.*, hither, [here.

herab'hängen, *tr.*, hang down.

herab'lassen (ie, a), *tr.*, let down; *reflex.*, condescend.

herab'steigen (ie, ie), *intr.*, ſ., descend.

herab'stürzen, *tr.*, hurl down; *intr.*, ſ., plunge.

herab'werfen (a, o), *tr.*, throw down.

herauf, *adv. and sep. pref.*, up here, hereupon.

herauf'steigen (ie, ie), *intr.*, ſ., ascend, climb.

heraus, *adv. and sep. pref.*, out here, out of, forth, from, out.

herbei'bringen, -brachte, -gebracht, *tr.*, bring on, produce.

herein, *adv. and sep. pref.*, in hither, in here, in.

herein'dringen (a, u), *intr.*, ſ., press in.

herein'kommen, -kam, -gekommen, *intr.*, ſ., enter, come in.

herein'stürzen, *intr.*, ſ., rush in, burst in.

herein'treten (a, e), *intr.*, ſ., step in, enter, come in.

herkömmlich, customary, usual.

hernieder, *adv. and sep. pref.*, down, down hither.

hernie'derfahren (u, a), *intr.*, ſ., descend; float down, 3658.

Herold, *m.*, herald.

Herr, *m.*, -n, -en, lord, master, sir; the Lord.

herrlich, splendid, glorious.

Herrlichkeit, *f.*, splendor, *as a title,* Excellency, Lordship.

Herrschaft, *f.*, sovereignty.

herrschen, *intr.*, rule, govern, prevail.

Herrscher, *m.*, ruler, sovereign.

Herrscherin, *f.*, -innen, sovereign.

Herrscherwort, *n.*, -e, word of command.

Herrscherzügel, *m.*, reins of government.

herrschwütig, imperious, despotic.

her'tragen (u, a), *tr.*, bear.

herum, *adv. and sep. pref.*, about, round, around.

herum'gehen, -ging, -gegangen, *intr.*, ſ., go about.

herum'treiben (ie, ie), *intr.*, roam about, drive around.

herunter, *adv. and sep. pref.*, down, downwards.

herun'terlassen (ie, a), let down; *reflex.*, condescend.

herun'tersteigen (ie, ie), *intr.*, s., descend.

herun'terstoßen (ie, o), *tr.*, thrust down.

hervor, *adv. and sep. pref.*, out, forth, forward.

hervor'gehen, –ging, –gegangen, *intr.*, s., go forth, proceed.

hervor'treten (a, e), *intr.*, s., step forth, come forward.

hervor'ziehen, –zog, –gezogen, *tr.*, draw forth.

her'wogend, surging on.

Herz, *n.*, –ens, –en, heart; — ... fassen, *see* 173, *note.*

herzerschütternd, heart-rending, appalling.

her'ziehen, –zog, –gezogen, *intr.*, s., march, draw near.

Heuchelschein, *m.*, hypocrisy.

heut(e), to-day.

heutig, of to-day, to-day's, present.

hier, here.

hierauf, thereupon, then, after this.

hie(r)her, hither.

Hifthorn, *n.*, "er, bugle, hunting-horn.

Hilfe (Hülfe), *f.*, help.

Hilfeflehende, *f.* (*dec. as adj.*), suppliant.

Himmel, *m.*, heaven.

Himmeldecke, *f.*, canopy (of state).

Himmelreich, *n.*, kingdom of heaven, heavenly realm.

Himmelsbote, *m.*, –n, –n, heavenly messenger.

Himmelskraft, *f.*, "e, heavenly power.

Himmelspeise, *f.*, bread of the sacrament, Holy Communion, manna.

Himmelsschoß, *m.*, –es, "e, heaven's canopy *or* expanse, 2091.

Himmelssegen, *m.*, heaven's blessing.

Himmelsthüre, *f.*, door of heaven.

himmlisch, heavenly, celestial.

hin, *adv. and sep. pref.*, away, hence.

hinab, *adv. and sep. pref.*, down (there).

hinab'schreien (ie, ie), *intr.*, shriek down.

hinab'steigen (ie, ie), *intr.*, s., descend.

hinab'stürzen, *tr.*, precipitate.

hinaus, *adv. and sep. pref.*, out, away, forth, hence; wo man — will, where they will end, 590.

hinaus'treiben (ie, ie), *tr.*, drive out, expel.

hindern, *tr.*, hinder, prevent.

hinein, *adv. and sep. pref.*, in, into, into it (away from speaker).

hinein'gehen, –ging, –gegangen, *intr.*, s., go in.

hinein'legen, *tr.*, lay in, insert, interpolate, interpose.

hinein'reißen (i, i), *tr.*, drag in *or* into, involve.

hinein'sehen (a, e), *intr.*, look in.

hin'fahren (u, a), *intr.*, s., go hence; fahr hin, be gone, 2437.

hin'fliehen (o, o), *intr.*, s., flee from here.

hin'führen, *tr.*, conduct, lead thither.

hin'geben (a, e), *tr.*, resign, give away, surrender.

hin'gehen, –ging, –gegangen, *intr.*, s., go hence, die, pass away.

hin'nehmen (a, o), *tr.*, take, receive.

hin'raffen, *tr.*, snatch away; carry off *or* kill, 1008.

hin'reichen, *tr.*, extend.

hin'reißen (i, i), *tr.*, carry away, transport.

Hinrichtung, *f.*, execution.

hin'schmelzen (o, o), *intr.*, s., melt away, languish.

hin'sehen (a, e), *intr.*, look toward.

hin'sinken (a, u), *intr.*, s., sink down.

hin'stellen, *tr.*, put, place; *reflex.*, take one's place.

hinten, behind, in the rear.

hinter, behind, after.

hinterge'hen, –ging, –gangen, *tr.*, deceive, delude.

Hintergrund, *m.*, –es, ⁼e, background.

hinterlas'sen (ie, a), *tr.*, leave behind.

hinterlistig, deceitful, artful, insidious.

hin'tragen (u, a), *tr.*, carry to.

hin'treten (a, e), *intr.*, s., approach.

hinüber, *adv. and sep. pref.*, over, across.

hinü'berlaufen (ie, au), *intr.*, s. *and* h., run over.

hinweg, away.

hinweg'führen, *tr.*, lead away, remove.

hin'werfen (a, o), *tr.*, throw away, discard, throw out (a remark).

hinzu, *adv. and sep. pref.*, to, towards, in addition to.

hinzu'fügen, *tr.*, add.

Hirtin, *f.*, –innen, shepherdess.

hoch, high.

Hochamt, *n.*, high mass.

Hochland, *n.*, –e, highland.

Hochmut, *m.*, arrogance, pride.

Hochverrat, *m.*, high treason.

Hochverräter, *m.*, arch-traitor.

hochwürdig, venerable, reverend; *as noun,* the Host (in the sacrament), 290.

Hochzeitsfackel, *f.*, nuptial torch.

Hof, *m.*, ⁼e, court, yard.

Hofdiener, *m.*, servant of the court.
Hoffahrt, *f.*, pride, haughtiness.
hoffen, *tr.*, hope, look for, anticipate.
Hoffen, *n.*, hope.
Hoffnung, *f.*, hope.
hoffnungslos, hopeless.
Höfling, *m.*, courtier, courtling.
Höhe, *f.*, height.
Hoheit, *f.*, highness, eminence, nobility; *as title,* Highness.
hohl, hollow.
Höhle, *f.*, cavern, den.
Hohn, *m.*, scorn, defiance, derision.
höhnend, scornful.
Hohngelächter, *n.*, scornful *or* jeering laughter.
höhnisch, scornful, mocking, sarcastic.
holen, *tr.*, fetch, get; holte Rat, took counsel, 526.
Hölle, *f.*, hell.
Höllenangst, *f.*, direst anxiety, anguish of hell.
Höllengeist, *m.*, –er, infernal spirit; Furies, 2187.
Höllenkunst, *f.*, ¨e, infernal *or* hellish art, diabolic skill.
Höllenpforte, *f.*, gate of hell.
Höllenschlange, *f.*, infernal serpent.
Höllenwaffe, *f.*, weapon of hell.
horchen, *intr.*, listen.
hören, *tr.*, hear.
Horn, *n.*, ¨er, horn.
Hostie, *f.*, Host, sacred wafer.
Hotel, *n.*, –s, –s, mansion.
Huldigung, *f.*, homage.
hundert, hundred.
hurtig, quick; machet —, make haste, 3445.
Hut, *f.*, guard, keeping, care.
hüten, *tr.*, watch, guard.
Hüter, *m.*, keeper, guardian.

I

ich, *pl.* wir, I.
ihr, her, hers, their, theirs.
ihretwillen (um), for her sake, *cf.* 78, *note.*
ihrige (**der, die, das**), hers, theirs; der Ihrigen, of her friends, 3357.
Ihro, Her, Your, His; *cf.* 2642, *note.*
immer, always, ever.
immerdar, ever, always.
immerhin, constantly, nevertheless, at any rate.
in, in, into.
indem, while.
indes, meanwhile.
indessen, meantime, while.
Inhalt, *m.*, tenor, purport (of a letter), contents.
in'nehalten (ie, a), *intr.*, pause.
innen, within, in, inside.
inner, inner, interior; heart,

mind, soul; *neut. sup. as noun,* very soul, inmost being, 2966, 3192.

Innere, *n.* (*dec. as adj.*), heart, soul, interior.

Inquisitionsgericht, *n.,* court of inquisition.

Insel, *f.,* island.

irdisch, earthly.

irgend, some, any.

irre, confused, delirious.

Irre, *f.,* wandering; in der — leitet, *see* 478, *note.*

irren, *intr.,* err, be wrong; *reflex.,* be mistaken.

Irrtum, *m.,* ¨er, error, erroneous views.

J

ja, yes, aye; surely, indeed.

Jagd, *f.,* hunt.

Jagdgefolge, *n.,* –s, –, hunting retinue *or* train.

jagen, *tr.,* drive, pursue, hunt; *intr.,* be hunting, hurry on, gallop.

Jagen, *n.,* hunting.

Jahr, *n.,* year.

jahrelang, for years.

Jahrestag, *m.,* anniversary.

Jammer, *m.,* grief, lamentation.

jammernswürdig, pitiable, miserable, worthy of pity.

jammervoll, wretched, lamentable.

Jawort, *n.,* –e, assent, consent.

je, ever, always; von —, always, 763.

jeder, –e, –es, each, every, each one, *etc.*

jedermann, every one, everybody.

jedoch, nevertheless, yet, however.

jedweder, –e, –es, each, every one.

jeglicher, –e, –es, *see* jeder.

jemand, some one.

jener, –e, –es, that one, he, she, it, the former.

Jesus, *gen.* –su, *dat. and acc.* –um, Jesus.

jetzo, *see* jetzt.

jetzt, now.

Joch, *n.,* yoke.

Jubel, *m.,* rejoicing, mirth.

jubeln, *intr.,* exult, rejoice, triumph.

Jugend, *f.,* youth.

Jugendkraft, *f.,* ¨e, youthful strength, vigor of youth.

Jugendland, *n.,* land of one's youth.

jugendlich, youthful, young.

Jugendlust, *f.,* youthful joy.

jung, young.

jungfräulich, maidenly, virgin.

Jüngling, *m.,* youth, young man.

jüngst, lately.

Juwel', *n.,* –s, –en, jewel.

K

kahl, bare, naked.
Kahn, *m.*, ¨e, boat, skiff.
kalt, cold.
Kammer, *f.*, chamber, room.
Kämmerer, *m.*, chamberlain.
Kammerfrau, *f.*, lady in waiting.
Kampf, *m.*, ¨e, contest, struggle, conflict.
kämpfen, *intr.*, struggle, fight.
Kanzler, *m.*, chancellor.
Kapelle, *f.*, chapel.
Kardinal′, *m.*, ¨e, cardinal.
Karte, *f.*, card.
katho′liſch, Catholic.
kaufen, *tr.*, buy.
kaum, hardly, scarcely.
Kavalier′, *m.*, –e, cavalier.
keck, bold, daring, forward, impudent.
kehren, *intr.*, ſ., turn.
kein, –e, –, no, none, not any, not one.
keineswegs, by no means, not at all.
Kelch, *m.*, cup; chalice, communion cup.
kennen, kannte, gekannt, *tr.*, know, be acquainted with.
Kerker, *m.*, prison, jail, dungeon.
Kerkerelend, *n.*, wretchedness of prison.
Kerkerhaft, *f.*, confinement in prison; in enger —, as a close prisoner, 91.
Kerkermauer, *f.*, prison wall.
Kerkermeiſter, *m.*, jailer.
Kerkerſchmach, *f.*, ignominy *or* dishonor of prison.
Kerze, *f.*, candle.
Kette, *f.*, chain, bondage; *pl.*, fetters.
keuſch, chaste, pure, modest.
Kind, *n.*, –er, child.
Kindheit, *f.*, childhood.
kindiſch, childish.
Kirche, *f.*, church.
Kirchenfeſt, *n.*, church festival.
Kirchenſtrafe, *f.*, penance.
Kiſſen, *n.*, cushion.
Klageartı′kel, *m.*, complaint, indictment.
Klage, *f.*, lament, complaint.
klagen, *intr.*, complain, lament.
Klagepunkt, *m.*, count (of an indictment), charge.
Kläger, *m.*, plaintiff, accuser.
klar, clear, evident.
Kleid, *n.*, –er, dress, gown.
kleiden, *tr.*, dress, clothe, deck.
klein, small, little, petty.
Kleinod, *n.*, –e, *or* –o′dien, jewel, ornament, treasure.
klingeln, *intr.*, ring the bell.
klingen (a, u), *intr.*, sound.
Kloſter, *n.*, ¨, cloister, convent.
Kluft, *f.*, ¨e, cleft, cavern; cell *or* dungeon, 3926.
Klugheit, *f.*, prudence, discretion, wisdom.
klüglich, discreetly, sagely.

Knabe, *m.*, –n, –n, boy.
Knecht, *m.*, servant.
Knechtſchaft, *f.*, servitude, bondage.
Knie, *n.*, –s, –e, knee.
knieen, *intr.*, kneel.
knüpfen, *tr.*. unite, knit, join (closely).
Koloſſeum, *n.*, Colosseum, i.e., the Flavian amphitheatre at Rome, 427.
kommen (a, o), *intr.*, ſ., come.
Kommiſſa'rius, *m.*, –, –ien, commissioner.
König, *m.*, king.
Königin, *f.*, –innen, queen.
königlich, kingly, royal.
Königreich, *n.*, kingdom.
Königsblut, *n.*, royal blood.
Königsmord, *m.*, murder of a king, regicide.
Königspflicht, *f.*, royal *or* sovereign duty.
Königsſohn, *m.*, ¨e, prince.
Königstitel, *m.*, royal title.
Königswille(n), *m.*, –ns, –n, royal will *or* purpose.
Königswürde, *f.*, royal *or* kingly dignity.
können, konnte, gekonnt, *tr. and modal aux.*, can, be able, may.
konſekrie'ren, *tr.*, consecrate.
Konzept', *n.*, rough drafts, outlines.
Kopie', *f.*, copy.
körperlos, bodiless, incorporeal.
koſtbar, precious, valuable.
Koſtbarkeit, *f.*, costliness; *pl.*, jewels, trinkets.
koſten, *tr.*, cost.
köſtlich, costly, precious.
Kraft, *f.*, ¨e, strength, force, power.
kraft, *prep. with gen.*, by virtue of.
kraftvoll, powerful.
krank, ill, sick.
Krankheit, *f.*, illness.
Kränkung, *f.*, mortification, grief.
Kranz, *m.*, ¨e, wreath, garland.
kreden'zen, *tr.*, present; *see* 630, *note*.
Kreis, *m.*, circle.
Kreuz, *n.*, cross.
kreuzigen, *tr.*, crucify; der Gekreuzigte, the Crucified, 3539.
Krieg, *m.*, war.
Krone, *f.*, crown.
krönen, *tr.*, crown.
krümmen, *tr.*, bend; gekrümmt, writhing, 3923.
Kruzifix, *n.*, crucifix.
Kugel, *f.*, bead.
kühn, bold, daring, hardy.
Kühnheit, *f.*, boldness, daring.
Kummer, *m.*, sorrow, grief, affliction.
kümmern, *tr.*, grieve, concern.
kund (*indec.*), known; — geben *or* thun, manifest, make known.

Kunde, *f.*, information, report.
kundig, familiar with, versed in.
Kundschaft, *f.*, information, knowledge.
künftig, future.
Kunst, *f.*, ¨e, art.
kunstfertig, skilled, skillful.
kurz, short, brief, concise.
Kuß, *m.*, –sses, ¨sse, kiss.
küssen, *tr.*, kiss.
Küste, *f.*, coast, shore.

L

Lächeln, *n.*, smile.
laden (u, a), *tr.*, load, burden.
Lady, *f.* (*Eng.*), –ies, lady; *cf.* 1, *note.*
Lager, *n.*, –, *or* ¨, couch, bed.
lähmen, *tr.*, lame, paralyze.
Lamm, *n.*, ¨er, lamb.
lammherzig, faint-hearted, meek.
Land, *n.*, –e *and* ¨er, land, country.
landen, *intr.*, s., land, disembark.
länderlos, landless.
Landesrecht, *n.*, law of the land.
Landsitz, *m.*, country-seat.
Landsmannschaft, *f.*, club, association; muntre Landsmannschaften, merry societies, 461.
lang, long.
lange, for a long while.
langentbehrt, long wanted *or* dispensed with.
langsam, slow.
längst, long since, long ago.
langverhalten, long suppressed.
Larve, *f.*, mask, disguise; face, 1996.
lassen (ie, a), *tr.*, let, allow, permit; *with dep. inf.*, cause *or* have, suffer.
lasten, *intr.*, weigh upon (auf), burden, oppress.
Laster, *n.*, crime, vice.
lasterhaft, vicious, wicked.
Lästerung, *f.*, abuse, calumny, blasphemy.
lastervoll, profligate, abandoned.
lauern, *intr.*, be on the watch, lie in ambush; lauernd, covertly, 1751.
Lauf, *m.*, ¨e, course, way; pace, 2072 +.
laufen (ie, au), *intr.*, s. *and* h., run.
laut, loud, aloud.
Laute, *f.*, lute.
leben, *intr.*, live; jene hat gelebt, her race is run, 3277; lebt wohl, farewell, 3580.
Leben, *n.*, life.
leben'dig, living, alive.
Lebensgott, *m.*, ¨er, god of life; — der Freuden, god of life and joy, 2557.
Lebensteppich, *m.*, life's tapestry; *cf.* 451-3, *note.*

Lebewohl, *n.*, farewell.
lebhaft, quick, animated, lively.
ledig, free, freed, exempt.
leer, empty, void.
Legat', *m.*, –en, –en, (papal) legate.
legen, *tr.*, lay, put, place; *reflex.*, subside, be stilled.
lehnen, *tr.*, *intr.*, *and reflex.*, lean.
lehren, *tr.*, teach, instruct.
Leib, *m.*, –er, body, life; angeklagt auf — und Leben, *cf.* 95-97, *note.*
Leibarzt, *m.*, ⸚e, court physician.
Leibeserbe, *m.*, –n, –n, offspring, descendant, heir.
Leibwache, *f.*, body-guard.
Leichnam, *m.*, corpse, dead body.
leicht, light, easy.
leichtbedeckt, lightly covered.
Leichtsinn, *m.*, frivolity, levity.
leichtsinnig, frivolous, fickle, wanton.
leid, sorrowful; es thut mir —, I am sorry for it.
leiden, litt, gelitten, *tr. and intr.*, suffer; leidend, passively, 1837.
Leiden, *n.*, sorrow, suffering, affliction.
Leidende, *m. and f.* (*dec. as adj.*), sufferer.
Leidenschaft, *f.*, passion, emotion.
leidenschaftlich, impassioned, eager, pathetic.
Leidensprobe, *f.*, test of suffering, trial, affliction.
leihen (ie, ie), *tr.*, lend.
leise, low, soft.
leisten, *tr.*, do, perform, render.
leiten, *tr.*, lead, guide; manage, 1883.
Leiter, *f.*, ladder.
Leitung, *f.*, lead, guidance, direction.
lenken, *tr.*, guide, direct.
lernen, *tr. and intr.*, learn.
lesen (a, e), *tr. and intr.*, read.
Lesen, *n.*, reading.
letzt, last.
leuchten, *intr.*, shine, gleam; leuchtend, radiant, 443.
leugnen, *tr.*, deny, disclaim.
Leutnant, *m.*, –s, –s or –e, lieutenant.
Licht, *n.*, –er, light.
Lichterscheinung, *f.*, radiant vision.
lieb, dear, beloved.
Liebe, *f.*, love.
lieben, *tr.*, love, like, be fond of.
liebenswert, lovable, amiable.
liebenswürdig, amiable, lovely.
lieber, rather, sooner.
Liebesband, *n.*, bond *or* tie of love.
Liebesbitte, *f.*, request of love.

Liebesbote, *m.*, –n, –n, messenger of love.
Liebesfackel, *f.*, torch of love.
Liebesglut, *f.*, passion, ardor of love.
liebkosen, *tr.*, fondle, caress, favor.
Liebling, *m.*, favorite, darling.
Lied, *n.*, –er, song.
liegen (a, e), *intr.*, h. *and* s., lie, be, be situated.
Lilie, *f.*, lily, fleur-de-lis.
Lippe, *f.*, lip.
List, *f.*, craft, artifice, stratagem, wile.
listig, crafty, artful.
Lob, *n.*, praise.
loben, *tr.*, praise.
lobenswürdig, praiseworthy.
Locke, *f.*, curl, lock (of hair).
locken, *tr.*, allure, entice, tempt.
Lohn, *m.*, ⁼e, reward.
lohnen, *tr.*, reward, recompense, requite.
Lond(o)ner, *indec.*, London; — Straßen, on the road to London, 2604.
Lord, *m.*, –s, –s, lord.
Lordmarschall, *m.*, Lord Marshal.
Los, *n.*, lot.
lösen, *tr.*, loose; löst sich, gives up, 3403.
Löseschlüssel, *m.*, key of absolution.
los'sprechen (a, o), *tr.*, acquit of (*gen.*).
Losung, *f.*, watchword.
Loth'ringen, Lorraine.
Loth'ringer, *m.*, Lothringian.
loth'ringisch, of Lorraine.
Luft, *f.*, ⁼e, air, breeze.
Lüge, *f.*, lie, falsehood; mich Lügen strafen, give me the lie, 3980.
lügen (o, o), *intr.*, lie, tell an untruth.
Lust, *f.*, ⁼e, joy, desire; lust.
lüsten, *imp.*, wish, desire.
Lüstling, *m.*, voluptuary.

M

machen, *tr.*, make, do; *reflex.*, sich . . . machend, *see* 7 +, *note.*
Macht, *f.*, ⁼e, might, power; Mächte des festen Landes, powers of the continent, 3214.
mächtig, mighty, powerful; *with gen.*, master of.
Madrigal, *n.*, madrigal.
Majestät', *f.*, –en, majesty.
majestätisch, majestic.
Mal, *n.*, time; mit einem —, at once, 3403.
man, one, they, people; *often rendered by passive voice.*
Mangel, *m.*, ⁼, want, hardship, poverty.
mangelhaft, incomplete.
mangeln, *intr.*, *imp. with dat.*, want, be lacking; *cf.* 39, *note.*

Mann, *m.*, ¨er, man.
Männerkraft, *f.*, ¨e, manly power, energy.
Männerschönheit, *f.*, manly beauty.
Männerwille(n), *m.*, –ns, –n, manly will.
männlich, manful.
Mantel, *m.*, ¨, mantle, cloak.
Märchen, *n.*, tale, story, fable.
Marschall, *m.*, ¨e, marshal.
Märtyrkrone, *f.*, martyr's crown.
Märtyrtum, *n.*, martyrdom.
Maß, *n.*, measure.
mäßigen, *tr.*, temper, control; *reflex.*, keep one's temper.
Mäßigung, *f.*, self-control, restraint.
Mauer, *f.*, wall.
Meer, *n.*, sea.
mehr, more; more than one, *cf.* 613, *note.*
mein, –e, –, my, mine; die Meinen, my kindred, my own, 3519.
meinen, *tr. and intr.*, think, mean, suppose.
meinesgleichen, *indec.*, my equals, 172, *note.*
Meinung, *f.*, (public) opinion, belief, intention, meaning.
Meister, *m.*, master.
Menge, *f.*, crowd, throng.
Mensch, *m.*, –en, –en, man, human being; *pl.*, people, mankind.
Menschenangesicht, *n.*, –er, human face.
Menschheit, *f.*, humanity.
menschlich, human, humane.
Menschlichkeit, *f.*, humanity.
Merkmal, *n.*, mark, sign.
Messediener, *m.*, ministrant, acolyte.
messen (a, e), *tr. and intr.*, measure; *reflex.*, compete [(with).
Messer, *n.*, knife.
Meßgewand, *n.*, ¨er *or* –e, vestment, chasuble.
Meuchelmörder, *m.*, –s, –, assassin.
Meuchelrotte, *f.*, band of assassins.
Miene, *f.*, air, look, countenance.
mild, mild, gentle, generous, merciful.
Milde, *f.*, clemency, leniency.
mildern, *tr.*, modify, extenuate, mitigate.
minder, less, lesser.
Minutenzeiger, *m.*, minute hand *or* pointer.
mischen, *tr.*, mingle, blend, mix.
Mission, *f.*, mission, missionary.
mißbrau'chen, mißbrauchte, mißbraucht *and* gemißbraucht, *tr.*, abuse, misuse.
mißgön'nen, *tr.*, envy, grudge, be jealous of.
mißhan'deln, *tr.*, **maltreat,** misuse.

Mißhandlung, *f.*, ill-usage, cruelty.

mißtrau'en, *intr. with dat.*, distrust, question.

Mißtrauen, *n.*, distrust.

mit, *prep., adv. and sep. pref.*, with, together, by, on, in, along.

Mitgefangene, *m.* (*dec. as adj.*), fellow-prisoner.

Mitleid, *n.*, sympathy, pity.

mitleidig, compassionate, sympathetic.

mitleidsvoll, sympathetic, tender.

Mittag, *m.*, noon; the south, 2096.

Mitte, *f.*, midst, middle.

Mittel, *n.*, means, expedient, way.

mitten, in the middle.

Mitwisser, *m.*, accessory, accomplice.

mögen, mochte, gemocht, *tr. and modal aux.*, may, can, be able; like.

möglich, possible.

Moment', *m.*, moment.

Monarch', *m.*, –en, –en, monarch.

Monarchie', *f.*, monarchy.

Monar'chin, *f.*, –innen, monarch, queen.

Monat, *m.*, month.

Mönch, *m.*, monk.

Mond, *m.*, moon; seit wenig Monden, a few months ago, 3314.

Monsieur, *Fr.*, –s, monsieur; *cf.* 1104, *note.*

Mord, *m.*, murder.

Mordanstifterin, *f.*, –innen, inciter *or* abettor of murder.

Mordblick, *m.*, murderous glance.

morden, *tr.*, murder.

Mörder, *m.*, murderer, assassin.

Mörderhand, *f.*, ″e, murderous hand, assassin's hand.

Mörderhilfe, *f.*, murderous help.

Mörderin, *f.*, –innen, murderess.

Mörderstreich, *m.*, fatal *or* mortal thrust.

Mordgerüst, *n.*, murderous scaffold.

Mordgesell, *m.*, –en, –en, accomplice in murder, fellow-murderer.

Mordstreich, *m.*, murder, deadly thrust.

Morgen, *m.*, morning.

morgen, to-morrow.

müde, weary, tired.

Mühe, *f.*, difficulty, pains.

Mund, *m.*, –e *or* ″er, mouth; voice, 690; spokesman, 3637.

mündig, of age, mature, 1575.

munter, cheerful, happy, merry.

Musik', *f.*, music.

müssen, mußte, gemußt, *intr. and modal aux.*, must, ought, be obliged *or* forced.

müßig, idle, vain, leisure.
Muster, *n.*, pattern, model, example.
Mut, *m.*, courage, spirit.
mutig, courageous, spirited.
mutlos, desponding, discouraged, dejected.
mutvoll, courageous.
mutvollstark, strong and brave; *sup. as noun,* 1371.
Mutter, *f.*, ", mother.

N

nach, after, to, toward, according to, about.
nach'ahmen, *tr.*, imitate.
nachdem, after, afterwards.
nach'denken, –dachte, –gedacht, *intr.*, reflect, meditate; nachdenkend, thoughtful, meditating.
Nachdenken, *n.*, thought, reflection.
nach'eilen, *intr.*, s., hasten after.
Nachen, *m.*, skiff, (small) boat.
nach'geben (a, e), *intr.*, yield to, give way.
nachläs'sig, careless, remiss.
nach'reißen (i, i), *tr.*, drag after.
Nachruhm, *m.*, posthumous renown, good name.
nach'schallen, *intr.*, echo, resound.
nach'schlagen (u, a), *intr.*, refer to, look into, consult.
nach'sehen (a, e), *intr.*, look after.
Nachsicht, *f.*, indulgence, forbearance.
nächst, next, (*superl. of* nah), nearest, readiest.
Nacht, *f.*, "e, night.
nächtlich, nightly, dark, sable.
nachts, at night, by night.
Nacken, *m.*, neck.
nagen, *tr.*, gnaw, sting, consume.
nahe, near.
Nähe, *f.*, nearness, presence, vicinity; in der —, near by.
nahen, *reflex.*, approach.
nähern, *tr.*, bring near; *reflex.*, approach, come near.
nähren, *tr.*, foster, nourish, cherish.
Name, *m.*, –ns, –n, name.
namenlos, nameless, unspeakable.
nämlich, (the very) same.
Nation', *f.*, nation.
Natter, *f.*, adder, viper.
Natur', *f.*, nature.
Naturzweck, *m.*, intent of nature.
Nebelberg, *m.*, misty *or* hazy mountain.
neben, near, by, beside.
nebst, by, beside, near, close.
Neffe, *m.*, –n, –n, nephew.
nehmen (a, o), *tr.*, take.

Neid, *m.*, envy.
neidisch, envious.
neigen, *tr.*, bend, incline; *reflex.*, bow.
Neigung, *f.*, inclination, affection, disposition.
nein, no.
nennen, nannte, genannt, *tr.*, name, call, mention.
Netz, *n.*, net, snare.
neu, new, late *or* recent; von neuem, anew.
neulich, recently, lately.
Neumond, *m.*, new moon.
nicht, not; *sometimes redundant, cf.* 1449.
nichts, nothing.
nichtswürdig, worthless, base, contemptible.
nie, never.
nieder, *adv. and sep. pref.*, down.
nie'derfallen (ie, a), *intr.*, s., fall down, descend.
nie'dergehen, –ging, –gegangen, *intr.*, s., go down; auf- und niedergehend, walking back and forth, 3894 +.
nie'derknieen, *intr.*, kneel (down).
nie'derlassen (ie, a), *tr.*, let down; *reflex.*, fall.
nie'derlegen, *tr.*, lay down, abdicate.
nie'derschlagen (u, a), *tr.*, strike down, fell, cast down, dishearten; refute, confute.
nie'derschreiben (ie, ie), *tr.*, write down, set down in writing.
nie'dersehen (a, e), *intr.*, look down.
nie'derstürzen, *tr.*, precipitate; *intr.*, s., fall down, plunge.
nie'derwerfen (a, o), *tr.*, throw down; *reflex.*, prostrate one's self.
niedlich, neat, nice, pretty.
niedrig, base, low; *cf.* 155, *note.*
niemals, never.
niemand, no one.
nimmer, never.
nimmermehr, by no means, never, nevermore.
nirgends, nowhere.
noch, yet, still, besides.
Norden, *m.*, north.
Not, *f.*, ¨e, need, exigency, necessity; not thun, be necessary.
Nota'rius (*Lat.*), *m.*, –, –ta'rien, notary.
Notdurft, *f.*, need, necessity.
nötigen, *tr.*, constrain, compel, necessitate.
notwendig, necessary, needful, requisite.
Notwendigkeit, *f.*, necessity.
nun, now; since, *cf.* 2236, *note; as interj.*, now.
nunmehr, now, by this time.
nur, only, merely, even.
Nutzen, *m.*, use, profit.

O

O, oh! O!

ob, *prep., adv., and sep. pref.,* over, above; *conj.,* whether, if; ob...ob, whether... or, 716; to see if, 1480.

ober, upper.

Oberhaus, *n.,* upper house, House of Lords.

Oberrichter, *m.,* superior judge, lord chief justice.

obgleich, although; *sometimes* ob...gleich, 1920.

ob'liegen (a, e), *impers. with dat.,* devolve upon, be incumbent upon.

ob'siegend, victorious, triumphant.

oder, or.

offen, open, sincere.

offenbar, evident, public, openly.

offenba'ren, *tr.,* reveal, disclose.

öffentlich, public, open.

Offizier', *m.,* officer.

offiziös', semi-official; in official tone, 2666.

öffnen, *tr.,* open; *reflex.,* open, unbosom one's self.

oft, oft, often.

Oheim, *m.,* uncle.

Ohm, *see* Oheim.

Öhm, *see* Oheim.

ohne, without.

ohngefähr, *see* ungefähr; von —, by chance, 2062.

ohnlängst, *see* unlängst.

Ohnmacht, *f.,* weakness, impotency.

ohnmächtig, weak, powerless, fainting.

Ohr, *n.,* –en, ear.

Ölbaum, *m.,* ⁻e, olive tree, *the symbol of peace,* 831.

Opfer, *n.,* sacrifice.

opfern, *tr.,* offer, sacrifice.

Ora'kel, *n.,* oracle.

Orden, *m.,* order (of nobility).

Ordnung, *f.,* order, arrangement.

Organ', *n.,* organ; tool, 740.

Ort, *m.,* –e *and* ⁻er, place.

Ozean, *m.,* ocean.

P

Page, *m.,* –n, –n, page.

Paket', *n.,* package, packet.

Palast, *m.,* ⁻e, palace.

Papist', *m.,* –en, –en, papist.

Papis'tin, *f.,* –innen, (woman) papist.

Papst, *m.,* ⁻e, pope.

Papsttum, *n.,* papacy.

Park, *m.,* –e *and* –s, park.

Parlament', *n.,* parliament.

Partei', *f.,* party.

Partei'enhaß, *m.,* –sses, party rage, factional hate.

Paß, *m.,* –sses, ⁻sse, pass, passport.

Papier', *n.,* paper; *in pl.,* papers, documents.

Pause, *f.*, pause.

Peer (*Eng.*), –s, –s, peer.

peinigen, *tr.*, torment; importune, 2023.

peinlich, painful.

Perle, *f.*, pearl.

Person', *f.*, person, rôle, character.

Pfand, *n.*, ⁿer, pledge, token, security; symbol, 3602.

Pfeil, *m.*, arrow, shaft.

pflanzen, *tr.*, plant.

pflegen (o, o, *and weak*), *tr.*, administer, attend to, conduct; *intr.*, be wont to, be in the habit of; enjoy.

Pflegerin, *f.*, –innen, attendant, nurse.

Pflicht, *f.*, duty, obligation.

Pforte, *f.*, gate, door.

Pilgerschar, *f.*, crowd *or* band of pilgrims.

Plagegeist, *m.*, –er, tormenting spirit.

Plan, *m.*, –e *or* ⁿe, plan, plot, scheme.

planvoll, carefully planned, systematically.

Platz, *m.*, ⁿe, place, situation, station.

Plauderer, *m.*, tattler, prattler.

plötzlich, suddenly, abruptly.

Pöbel, *m.*, rabble, populace, mob.

pochen, *tr. and intr.*, knock; pocht ... auf, boast of, 2022.

Pochen, *n.*, knocking, pounding.

Possenspiel, *n.*, farce.

Post, *f.*, post, relay.

Posten, *m.*, post, place.

Pracht, *f.*, splendor, magnificence.

Prachtgerät, *n.*, splendid plate, state service (of silver).

prächtig, splendid.

prägen, *tr.*, stamp; enact, 779.

Prahler, *m.*, boaster, braggart.

prangen, *intr.*, shine, be splendid; sein prangend Los, his brilliant lot, 304.

Prediger, *m.*, preacher.

Predigtstube, *f.*, meeting-room, conventicle.

Preis, *m.*, reward, prize.

preisen (ie, ie, *and weak*), *tr.*, praise; das gepriesene Italien, far-famed Italy, 416; glücklich —, count happy.

preis'geben (a, e), *tr.*, give over, expose.

pressen, *tr.*, press.

Priester, *m.*, priest.

priesterlich, priestly.

Primas, *m.*, *indec. in sing. or like pl.*, –maten, primate, archbishop, 751.

Probe, *f.*, proof, test.

prophezei'en, *tr.*, predict, prophesy.

Protestant', *m.*, –en, –en, Protestant.

Prozeß', *m.*, –sses, –sse, action, case, suit.

prüfen, *tr.*, try, test, examine.

Prüfung, *f.*, trial, test.

Prüfungsjahr, *n.*, period of probation.
Prunk, *m.*, pomp, parade.
Pult, *n. and often m.*, desk.
Punkt, *m.*, point.
Puritaner, *m.*, Puritan.
Putz, *m.*, dress, finery, ornament.

Q

Qual, *f.*, torture.
quälen, *tr.*, torment, torture, afflict, grieve, worry.
Quelle, *f.*, spring, source, fountain.
quellen (o, o), *intr.*, s., stream, spring, well forth.

R

Rache, *f.*, revenge.
racheforderud, demanding vengeance.
Rachegeist, *m.*, –er, avenging spirit.
rächen, *tr.*, avenge, revenge.
Rächer, *m.*, avenger.
Rachegedanke, *m.*, –ns, –n, vengeful thought.
ragen, *intr.*, stand out, tower.
Rand, *m.*, ¨er, border, verge, brim.
Rank, *m.*, ¨e, intrigue, trick.
ränkespinnend, plotting intrigues, intriguing.
ränkevoll, artful, wily.
rasch, quick, swift, prompt.
rasen, *intr.*, rage, rave, rant.
Rasende, *m., f., and n.* (*dec. as adj.*), madman, 2614; mad deed, 2624.
Raserei, *f.*, madness, fury.
Rat, *m.*, ¨e, council, advice, plan, counsel, counsellor.
raten (ie, a), *tr.*, advise, counsel.
ratlos, helpless.
Rätsel, *n.*, riddle, enigma.
Raub, *m.*, robbery.
rauben, *tr.*, rob, plunder.
Räuberin, *f.*, –innen, (woman) robber, usurper.
rauh, rough, rude, coarse.
Raum, *m.*, ¨e, room, place, scope, occasion, opportunity.
räumen, *tr.*, remove, quit, leave.
Rechenschaft, *f.*, account, responsibility.
Rechnung, *f.*, account.
recht, right; die . . . Rechte, your royal right hand, 2255.
Recht, *n.*, right, just claim, justice, law; das ist . . . Rechtens; *cf.* 915, *note.*
recht'fertigen, *tr.*, justify, vindicate.
Rechtsanspruch, *m.*, ¨e, just title, lawful claim.
Rechtsform, *f.*, legal process.
Rechtsgelehrte, *m.* (*dec. as adj.*), jurist.

Rechtsspruch, *m.*, ″e, verdict, sentence.

Rechtsstreit, *m.*, lawsuit, legal controversy.

Rede, *f.*, speech; mich ... — stehen lassen, made me appear and answer, 224.

reden, *intr.*, speak, talk.

redlich, honest, candid, just.

Redlichkeit, *f.*, candor, honesty, integrity.

Redner, *m.*, public speaker, orator.

Rednerkunst, *f.*, ″e, speaker's art, oratory.

regen, *tr.*, stir, move; *reflex.*, be moved, move.

Regen'tenstamm, *m.*, ″e, reigning family, royal line.

regieren, *tr.*, rule, reign.

Regierung, *f.*, reign, government.

Regung, *f.*, agitation, emotion.

reich, rich.

Reich, *n.*, realm, kingdom, empire.

reichen, *tr.*, reach, extend, offer; *intr.*, extend.

Reichsgesetz, *n.*, law of the land, law.

Reichsreligion, *f.*, religion established by law of the realm; national faith, 1106.

Reichsschluß, *m.*, –sses, ″sse, royal decree, act of parliament.

Reichsverräter, *m.*, traitor to the realm, traitor.

Reichtum, *n.*, ″er, riches, wealth, treasure.

Reif, *m.*, band, circle, hoop.

reihen, *tr.*, set in a row; *reflex.*, range one's self.

reimen, *tr.*, reconcile *or* explain, 2129.

rein, pure, spotless, clean, innocent.

reinigen, *tr.*, clear, purge, cleanse.

Reise, *f.*, journey.

reisen, *intr.*, h. *and* s., travel.

reißen (i, i), *tr.*, snatch, tear, rescue, drag, carry.

Reiz, *m.*, charm, grace.

reizen, *tr.*, provoke, irritate, incite, charm, attract; reizend, charming, attractive, 1948.

Reizung, *f.*, charm, allurement.

Religion, *f.*, religion.

rennen, rannte, gerannt, *intr.*, s. *and* h., run.

Ressort (*pr.* ressohr'), *m.*, –s, –s, drawer, compartment; *cf.* 18, *note.*

Rest, *m.*, rest, remainder.

retten, *tr.*, rescue, save.

Retter, *m.*, savior, deliverer.

Rettung, *f.*, deliverance, escape, rescue.

Rettungsbrücke, *f.*, bridge of rescue.

Rettungshand, *f.*, ″e, rescuing hand.

Reue, *f.*, repentence, penitence.

reuen, *tr., impers.,* rue, repent; mich reuet, I regret, 1616.

reuevoll, penitently.

richten, *tr.,* direct, turn, judge; ins Werk gerichtet, performed *or* accomplished, 2958.

Richter, *m.,* judge.

Richterhof, *m.,* ¨e, court of judgment, tribunal.

Richterschwert, *n.,* –er, sword of judgment.

Richterspruch, *m.,* ¨e, judicial sentence, judgment, sentence.

Richterstuhl, *m.,* ¨e, judgment seat, bench, tribunal.

Riegel, *m.,* bolt, bar.

Riesenkraft, *f.,* gigantic strength.

Ring, *m.,* ring.

ringen (a, u), *intr.,* struggle, wrestle; *tr.,* wring.

rings, round about.

Ritter, *m.,* knight.

ritterlich, chivalrous, gallant, brave.

Ritterschaft, *f.,* chivalry, (knightly) exploit.

Ritterspiel, *n.,* tournament.

roh, rude.

Rohr, *n.,* –e *or* ¨e, reed.

Rolle, *f.,* rôle, character, part.

Rom, *n.,* Rome.

römisch, Romish.

Rose, *f.,* rose.

Rosenkranz, *m.,* ¨e, rosary.

Roß, *n.,* –sses, –sse, charger, steed.

ruchlos, depraved, vicious; *cf.* 1636, *note.*

rücken, *tr. and intr.,* h. *and* s., move.

Rücken, *m.,* back.

Rückfall, *m.,* ¨e, relapse.

rückwärts, backward.

Rückweg, *m.,* journey home, return.

Ruf, *m.,* call, reputation, report; peal, 2135.

rufen (ie, u), *tr.,* call, summon.

Ruhe, *f.,* rest, quiet.

ruhen, *intr.,* rest.

ruhig, quiet, calm.

Ruhm, *m.,* fame, renown, glory.

ruhmbegierig, ambitious.

rühmen, *tr.,* praise; *reflex.,* boast, vaunt.

ruhmvoll, renowned, glorious.

rühren, *tr.,* stir, touch, affect; rührend, touching.

rüsten, *tr.,* equip, arm.

Rüsthaus, *n.,* ¨er, arsenal.

S

Saal, *m.,* Säle, room, hall.

Sache, *f.,* thing, matter, affair, concern, case, cause.

Säge, *f.,* saw.

sagen, *tr.,* say, tell.

Sakrament', *n.,* sacrament.

sammeln, *tr.*, collect, gather, rally; *reflex.*, gather, collect one's thoughts.
sanft, mild, gentle.
Sänfte, *f.*, litter, sedan-chair.
Sanftmut, *f.*, gentleness, meekness.
Sänger, *m.*, singer, poet.
Sankt, *used before proper nouns,* Saint, St.
Sarg, *m.*, "e, coffin.
Säule, *f.*, column, pillar.
säumen, *intr.*, tarry, delay.
Säumen, *n.*, delay.
Schade *or* Schaden, *m.*, –s (*sometimes* –n), ", harm, mischief; *as exclamation only* schade, pity, too bad, 2736.
schaden, *intr. with dat.*, harm, injure.
schaffen (u, a), *tr.*, create, make, get.
schaffen, *tr.*, do, procure; *intr.*, be at work.
Schafott', *n.*, scaffold.
Schale, *f.*, dish; paten, 3648+.
Schall, *m.*, "e, sound.
schalten, *intr.*, rule, dispose of (über), 3544.
Scham, *f.*, shame.
Schamerröten, *n.*, blush of shame.
schamhaft, bashful, modest, chaste.
schamlos, shameless.
Schande, *f.*, shame, disgrace; zu Schanden machte, baffled *or* confounded, 2659.
schänden, *tr.*, disgrace.
schändlich, shameful, infamous, base.
Schandthat, *f.*, infamous action, infamy.
Schar, *f.*, troop, throng, host.
scharf, sharp, keen, piercing.
Scharfblick, *m.*, penetration, acute perception, acuteness.
schärfen, *tr.*, sharpen.
Schatten, *m.*, shadow, shade, phantom.
Schatz, *m.*, "e, treasure.
schätzen, *tr.*, value, appreciate, estimate.
Schatzmeister, *m.*, treasurer.
Schau, *f.*, show; stelltet . . . zur —, openly displayed, 345.
Schauder, *m.*, shudder, dread, terror.
schauderhaft, terrible, dreadful.
schaudern, *intr.*, shudder.
schauen, *tr.*, see, behold; *intr.*, look.
Schauspiel, *n.*, spectacle, sight, drama.
Scheide, *f.*, sheath, scabbard.
scheiden (ie, ie), *tr.*, cut off, separate; es muß geschieden sein, we must part; *intr.*, s., depart.
Schein, *m.*, light, splendor, appearance, pretence; den — . . . retten, save appearances, 1998.
scheinen (ie, ie), *intr.*, seem, appear.

schelten (a, o), *tr.*, chide, blame, reproach.
Schemel, *m.*, bench, low stool.
schenken, *tr.*, give, present.
Schergenamt, *n.*, ⸗er, beadle's office; jailer's task; *cf.* 1054, *note.*
Scherz, *m.*, jest.
scheu, shy, timid.
Scheu, *f.*, shyness, timidity.
scheuchen, *tr.*, frighten away, intimidate.
scheuen, *tr.*, shun, fear, dread.
schicken, *tr.*, send.
Schicksal, *n.*, fate, destiny, fortune, doom.
Schickung, *f.*, God's sending, divine dispensation, fate.
schießen (o, o), *tr.*, shoot, dart.
Schiff, *n.*, ship.
Schiffbruch, *m.*, ⸗e, shipwreck.
schiffen, *intr.*, s. *and* h., sail.
schildern, *tr.*, depict, describe, paint.
Schilderung, *f.*, description, portrayal.
Schimmer, *m.*, glimmer, glitter, splendor.
schimmerlos, quiet, unostentatious.
schimmern, *intr.*, glisten, sparkle.
schimpflich, disgraceful, ignominious, shameful; insolent, 2304.
Schlachtopfer, *n.*, sacrifice, victim.
Schlaf, *m.*, sleep.
Schläfe, *f.*, temple.
schlafen (ie, a), *intr.*, sleep; *with cog. acc.*, 3510.
Schlag, *m.*, ⸗e, blow, stroke.
schlagen (u, a), *tr.*, beat, strike.
Schlange, *f.*, snake, viper.
Schlangenhaar, *n.*, snaky hair.
schlau, cunning.
schlaugefaßt, craftily devised, cunningly drawn.
schlecht, bad, mean, lowly; humble *or* plain, 35.
schleichen (i, i), *intr.*, s., creep, steal away.
Schleier, *m.*, veil.
schleifen, *tr.*, drag.
schleudern, *tr.*, hurl.
schleunig, prompt, quick, speedy.
schlicht, plain, homely.
schließen (o, o), *tr.*, shut, close; *intr.*, finish, end, conclude; *reflex.*, join, attach one's self to (an), 459.
schlimm, bad, evil.
Schloß, *n.*, –sses, ⸗sse, castle, palace.
schluchzen, *intr.*, sob.
Schlummer, *m.*, slumber.
Schlund, *m.*, ⸗e, abyss, gulf.
schlüpfrig, slippery, dangerous.
Schluß, *m.*, –sses, ⸗sse, end, conclusion, resolution, decree.

Schlüssel, *m.*, key.

Schmach, *f.*, ignominy, dishonor, disgrace.

schmachvoll, ignominious, disgraceful.

schmachten, *intr.*, languish, pine.

schmählich, ignominious, outrageous.

schmal, narrow, small.

schmeicheln, *intr. with dat.*, flatter, coax; *inf. as noun*, 1804.

Schmeichelrede, *f.*, flattering speech.

Schmeichler, *m.*, flatterer.

schmeichlerisch, flattering, cajoling, adulatory.

schmeidigen, *tr.*, make soft; geschmeidigt, made pliant *or* softened, 2244.

schmelzen (o, o), *intr.*, f., melt, dissolve; *tr. and weak*, melt; die ... schmelzt, who are softened by a woman's deceitful tears, 258.

Schmerz, *m.*, –es, –en, pain grief, sorrow.

schmerzenvoll, painful, sorrowful.

schmerzlich, painful.

schmerzvoll, painful, sorrowful.

schmieden, *tr.*, forge, devise, fabricate.

Schmuck, *m.*, –e, *or* Schmucksachen, ornament, trinket.

schmücken, *tr.*, adorn, grace.

Schmuckkästchen, *n.*, jewel-casket.

schneiden (i, i), *tr.*, cut.

schnell, fast, quick, swift.

schon, already, indeed.

schön, beautiful, fair, handsome.

schonen, *tr. and intr. with gen.*, spare.

Schönheit, *f.*, beauty.

Schönheitsgarten, *m.*, ", garden of beauty.

Schönheitsglanz, *m.*, radiant beauty.

Schonung, *f.*, mercy.

schonungslos, pitiless, unsparing.

Schöpfung, *f.*, creation.

Schoß, *m.*, "e, lap, bosom.

Schotte, *m.*, –n, –n, Scotchman.

schottisch, Scotch.

Schottland, *n.*, Scotland.

Schrank, *m.*, "e, cabinet, desk.

Schranke, *f.*, barrier, bar; *pl.*, tribunal, 218; due limits, 1558; des Gerichtes Schranken, the bar of justice, 95.

schrecken, *tr.*, frighten, terrify, affright.

Schrecken, *m.*, fright, panic, alarm.

Schreckensauftrag, *m.*, "e, dreadful errand.

Schreckenskraft, *f.*, power of terror.

schreckenvoll, frightened, terrified.

schrecklich, fearful, dreadful.
Schrecknis, *n.*, –sses, –sse, horror, terror, terrific object *or* event.
schreiben (ie, ie), *tr. and intr.*, write.
Schreiben, *n.*, writing, document, letter.
Schreiber, *m.*, secretary, writer, clerk.
schreien (ie, ie), *intr.*, cry, scream.
schreiten (i, i), *intr.*, s., stride.
Schrift, *f.*, writing, document.
schriftlich, written, in writing.
Schritt, *m.*, step.
schroff, harsh.
Schuld, *f.*, guilt, blame, fault, debt; man gab euch —, they accused you, 1496.
schuldig, guilty; schuldigst, dutifully, 2664; — sein, owe; ihr Schuldig, their "guilty," 589.
schuldlos, guiltless, innocent.
Schuldnerin, *f.*, –innen, debtor.
Schule, *f.*, school.
Schulter, *f.*, shoulder.
schütteln, *tr.*, shake.
Schutz, *m.*, protection, defense.
Schütze, *m.*, –n, –n, archer, marksman.
schützen, *tr.*, protect, guard, defend.
schwach, weak.
Schwäche, *f.*, weakness, frailty.
Schwachheit, *f.*, weakness, frailty.
Schwager, *m.*, ¨, brother-in-law.
schwank, wavering, unstable.
schwärmen, *intr.*, revel, dream, rave.
Schwärmer, *m.*, enthusiast, visionary, fanatic.
Schwärmereifer, *m.*, fanaticism.
schwarz, black.
schwärzen, *tr.*, blacken.
schwatzen, *intr.*, prattle, prate, talk.
schweben, *intr.*, hover, soar.
schweigen (ie, ie), *intr.*, be silent, keep silence.
Schweigen, *n.*, silence.
Schwelle, *f.*, threshold.
schwer, heavy, difficult, hard, grievous, heinous.
Schwermut, *m.*, melancholy, dejection.
Schwert, *n.*, –er, sword.
Schwester, *f.*, sister.
schwesterlich, sisterly.
schwierig, difficult.
schwimmen (a, o), *intr.*, h. *and* s., swim.
Schwindel, *m.*, dizziness, vertigo.
schwinden (a, u), *intr.*, s., vanish, disappear; fail (in health), 1059.
Schwinge, *f.*, wing, pinion.
schwingen (a, u), *intr.*, swing; *tr.*, swing, brandish; *reflex.*, soar.
schwören (o *or* u, o), *tr. and intr.*, take an oath, swear.

Schwur, *m.*, ¨e, vow, protestation, oath.
Seele, *f.*, soul.
Segen, *m.*, blessing, benediction, sign of the cross, 3736 +.
segenbringend, beneficent.
segenvoll, blessed, blissful.
Segler, *m.*, sailor, voyager.
segnen, *tr.*, bless.
Segnung, *f.*, blessing.
sehen (a, e), *tr. and intr.*, see, perceive; *imp. as exclamation*, see! look!
sehr, very, much, greatly.
seiden, silken, of silk.
sein, war, gewesen, *intr.*, s., be, exist; *as aux.*, be, have.
sein, –e, –, his, its.
seinesgleichen, *indec.*, his equals.
seit (*with dat.*), since.
seitdem, *adv. and conj.*, since.
Seite, *f.*, side.
Seitenthüre, *f.*, side-door.
selber, *indec.*, self, myself, himself, *etc.*
selbst, *indec.*, self, even.
selbständig, independent.
selbsteigen, own (*used for great emphasis*).
Selbstsucht, *f.*, selfishness.
Selbstvergessen, *n.*, self-forgetfulness, oblivion.
selig, happy, blessed.
seltsam, strange, rare.
Senat', *m.*, senate.
senden, sandte, gesandt (*or reg.*), *tr.*, send.
Seneschall, *m.*, Lord Steward.
Sentenz', *f.*, sentence.
Serail', *n.*, –s, –s (*pr.* szerálj), seraglio, harem.
setzen, *tr.*, put, place; *reflex.*, be seated, take a seat; gesetzt, granted, conceded, 936.
seufzen, *intr.*, sigh.
Scheriff (*Eng.*), –s, –s, sheriff.
sich, *indec.*, *reflex. of third person*, himself, herself, itself, themselves.
sicher, sure, safe, secure.
Sicherheit, *f.*, safety, security.
sichtbar, visible.
sie, *pl.* sie, she, they; Sie, *with pl. vb.*, you.
sieben, seven.
Sieg, *m.*, victory, triumph.
Siegel, *m.*, seal.
siegen, *intr.*, conquer, triumph; siegend, victorious.
Siegesbogen, *m.*, triumphal arch.
silbern, silver.
sinken (a, u), *intr.*, s., sink.
Sinn, *m.*, sense, thought, mind, meaning, purport; von Sinnen war, had lost his wits, 3948.
sinnen (a, o), *intr.*, think, reflect.
Sitte, *f.*, custom; *pl.*, manners.
Sitz, *m.*, seat.
Sitzung, *f.*, session; council, 482.

Sklave, *m.*, –n, –n, slave.
Sklavendemut, *f.*, servile humility.
Sklaverei', *f.*, slavery.
so, so, thus, as.
sobald, *adv. and conj.*, so soon; as soon as.
sogar, even.
sogleich, at once, immediately.
Sohn, *m.*, ¨e, son.
solang(e), as long as.
solch, **–er**, **–e**, **–es**, such.
sollen, *intr. and modal aux.*, shall, ought, must; to be, be said to, be intended to.
sondergleichen, without equal, unparalleled.
Sonne, *f.*, sun.
sonst, otherwise, formerly.
Sorge, *f.*, care, anxiety, sorrow.
sorgen, *intr.*, care for, see to, fear, be afraid *or* anxious.
sorgenvoll, anxious.
Souverän', *m.*, sovereign.
Späher, *m.*, spy.
Spähertritt, *m.*, spying footsteps.
Spanien, Spain.
spanisch, Spanish.
Spannung, *f.*, suspense.
sparen, *tr.*, spare, save.
spärlich, scanty.
spät, late.
Speise, *f.*, food, nourishment.
speisen, *tr.*, give to eat; treated *or* served, 37.
sperren, *tr.*, close, shut, bar.
Spiegel, *m.*, mirror, looking-glass.
Spiel, *n.*, play, game.
spielen, *tr. and intr.*, play.
Spielzeug, *n.*, plaything, toy.
spinnen (a, o), *tr.*, spin, plan, devise.
Spitze, *f.*, point, head.
Spott, *m.*, scorn, mockery; — mit mir zu treiben, to mock me, 2821.
spotten, *intr.*, mock, deride, ridicule.
Sprache, *f.*, language.
sprachlos, speechless.
sprechen (a, o), *intr. and tr.*, speak; pronounce.
sprengen, *tr.*, burst.
spröde, brittle; shy, coy, stubborn, reserved, prudish.
Spruch, *m.*, ¨e, saying, sentence, decree, judgment.
Spur, *f.*, trace, track, footprint.
Spürkunst, *f.*, sagacity, astuteness.
Staat, *m.*, –es, –en, state.
Staatsamt, *n.*, ¨er, office (of state).
Staatskunst, *f.*, statecraft.
Staatsmann, *m.*, ¨er, statesman.
Staatsrat, *m.*, council of state, privy council.
Staatsverbrechen, *n.*, crime against the state.
Staatsvorteil, *m.*, common weal, advantage of the state.

Stab, *m.*, ⁻̈e, staff, rod, support, prop; brecht den —, pass sentence, 1069.
Stachel, *m.*, –s, –n, sting.
Stadt, *f.*, ⁻̈e, city.
Stamm, *m.*, ⁻̈e, stock, lineage, family.
Stammbaum, *m.*, ⁻̈e, family tree, pedigree, genealogy.
stampfen, *intr.*, stamp.
Stand, *m.*, ⁻̈e, station, rank, condition.
standhaft, steadfast, firm.
stark, strong.
Stärke, *f.*, strength.
stärken, *tr.*, strengthen.
starr, rigid, stiff, inflexible, stern, fixed.
Statthalter, *m.*, vicar, vice-regent.
Staub, *m.*, dust.
staunen, *intr.*, be amazed *or* astonished, wonder.
stecken, *tr.*, stick, put; *intr.*, be, be hidden.
stehen, stand, gestanden, *intr.*, h. *and* s., stand, be.
stehlen (a, o), *tr.*, steal; *reflex.*, insinuate one's self; *cf.* 1480, *note*.
steigen (ie, ie), *intr.*, s., mount, ascend, rise.
Stein, *m.*, stone, gem.
stellen, *tr.*, place, put; *reflex.*, feign, make believe, affect.
Stellung, *f.*, position, attitude.
sterben (a, o), *intr.*, s., die.
Sterben, *n.*, death, dying.
sterblich, mortal.
Sterbliche, *m. and f.* (*dec. as adj.*), mortal.
Sterblichkeit, *f.*, mortality.
Stern, *m.*, star.
stets, ever, always.
sticken, *tr.*, embroider.
stiften, *tr.*, found, institute.
Stifter, *m.*, founder, instigator.
Stifterin, *f.*, –innen, author, instigator.
still, quiet, still.
stillen, *tr.*, appease, quiet, still.
still'schweigen (ie, ie), *intr.*, keep silence; stillschweigend, silently, 1423.
Stillschweigen, *n.*, silence.
Stimme, *f.*, voice, vote.
stimmen, *intr.*, vote.
Stimmenmehrheit, *f.*, majority of votes.
Stimmung, *f.*, mood, temper.
Stirn(e), *f.*, brow, face, front; — gegen —, face to face, 883.
Stirnband, *n.*, ⁻̈er, diadem.
Stock, *m.*, story (of a house); stick, cane.
stocken, *intr.*, s., falter, hesitate.
stolz, proud, haughty.
Stolz, *m.*, pride.
Stoß, *m.*, ⁻̈e, thrust, blow.
stoßen (ie, o), *tr.*, thrust.
Strafe, *f.*, punishment.
strafen, *tr.*, punish.

straflos, unpunished; *as adv.*, with impunity.

Strahl, *m.*, –es, –en, beam *or* flash of lightning, thunderbolt.

stranden, *intr.*, s., be wrecked; der Strandende, the wrecked *or* stranded mariner, 2270.

Straße, *f.*, street, highroad.

streben, *intr.*, strive.

strecken, *tr.*, stretch, stretch out.

Streich, *m.*, stroke, blow.

Streit, *m.*, contention, dispute, strife.

streiten (i, i), *intr.*, dispute, contest.

streng, severe, strict, austere, hard.

Strenge, *f.*, severity, rigor.

streuen, *tr.*, scatter, spread, disseminate, sow.

Strom, *m.*, ¨e, stream.

strömen, *intr.*, h. *and* s., flow, stream, gush.

Stufe, *f.*, step.

Stuhl, *m.*, ¨e, chair.

stumm, silent, mute, dumb.

Stunde, *f.*, hour, time.

Sturm, *m.*, ¨e, storm, assault.

stürmen, *intr.*, storm; *tr.*, assault, carry by storm.

stürmevoll, stormy.

Sturz, *m.*, ¨e, fall.

stürzen, *intr.*, s., fall, rush; *tr.*, overthrow, plunge, hurl down; *reflex.*, plunge; gestürzt, undone.

Stütze, *f.*, prop, support.

Suada, *f.*, persuasiveness, persuasion.

suchen, *tr.*, seek, search for.

Suchen, *n.*, search.

Sultanslaune, *f.*, sultan's caprice, despotic whim.

Sünde, *f.*, sin.

Sünderin, *f.*, –innen, (woman) sinner.

sündig, sinful.

süß, sweet.

Szene, *f.*, scene, stage setting, scenery.

T

Tadel, *m.*, blame, reproach.

tadeln, *tr.*, blame, criticise.

Tafel, *f.*, table.

Tag, *m.*, day.

tagen, *intr.*, dawn.

Tagesanbruch, *m.*, break of day.

Tand, *m.*, trifles.

tapfer, brave, gallant, courageous.

Tapferkeit, *f.*, bravery, valor.

Tasche, *f.*, pocket.

Tausch, *m.*, exchange.

täuschen, *tr.*, delude, cheat, disappoint.

Täuschung, *f.*, deception.

tausend, thousand; *as pl. noun*, 488.

Teil, *m.*, part, share, lot; zu teil werden, fall to one's lot, be given one.

teilen, *tr.,* divide.
Tempel, *m.,* temple.
Teppich, *m.,* carpet.
Testament', *n.,* will, testament.
teuer, dear, beloved, precious.
teuflisch, devilish, fiendish.
That, *f.,* deed; in der —, really, 1760.
Thäter, *m.,* doer, author.
thätig, active.
Thor, *m.,* –en, –en, fool.
Thor, *n.,* –es, –e, gate.
Thorheit, *f.,* foolishness, folly.
thöricht, absurd, silly, foolish.
Thräne, *f.,* tear.
Thron, *m.,* throne.
thun, that, gethan, *tr. and intr.,* do, act; so stolz gethan, been so proud of (mit), 2021; *cf. note.*
Thun, *n.,* action, conduct.
Thüre, *f.,* door.
tief, deep.
Tiefe, *f.,* depth.
tiefgebeugt, bowed down, humbled.
tiefgefallen, deeply fallen, *as noun,* 1547.
tiefsinnig, thoughtful, pensive.
Tiger, *m.,* tiger.
tilgen, *tr.,* blot out, erase, remove.
Tisch, *m.,* table.
Titel, *m.,* title.
toben, *intr.,* rage, roar; tobend, furious.
Tod, *m.,* death.
Todesmacht, *f.,* ⁿe, power of death.
Todesnetz, *n.,* snare of death, fatal snare.
Todesopfer, *n.,* victim.
Todespost, *f.,* fatal news.
Todesstunde, *f.,* hour of death.
Todesurteil, *n.,* sentence of death, death warrant.
Todesweg, *m.,* way to death.
tödlich, deadly, fatal.
Tollkühnheit, *f.,* foolhardiness.
Ton, *m.,* ⁿe, tone.
tönen, *intr.,* sound.
tot, dead.
töten, *tr.,* kill, put to death.
Trabant', *m.,* –en, –en, guardsman.
tragen (u, a), *tr.,* bear, carry, wear.
trauen, *intr.,* trust, confide in.
Trauer, *f.,* mourning.
Trauerflor, *m.,* veil of crape, mourning crape.
Trauerkleid, *n.,* –er, mourning dress.
trauern, *intr.,* grieve, mourn.
Traum, *m.,* ⁿe, dream.
träumen, *tr., intr., and imp.,* dream.
traurig, sad, sorrowful, dismal, mournful.
treffen (a, o), *tr. and intr.,* strike, hit, fall upon, meet, fall in with; Anstalt ist ... getroffen, preparations are made, 1843.

trefflich, excellent, eminent.
treiben (ie, ie), *tr.*, drive, impel, prompt, do, carry on; bear, put forth.
trennen, *tr.*, separate, part.
Trennung, *f.*, separation.
Treppe, *f.*, stairway.
treten (a, e), *intr.*, ſ., tread, step.
treu, faithful, loyal, true.
Treubruch, *m.*, ¨e, perfidy, breach of faith.
Treu(e), *f.*, fidelity, loyalty, truth.
treulos, faithless, perfidious, false.
Trieb, *m.*, instinct, impulse, motive.
trinken (a, u), *tr.*, drink.
Triumph', *m.*, triumph.
trocknen, *tr.*, dry, wipe.
Trost, *m.*, comfort, consolation.
trösten, *tr.*, console, comfort.
trostlos, comfortless, inconsolable.
Trotz, *m.*, defiance, scorn, spite.
trotz (*with gen. or dat.*), in spite of.
trotzen, *intr.*, defy; — auf, insist (defiantly) upon.
Trübsal, *f.*, –e *or* –en (*or n.*, –s, –e), sorrow, affliction.
trunken, drunk, intoxicated; delighted, 1144.
Trunkenheit, *f.*, intoxication.
Tuch, *n.*, ¨er, cloth, kerchief.
Tugend, *f.*, virtue.
Tugendruf, *m.*, reputation for virtue.
Tumult, *m.*, tumult.
Turm, *m.*, ¨er, tower.
Turnier'platz, *m.*, ¨e, lists.
Tyrann', *m.*, –en, –en, tyrant.
Tyrannei', *f.*, tyranny.
Tyrannenmacht, *f.*, tyrant's power, despotism.
tyrannisch, tyrannical, despotic.

U

üben, *tr.*, exercise, practice.
über, *prep.*, *adv.*, *sep. and insep. pref.*, over, above, across, concerning, beyond.
ü'berbleiben (ie, ie), *intr.*, ſ., survive; *commonly* übrig bleiben.
überbring'en, überbrachte, überbracht, *tr.*, deliver.
überei'len, *tr.*, over-hasten, hurry; *intr.*, use undue haste.
übereilt, precipitate, rash, hasty.
überfal'len (ie, a), *tr.*, attack suddenly, surprise.
Überfluß, *m.*, –ſſes, surplus, abundance.
überfüh'ren, *tr.* (*with gen.*), convict of.
überge'ben (a, e), *tr.*, surrender, give over, deliver.

ü'bergehen, –ging, –gegangen, *intr.*, ſ., go over, pass over.

überhe'ben (o *or* u, o), *reflex. with gen.*, presume upon, boast of.

überlaſ'ſen (ie, a), *tr.*, give up, resign, relinquish, abandon. [portunate.

überläſtig, troublesome, im-

überle'gen *tr.*, ponder, deliberate, reflect.

überlie'fern, *tr.*, deliver.

Übermut, *m.*, arrogance, haughtiness.

übermütig, arrogant, insolent.

überneh'men (a, o), *tr.*, accept, take upon one's self.

überraſch'en, *tr.*, surprise, take unawares.

überre'den, *tr.*, persuade.

überrei'chen, *tr.*, hand to, present.

überſchrei'ten (i, i), *tr.*, overstep, violate, exceed.

überſtrah'len, *tr.*, outshine.

übertra'gen (u, a), *tr.*, commit, entrust to, assign to.

überwäl'tigen, *tr.*, overpower.

überwunden, vanquished, conquered.

überzeu'gen, *tr.*, convince.

Überzeugung, *f.*, conviction, assurance.

überzieh'en (o, o), *tr.*, cover over, drape.

übrig, over, left, remaining; *as noun*, the rest.

Übung, *f.*, practice, exercise.

Ufer, *n.*, shore.

um, *adv.*, *sep. and insep. pref.*, *and prep.*, around, about, for, concerning; — . . . willen, for the sake of.

umar'men, *tr.*, embrace.

Umarmung, *f.*, embrace.

umfang'en (i, a), *tr.*, encircle, surround.

umfaſ'ſen, *tr.*, embrace, comprise, surround.

umflech'ten (o, o), *tr.*, twist around, entwine.

umflie'ßen (o, o), *tr.*, flow around, encompass.

umge'ben (a, e), *tr.*, surround; ſie nicht königlich — ſei, her surroundings are not royal, 2055.

um'gehen, –ging, –gegangen, *intr.*, ſ., go around.

umgeh'en, umging, umgangen, *tr.*, avoid, evade.

umgit'tern, *tr.*, surround with bars *or* grating .

umglän'zen, *tr.*, make radiant, surround with splendor.

um'hangen, *tr.*, put on, hang about.

umher, *adv. and sep. pref.*, around, about.

umher'blicken, *intr.*, look about.

umher'gehen, –ging, –gegangen, *intr.*, ſ., go about.

umhül'len, *tr.*, veil, envelop.

umklam'mern, *tr.*, clasp.

um'kommen (a, o), *intr.*, ſ., die, perish.

umlach'en, *tr.*, surround with smiles, smile around.

umla'gern, *tr.*, beset, encompass.

umring'en, *tr.*, surround, beset; umrungen *as past part.*, 1369.

umschling'en (a, u), *tr.*, embrace, twine.

um'sehen (a, e), *reflex.*, look around.

umsonst, in vain, to no purpose, for nothing.

umsteh'en, umstand, umstanden, *tr.*, surround.

umstrah'len, *tr.*, shine around, illumine.

umstrick'en, *tr.*, entangle, ensnare.

um'wenden, –wandte, –gewandt (*or reg.*), *tr. and intr.*, turn round.

umzing'eln, *tr.*, surround on all sides, encircle.

unabsehbar, unbounded, incalculable.

unanständig, indecorous, unseemly, unbecoming.

unauflöslich, inextricable.

unbedachtsam, indiscreet, rash.

unbedeutend, insignificant, unimportant.

unbefleckt, unspotted, unsullied, spotless.

unbereitet, unprepared.

unberufen, uncalled for, officious, meddling.

unbescholten, unimpeachable, blameless.

unbestechlich, incorruptible, not to be bribed.

unbewegt, unmoved.

unbezwinglich, invincible, unconquerable.

und, and.

uneingeschränkt, unlimited, unreservedly.

unendlich, endless, infinite, unending.

unentschlossen, irresolute, undecided.

unermüdet, unwearied.

unerschöpflich, inexhaustible.

unerträglich, unbearable, intolerable.

unerwartet, unexpected.

Ungeduld, *f.*, impatience.

ungeduldig, impatient.

ungefähr, about, nearly, almost; von —, by chance, accidentally.

ungeheuer, monstrous.

ungekränkt, unmolested.

ungelehrt, unlettered.

ungemessen, boundless.

ungenützt, unemployed.

ungerecht, unjust, wrongful.

ungesäumt, immediately, promptly.

ungeschehen, undone.

ungestraft, unpunished; with impunity, 2414.

ungestüm, impetuous, violent, vehement.

Ungestüm, *m. and n.*, vehemence, violence, impetuosity.

ungeteilt, undivided.
ungetreu, faithless, disloyal.
ungeweiht, unconsecrated, unordained.
Ungewißheit, *f.*, uncertainty.
ungleich, unlike, unequal.
Unglück, *n.*, misfortune, adversity.
unglücklich, unfortunate, unhappy.
Unglücksbrief, *m.*, fatal letter.
unglückselig, unhappy, unfortunate, ill-starred; der Unglückselige, that evil genius, 2743.
Unglücksthat, *f.*, fatal *or* unhappy deed.
unglücksvoll, unfortunate, unhappy.
Ungrund, *m.*, groundlessness.
Unheil, *n.*, mischief, evil, harm.
unheilbringend, bringing mischief, harmful, pernicious.
unheilbrütend, brooding evil.
unheilspinnend, spinning *or* plotting mischief; *cf.* 114, *note.*
unhold, unkind, ungracious.
unköniglich, unkingly.
unkundig, not knowing, unacquainted (with).
unlängst, recently, lately, not long ago.
unmäßig, immoderate, excessive.
Unmenschlichkeit, *f.*, inhumanity.
Unmut, *m.*, indignation.
Unrecht, *n.*, wrong, injustice.
Unruhe, *f.*, uneasiness, anxiety, agitation.
Unschuld, *f.*, innocence.
unser, –e, –, our, ours.
unsichtbar, invisible.
unsinnig, mad, insane, frantic.
unstät, unsteady.
unsterblich, immortal.
unten, below.
unter, *adv., prep., and sep. and insep. pref.*, under, beneath, amid, among.
unterbrech'en (a, o), *tr.*, interrupt.
unterdrück'en, *tr.*, oppress.
Unterdrückung, *f.*, oppression.
unter(e), lower.
unterfang'en (i, a), *reflex.*, venture, presume.
Untergang, *m.*, destruction.
un'tergehen, –ging, –gegangen, *intr.*, s., perish.
unterhal'ten (ie, a), *tr.*, amuse, entertain; *reflex.*, converse, talk.
unterhan'deln, *tr. and intr.*, negotiate.
Unterhandlung, *f.*, negotiation.
unterjoch'en, subjugate, subdue.
unterlie'gen (a, e), *intr.*, s., succumb, yield.
unterneh'men (a, o), *tr.*, undertake.
Unterredung, *f.*, interview.

unterschrei'ben (ie, ie), *tr.*, sign.
Unterschrift, *f.*, signature.
untersu'chen, *tr.*, investigate.
Untersuchung, *f.*, examination, investigation.
unterthan, subject (to).
Unterthan, *m.*, –s (*and* –en), –en, subject.
unterthänig, subject (to).
unterwegs *or* –weges, on the way.
unterwer'fen (a, o), *tr.*, subject, subdue; *reflex.*, submit, yield; *past part.*, subject to, 845.
Unterwerfung, *f.*, submission.
unterwürfig, submissive, subject.
unterzeich'nen, *tr.*, sign.
unverdient, unmerited, undeserved.
unverdrossen, unwearied, unremitting.
unvereinbar, irreconcilable, incompatible.
unverhofft, unexpected, unhoped for.
unverhohlen, unconcealed, open, plain.
unvermählt, unwed, unmarried.
unvermeidlich, inevitable, unavoidable.
unverschämt, impudent, insolent.
unversöhnlich, implacable, irreconcilable.
unversöhnt, implacable.
unverwahrt, unguarded.
unverwandt, unmoved, fixed.
unvollstreckt, unexecuted.
Unwille, *m.*, –ens, displeasure, anger.
unwillkürlich, involuntary.
unwürdig, unworthy, discreditable.
unzählig, countless.
Unziemlichkeit, *f.*, impropriety.
unzugänglich, inaccessible.
üppig, luxurious, wanton.
uralt, ancient, primeval.
Urlaub, *m.*, leave (of absence).
Urteil, *n.*, sentence, judgment, warrant.
urteilen, judge.
urteln, *see* urteilen.
Urtelsspruch, *m.*, ⁿe, judgment, sentence.

V

Vasall, *m.*, –en, –en, vassal.
Vater, *m.*, ⁿ, father.
Vaterland, *n.*, fatherland, native land.
Vatikan', *m.*, Vatican.
ver=, *unaccented insep. pref.*
verabscheuen, *tr.*, abhor, detest.
verachten, *tr.*, scorn, despise.
verächtlich, contemptible, despicable.

Verachtung, *f.*, contempt, disdain.

verachtungswert, despicable, contemptible.

verändern, *tr.*, change, alter.

Veränderung, *f.*, change, alteration.

verbannen, *tr.*, banish, exile, proscribe.

Verbannte, *m. or f.* (*dec. as adj.*), exile.

Verbannung, *f.*, exile, banishment.

verbergen (a, o), *tr.*, hide, conceal.

verbieten (o, o), *tr.*, forbid, interdict, prohibit.

verbinden (a, u), *tr.*, bind, bandage, blindfold; *reflex.*, unite *or* join one's self, 3753.

verblassen, *intr.*, turn pale.

verborgen, hidden, concealed.

Verbot, *n.*, prohibition.

verbrechen (a, o), *tr.*, commit a crime, transgress; *cf.* 3739, *note.*

Verbrechen, *n.*, crime, transgression.

Verbrecher, *m.*, criminal, offender.

verbreiten, *tr.*, spread; *reflex.*, be spread.

verbringen, verbrachte, verbracht, spend, pass (time).

verbuhlt, wanton, amorous.

verbünden, *reflex.*, be associated, ally.

verbürgen, *reflex.*, go bail, answer for.

Verdacht, *m.*, suspicion.

verdammen, *tr.*, damn, condemn; die Verdammten, the damned, 139.

Verdammnis, *f.*, perdition, damnation.

verdanken, *tr.*, owe, be indebted.

verderben (a, o), *tr.*, destroy, ruin; *intr.*, s., perish.

Verderben, *n.*, destruction.

verdienen, *tr.*, earn, merit, deserve; um England wenig Dank verdient, not deserved well of England, 2699.

Verdienst, *n.*, merit.

verehren, *tr.*, honor, respect, revere.

Verehrer, *m.*, worshiper.

Verein, *m.*, union, association.

vereinigen, *tr.*, unite, join.

vereiteln, *tr.*, baffle, thwart, frustrate.

verfahren (u, a), *intr.*, s. *and* h., proceed.

verfallen (i, a), *intr.*, s., fall, be forfeited, incur the penalty of.

verfassen, *tr.*, compose, draw up, write.

verfluchen, *tr.*, curse, execrate.

verflucht, cursed, accursed.

verfolgen, *tr.*, pursue, prosecute.

Verfolger, *m.*, pursuer, persecutor.

verfügen, *reflex.*, repair to, betake one's self (to).

Verfügung, *f.*, order, direction, disposition; — treffen über, dispose of, 200.

verführen, *tr.*, lead astray, corrupt, seduce.

Verführer, *m.*, seducer, corrupter.

verführt, misguided.

vergangen, (just) gone, past.

vergeben (a, e), *tr.*, give away, forgive; compromise, 701; *past part. as adj.*, vain, idle, 620.

vergeblich, fruitless, vain, useless.

Vergebung, *f.*, pardon, forgiveness.

vergehen, verging, vergangen, *intr.*, s., pass away, perish, be lost; *reflex.*, err, go astray.

vergessen (a, e), *tr.*, *also with gen.*, forget.

Vergessen, *n.*, forgetfulness, oblivion.

vergießen (o, o), *tr.*, spill, shed.

vergleichen (i, i), *tr.*, compare.

vergönnen, *tr.*, permit, not grudge, grant.

vergrößern, *tr.*, enlarge, magnify, exaggerate.

Vergünstigung, *f.*, permission, favor, privilege.

verhaften, *tr.*, arrest, seize, imprison.

verhandeln, *tr.*, discuss.

verhaßt, odious, hated.

verhehlen, *tr.*, hide, conceal.

verheimlichen, *tr.*, keep secret.

verheißen (ie, ei), *tr.*, promise.

verherrlichen, *tr.*, glorify.

verhindern, *tr.*, hinder, prevent.

verhöhnen, *tr.*, deride, mock, sneer at, scorn.

Verhör, *n.*, trial, hearing; ins — genommen, taken to task, 1790.

verhüllen, *tr.*, veil, cover.

verhüten, *tr.*, prevent, ward off.

verjagen, *tr.*, drive away, expel.

verjüngen, *tr.*, make young, rejuvenate; *reflex.*, grow young once more.

verkaufen, *tr.*, sell.

verklagen, *tr.*, accuse, indict.

verklären, *tr.*, transfigure, glorify; verklärt, radiant with bliss, 3756.

Verklärung, *f.*, transfiguration, glory.

verkünden, *see* verkündigen.

Verkünderin, *f.*, –innen, herald, harbinger.

verkündigen, *tr.*, announce, proclaim.

verkürzen, *tr.*, shorten.

verlangen, *tr.*, ask, demand, require, request.

Verlangen, *n.*, desire.
verlängern, *tr.*, make long, prolong.
verlassen (i, a), *tr.*, leave, abandon; *reflex.*, rely *or* depend upon (auf).
verlegen, perplexed, embarrassed.
Verlegenheit, *f.*, embarrassment.
verleihen (ie, ie), *tr.*, lend, grant, bestow, confer upon.
verleiten, *tr.*, mislead.
verletzen, *tr.*, wound, hurt, offend, outrage.
verleugnen, *tr.*, deny.
verlieren (o, o), *tr.*, lose.
verloren, lost, wasted.
Verlorene, *m. and f.* (*dec. as adj.*), outcast, reprobate.
Verlust, *m.*, –e *or* ¨e, loss.
Vermächtnis, *n.*, –sses, –sse, last will; legacy, 3557.
vermählen, *tr.*, marry, give in marriage.
Vermählung, *f.*, marriage.
vermeiden (ie, ie), *tr.*, avoid, shun, evade.
vermengen, *tr.*, confuse, confound.
vermessen (a, e), *reflex.*, presume, dare; *past part. as adj.*, presumptuous, insolent.
vermischen, *tr. and reflex.*, mix.
vermissen, *tr.*, miss.
vermögen, vermochte, vermocht, *tr.*, be able *or* have power to do.
vermummen, *tr.*, disguise.
vernehmen (a, o), *tr.*, hear, learn; ließ Euch darüber —, made answer thereto, 708.
vernichten, *tr.*, destroy, annihilate.
Vernichtung, *f.*, extermination, destruction.
Vernunft, *f.*, reason.
veröden, *tr.*, lay waste; *intr.*, s., become desolate.
verordnen, *tr.*, order, enact.
verpflanzen, *tr.*, transplant.
Verrat, *m.*, treachery, treason.
verraten (ie, a), *tr.*, betray.
Verräter, *m.*, traitor.
Verräterei', *f.*, treason.
verräterisch, treacherous, treasonable.
verrichten, *tr.*, do, perform.
verrinnen (a, o), *intr.*, s., elapse, pass.
Verrückte, *m.* (*dec. as adj.*), maniac.
verrufen (ie, u), *intr.*, decry, defame; *tr.*, abolish (as infamous), 779.
versagen, *tr.*, deny, refuse; *intr.*, fail.
versammeln, *tr. and reflex.*, assemble, meet; versammelt, collected *or* united.
Versammlung, *f.*, meeting.
verschaffen, *tr.*, procure, furnish, provide.
verscharren, *tr.*, bury.

verscheiden (ie, ie), *intr.*, s., die.

verschenken, *tr.*, give away, bestow.

verscheuchen, *tr.*, scare *or* frighten away.

verschieden, different.

verschleudern, *tr.*, fling away.

verschließen (o, o), *tr.*, shut, lock; verschlossen, locked.

verschlingen (a, u), *tr.*, swallow (up), devour.

verschmähen, *tr.*, disdain, scorn.

verschmerzen, *tr.*, bear patiently, brook, cease to grieve at.

verschonen, *tr.*, spare, excuse from.

Verschulden, *n.*, guilt, fault, offence.

verschweigen (ie, ie), *tr.*, keep secret, conceal; *intr.*, be silent.

verschwenderisch, lavish, prodigal.

verschwinden (a, u), *intr.*, s., disappear, pass away.

verschwören (o *or* u, o), *tr.*, abjure, forswear; *reflex.*, conspire; verschworen, joined in conspiracy.

Verschwörung, *f.*, conspiracy, plot.

versehen (a, e), *tr.*, provide with, supply.

Versehen, *n.*, error, blunder.

versichern, *tr.*, assure, certify.

Versicherung, *f.*, assurance.

versiegeln, *tr.*, seal, attest.

versinken (a, u), *intr.*, s., sink down *or* into, lapse into.

versöhnen, *tr.*, reconcile, propitiate, expiate.

versöhnt, reconciled, at peace.

Versöhnung, *f.*, reconciliation.

verspotten, *tr.*, scoff, deride.

versprechen (a, o), *tr.*, promise.

Versprechen, *n.*, promise.

verspritzen, *tr.*, spill, shed.

Verstand, *m.*, understanding, intellect.

verständigen, *reflex.*, arrange with, come to an understanding.

Verständnis, *n.*, –sses, –sse, understanding, comprehension.

verstatten, *tr.*, allow, permit.

verstecken, *tr.*, hide, conceal.

verstehen, verstand, verstanden, *tr.*, understand, comprehend.

Verstellung, *f.*, dissimulation.

verstohlen, secret, clandestine.

verstoßen (ie, o), *tr.*, expel, cast off.

verstricken, *tr.*, entangle.

verstummen, *intr.*, s., be dumb *or* speechless, keep silent.

versuchen, *tr.*, try, attempt, tempt.

vertauschen, *tr.*, exchange.

verteidigen, *tr.*, defend.

verteilen, *tr.*, distribute, divide.

vertilgen, *tr.,* exterminate.

Vertilgungskrieg, *m.,* war of extermination.

Vertrag, *m.,* ⸗e, treaty, agreement.

vertragen (u, a), *reflex.,* agree, become reconciled.

vertrauen, *tr.,* entrust, confide; *intr. with dat.,* trust (to *or* in); *past part. as adj.,* trusty, faithful.

Vertrauen, *n.,* confidence, trust.

vertrauern, *tr.,* spend in mourning, pass in sorrow.

vertraulich, confidential, intimate.

Vertraute, *m. and f.* (*dec. as adj.*), confidant, friend.

vertreiben (ie, ie), *tr.,* drive away, dispel.

Vertriebene, *m. and f.* (*dec. as adj.*), exile, banished one.

veruntreuen, *tr.,* prove false to, break faith.

verurteilen, *tr.,* condemn.

verwahren, *tr.,* keep, guard.

Verwahrung, *f.,* keeping, custody.

verwalten, *tr.,* administer; ein Amt —, fill an office, 1295.

verwandeln, *tr.,* change, transform; *reflex.,* be changed.

Verwandlung, *f.,* change; Transubstantiation, 3620.

Verwandte, *m. and f.* (*dec. as adj.*), relative, kinsman *or* kinswoman.

verwegen, bold, rash, venturesome, presumptuous, insolent; *as noun,* 8.

verwehren, *tr.,* hinder, prevent.

verweigern, *tr.,* deny, refuse.

verweilen, *reflex.,* stay, stop.

verweint, red with weeping.

verweisen (ie, ie), *tr.,* rebuke, reprove.

verwerfen (a, o), *tr.,* throw away, cast aside; reject, repudiate, deny, not acknowledge.

verwildert, dishevelled.

verwirken, *tr.,* forfeit, lose.

verwirren, *tr.,* confuse, confound.

Verworfene, *m. and f.* (*dec. as adj.*), reprobate, wretch.

verworren, confused.

verwunden, *tr.,* wound, hurt, sting.

verwundern, *tr.,* surprise, startle, astonish.

Verwunderung, *f.,* amazement, astonishment.

Verwünschung, *f.,* execration, cursing.

Verzeichnis, *n.,* –sses, –sse, list, inventory.

verzeihen (ie, ie), *tr.,* pardon, forgive.

Verzeihung, *f.,* forgiveness, pardon.

Verzweiflung, *f.,* despair, desperation.

verzweiflungsvoll, desperate, full of despair.

Vetter, *m.*, cousin.

viel (mehr, meist), much, many.

vielbedeutend, very significant, influential; full of meaning.

vielgeliebt, much-loved, well-beloved.

vielleicht, perhaps.

viermal, four times.

vierzig, forty.

Volk, *n.*, ¨er, people, nation; bewaffnet —, troops *or* men at arms, 2592.

Völkerhaß, *m.*, –sses, national hatred.

Völkerhirt, *m.*, –en, –en, shepherd of the people.

Völkerrecht, *n.*, law of nations, international law.

Völkerschaft, *f.*, nation.

Volksdienst, *m.*, popular service, service of the nation.

Volksgunst, *f.*, popularity.

voll, *adj.*, full, whole, complete; *sep. and insep. pref.*, fully, entirely.

vollbring'en, vollbrachte, vollbracht, *tr.*, perform, accomplish, carry out; *inf. as noun,* deed, performance, 3597.

vollen'den, *tr.*, finish, conclude.

vollfüh'ren, *tr.*, accomplish, carry out.

völlig, full, entire, complete.

vollkommen, complete, perfect.

Vollmacht, *f.*, authority, full power.

vollstreck'en, *tr.*, execute, carry out.

Vollstreckung, *f.*, performance, execution.

vollzieh'en, vollzog, vollzogen, *tr.*, fulfil, execute, carry out.

Vollziehung, *f.*, fulfillment, execution.

von, of, from, by.

vor, *prep., adv., and sep. pref.*, before, from, for, with, because of; *in expressions of time,* ago.

voran', *adv. and sep. pref.*, forward, before, in front of.

voran'gehen, –ging, –gegangen, *intr.*, s., precede, go before.

voraus', *adv. and sep. pref.*, before; nichts — vor, no prominence over, 1208; im —, in advance.

voraus'eilen, *intr.*, s., hasten on ahead of.

Vorbedeutung, *f.*, portent, omen, foreboding.

vorbei', *adv. and sep. pref.*, by, past, along.

vorbei'führen, *tr.*, lead past.

vorbei'kommen, –kam, –gekommen, *intr.*, s., come along, come past.

vor'bereiten, *tr.*, prepare, make ready.

Vorbereitung, *f.*, preparation.

Vorfahr, *m.*, –en, –en, predecessor; *pl.*, ancestors.

vor'fordern, *tr.*, summon, cite.

vor'führen, *tr.*, produce, bring before.

vor'geben (a, e), *tr.*, put forward, assert, plead.

vor'gehen, –ging, –gegangen, *intr.*, f., happen, come to pass, occur.

vor'greifen (i, i), *intr.*, anticipate, forestall.

Vorhang, *m.*, ⁻e, curtain.

vorher', *adv. and sep. pref.*, before, previously.

vorher'bedenken,–bedachte,–bedacht, *tr.*, plan in advance; vorherbedacht, premeditated, 2752.

vorhin, just now, recently, a little while ago.

vorig, former.

vor'leuchten, *intr.*, shine before; als Muster —, be a shining example, 1189.

vorn, in front, before, in the foreground.

Vorrecht, *n.*, privilege.

Vorsaal, *m.*, –säle, antechamber, hall.

Vorsatz, *m.*, ⁻e, purpose, design, intention.

Vorsicht, *f.*, foresight, caution, providence.

vor'stellen, *tr.*, place before, confront 910; represent, show.

Vorteil, *m.*, advantage; expediency, 1441; zu ihrem — sprechend, *cf.* 1352, *note.*

vor'tragen (u, a), *tr.*, bring before, lay before, 3187.

vor'treten (a, e), *intr.*, f., step forward, advance.

vorü'ber, *adv. and sep. pref.*, past, over, by.

vorü'berziehen, –zog, –gezogen, *intr.*, f., pass, move by.

Vorwand, *m.*, ⁻e, pretext.

vor'weisen (ie, ie), *tr.*, exhibit, produce.

vor'werfen (a, o), *tr.*, throw up to, reproach, upbraid.

Vorwurf, *m.*, ⁻e, reproach.

vor'ziehen, –zog, –gezogen, *tr.*, prefer.

Vorzimmer, *n.*, anteroom.

Vorzug, *m.*, ⁻e, preference, preëminence.

W

wach, awake; wird —, is roused, 1816.

Wache, *f.*, watch, sentry, guard.

wachsam, watchful.

Wachsamkeit, *f.*, watchfulness, vigilance.

wachsen (u, a), *intr.*, f., grow.

wachstehend, standing guard.

Wächter, *m.*, keeper, watchman, guard.

Waffe, *f.*, arms, weapon.

waffnen, *tr.*, arm; *reflex.*, take up arms.

wagen, *tr.*, risk, venture, dare; gewagt, risky, 2941.

Wag(e)ſtück, *n.*, venture, risk.

Wagnis, *n.*, –ſſes, –ſſe, hazard, chance, risk.

Wahl, *f.*, choice, option, alternative.

wählen, *tr.*, choose.

Wahn, *m.*, illusion, error, fancy, delusion.

wähnen, *intr.*, fancy, imagine.

Wahnbegriff, *m.*, false notion, erroneous idea.

Wahnſinn, *m.*, insanity, madness; fanaticism, 2341.

wahnſinnig, insane, mad, frantic.

Wahnwitz, *m.*, frenzy, madness, delirium.

wahr, true, real, genuine; — machen, fulfil, 137.

wahren, *tr.*, guard, watch over; des Siegels wahret, is keeper of the Seal, 752.

während, *prep.*, during; *conj.*, while.

wahrhaft, truthful, genuine, true.

Wahrheit, *f.*, truth, reality.

Wald, *m.*, ¨er, forest.

Wall, *m.*, ¨e, wall, rampart.

wallfah'ren, *intr.*, ſ., go on a pilgrimage.

walten, *intr.*, manage, dispose of, rule.

wälzen, *tr. and reflex.*, roll.

Wand, *f.*, ¨e, wall.

Wandel, *m.*, behavior, conduct.

wandelbar, unstable, inconstant, fickle.

wandeln, *intr.*, ſ. *and* h., wander, travel, go.

wandern, *intr.*, h. *and* ſ., wander.

Wanderung, *f.*, migration.

Wange, *f.*, cheek.

wankelmütig, fickle, inconstant.

wanken, *intr.*, h. *and* ſ., totter, waver, falter.

wann, when (*interrogative*).

Wappen, *n.*, coat of arms, scutcheon.

Wappenbuch, *n.*, ¨er, book of heraldry.

warm, warm.

warnen, *tr.*, warn; warnend, as a warning, 645.

Warnung, *f.*, warning.

Warnungsſtimme, *f.*, warning voice.

warten, *intr.*, wait, wait for, expect, await.

warum, why, wherefore.

was, *interrog. and rel. pron.*, what, whatever, that which, that, which; *used for* warum, 2000, 2491, *etc.*, *for* etwas, 252; — auch, whatever.

waſchen (u, a), *tr.*, wash.

Waſſer, *n.*, water.

Waſſerflut, *f.*, deluge, inundation.

weben (o, o, *also weak*), *tr.*, weave.

Wechsel, *m.*, change, vicissitude.

wecken, *tr.*, wake, awaken.

Weg, *m.*, way, road, path, track; den großen — gemacht, taken the grand tour, 1470.

weg, *adv. and sep. pref.*, away.

wegen, on account of.

weg'führen, *tr.*, carry off, remove.

weg'nehmen (a, o), *tr.*, take away.

weg'schleudern, *tr.*, fling away.

Weh, *n.*, woe, sorrow.

weh(e), woe! alas! wehe thut's, it hurts, 53.

Wehmut, *f.*, melancholy, dolefulness.

wehren, *tr.*, ward off, hinder, stop, prevent; avert, 2657.

wehrlos, unarmed, weak, defenseless.

Weib, *n.*, ⸚er, woman.

Weiberlist, *f.*, woman's craft.

Weiberthräne, *f.*, woman's tear.

weibisch, effeminate, womanish.

weiblich, womanly, feminine; ein — Bildnis, a woman's portrait, 503.

Weiblichkeit, *f.*, womanhood.

weich, soft, tender, gentle.

Weichbild, *n.*, –er, precincts, city domain.

weichen (i, i), *intr.*, s., yield, give way, retire; be inferior, 2011.

Weicherzogene, *f.* (*dec. as adj.*), delicately nurtured one.

weichgewohnt, used to softness; *cf.* 33, *note.*

weichlich, effeminate, weak, mawkish.

weiden, *tr.*, feed, feast; *reflex.*, revel in, gloat over.

weigern, *tr.*, refuse, deny.

Weihe, *f.*, consecration, ordination; *cf.* 3652, *note.*

weihen, *tr.*, consecrate, dedicate, devote; doom, 1524.

Weihrauch, *m.*, incense.

weil, because, since.

Weile, *f.*, while, space of time; leisure.

weilen, *intr.*, stay, linger, tarry.

Wein, *m.*, wine.

weinen, *intr.*, weep; *inf. as noun*, 3755.

weise, wise.

Weise, *f.*, mode, manner, wise, fashion, custom.

weisen (ie, ie), *tr.*, show, point out, teach; *intr.*, point to.

Weisheit, *f.*, wisdom.

weiß, white.

weit, far, distant, wide, broad.

weiten, *tr.*, broaden, widen.

weiter (*comp. of* weit), further.

welcher, **welche**, **welches**, *in-*

terrog. adj. and interrog. and rel. pron., who, which, what, that.

welken, *intr.*, ſ., fade, wither.

Welle, *f.*, wave.

Welt, *f.*, world.

Weltgeräusch, *n.*, noise of the world.

Weltlust, *f.*, wordly pleasure, worldliness.

Weltteil, *m.*, part of the world.

wenden, wandte, gewandt (*or reg.*), *tr.*, turn, avert; *reflex.*, turn, appeal; sich anders wendet, veers, 1328.

Wendung, *f.*, turn.

wenig, little, few; ein klein Weniges, a trifle, 2084; mit wenigem, briefly, 1741.

wenigstens, at least.

wenn, if, when; while, 1567.

wer, *indef. rel. and interrog. pron.*, who, he who, whoever.

werben (a, o), *intr.*, sue, woo for (um); *inf. as noun*, 1776.

werden, ward (*or* wurde), geworden, *intr.*, ſ., become, be, grow; *impers. with dat.*, be assigned to, 131, be done, 235; wie ward mir, what were my feelings, 425; wie wird Euch, what ails you, 2156; *aux. of future*, shall *or* will, *of passive voice*, be.

werfen (a, o), *tr.*, throw, fling away.

Werk, *n.*, work; ins — gerichtet, perform, bring about, 2958; zu — gehen, go about things, 238.

Werkzeug, *n.*, tool, instrument.

wert, worth, worthy, worthy of, dear.

Wert, *m.*, value, worth.

Wesen, *n.*, being, nature, manner, conduct, bearing.

weswegen, wherefore, why.

wetteifern, *intr.*, contend, vie with.

wichtig, weighty, important, momentous.

wider, *prep., adv., and insep. pref.*, against, in opposition to, contrary to.

widerlegen, *tr.*, refute.

widerrufen (ie, u), *tr.*, recall, revoke, retract.

Widerspruch, *m.*, ⁿe, contradiction; opposition, 1419.

widerstreben, *intr. with dat.*, resist, struggle against.

widerwärtig, repugnant, odious, offensive.

Widerwille, *m.*, –ns, dislike, aversion, reluctance.

widmen, *tr.*, dedicate.

widrig, repugnant, odious.

wie, *adv. and conj.*, like as, how, when; — auch, however.

wieder, *adv., sep. and insep. pref.*, again, once more.

wiederho'len, *tr.*, repeat.

wie'derkehren, *intr.*, ſ., return.

Wiedersehen, *n.*, meeting, reunion.
Wiege, *f.*, cradle.
Wiese, *f.*, meadow.
wild, wild, fierce, savage.
Wille(n), *m.*, –ns, will, design, purpose; letzter —, last will, testament, 191; willens sein, intend to, 160; um ... willen, for the sake of.
willenlos, without will, weak.
willfährig, complaisant, courteous.
willig, willing, ready.
willkommen, welcome.
Willkür, *f.*, arbitrariness, despotism, caprice.
wimmeln, *intr.*, swarm, be crowded.
Wind, *m.*, wind.
winken, *intr.*, beckon, make a sign to.
wir, we.
wirklich, real, actual, genuine; *as adv.*, indeed, truly, really.
wissen, wußte, gewußt, know, know how; manage, 64, *etc.*; sich ... gewußt, piqued herself, 2020, *note;* wissend, knowingly, 3710.
Wissenschaft, *f.*, knowledge.
Witwe, *f.*, widow.
wo, *adv. and conj.*, where, when; — nicht, if not, 2641.
wodurch, by which *or* what, whereby, through which *or* what.
Woge, *f.*, wave, billow.
wohin, whither, where.
wohl, well, indeed, perhaps, probably; wie mir — ist, how happy I am, 2455.
Wohl, *n.*, weal, welfare, interest.
wohlanständig, seemly, decent.
Wohlfahrt, *f.*, welfare, prosperity.
wohlfeil, cheap.
wohlriechend, fragrant, sweet-smelling.
Wohlthat, *f.*, good deed, boon, favor, kindness.
wohlthätig, beneficent.
wohnen, *intr.*, live, dwell.
Wohnplatz, *m.*, "e, dwelling-place.
Wohnung, *f.*, home, residence, lodging.
Wolke, *f.*, cloud.
wollen, wollte, gewollt, *tr. and modal aux.*, will, wish, want; require, 2048; *with inf.*, be on the point of; ich will nicht hoffen, I hope you've not, 3974.
Wollen, *n.*, will, volition, intention.
womit, wherewith, with which *or* what.
worin, wherein, in which *or* what.
Wort, *n.*, "er *or* –e, word; ins — fallen, interrupt, 696; red' ... das —, defend, 1363, *note.*

Wortgefecht, *n.*, dispute, debate.

worüber, over which *or* what, about what.

wovon, whereof, wherefrom, of *or* from *or* by which *or* what.

wovor, at which, before what.

wozu, whereto, for what purpose, wherefore.

Wunder, *n.*, miracle.

wundergroß, prodigious.

Wunderhand, *f.*, miraculous hand.

wundersam, wonderful.

wundervoll, wonderful.

Wunderwelt, *f.*, wonder-world.

Wunsch, *m.*, ⁻̈e, wish, desire.

wünschen, *tr.*, desire, wish.

Würde, *f.*, dignity, honor, position.

würdig, worthy of; *as a noun,* worthy.

würdigen, *tr.*, deem worthy, vouchsafe.

Wurm, *m.*, ⁻̈er, worm; *cf.* 3700, *note.*

Wut, *f.*, rage, madness, fury.

wüten, *intr.*, rage, be mad; wütend, furious, frantic, *masc. as noun,* madman, 3109.

Z

zaghaft, faint-hearted, timorous.

zählen, *tr.*, number; *intr.*, count upon (auf).

zart, tender, delicate.

zärtlich, tender, fond.

Zärtlichkeit, *f.*, tenderness, fondness.

Zauber, *m.*, magic, enchantment, spell, fascination.

Zauberkunst, *f.*, ⁻̈, magic art, witchcraft.

Zaubertrank, *m.*, ⁻̈e, magic potion, philter.

zaudern, *intr.*, delay, linger.

zehen, *see* zehn; *cf.* 548, *note.*

zehn, ten.

Zeichen, *n.*, token, sign.

zeihen (ie, ie), *tr.*, tax with, accuse of (*gen.*).

Zeit, *f.*, time; zu seiner —, at the proper time.

Zeitlang, *used adverbially,* for a time, a short time.

zeitlich, temporal; alles Zeitliche, all earthly matters, 3581.

Zeitung, *f.*, tidings, news.

Zepter, *more commonly* Scepter, *n.*, sceptre.

zer-, *unaccented insep. pref. giving idea of destruction, separation, etc.*

zermalmen, *tr.*, crush.

zerreißen (i, i), *tr.*, tear, rend; distract, 2317; dismember, 2690; break through, repudiate, 2683.

zerschlagen (u, a), *tr.*, beat, crush, smite.

zerstören, *tr.,* destroy.

zerstreuen, *tr.,* scatter, dissipate, dispel, divert.

Zeuge, *m.,* –n, –n, witness.

zeugen, *tr.,* beget; *intr.,* bear witness, testify.

Zeugnis, *n.,* –sses, –sse, testimony, evidence.

ziehen, zog, gezogen, *tr.,* draw; *intr.,* s., march, go, pass.

Ziel, *m.,* goal, end.

ziemen, *intr.* (*with dat.*), suit, become, befit, be suited to.

Zierde, *f.,* ornament, honor.

zieren, *tr.,* adorn, grace.

Ziffer, *m.,* cipher.

Zimmer, *n.,* room, apartment.

Zimmerer, *m.,* carpenter.

Zinn, *n.,* pewter.

zittern, *intr.,* tremble.

zögern, *intr.,* hesitate, delay.

Zorn, *m.,* anger, wrath.

zu, *prep., adv., and sep. pref.,* to, at, towards, with, for, besides, too.

zu'bereiten, *tr.,* prepare.

zucken, *intr.,* quiver, wince; zuckend, convulsive.

zu'denken, –dachte, –gedacht, *tr.,* intend for.

zu'eignen, *tr.,* appropriate; sich zuzueignen, make its own, 3603; seize.

zu'eilen, *intr.,* hasten to *or* towards.

zu'erkennen, –erkannte, –erkannt, *tr.,* adjudge, award.

zuerst, first, at first.

zu'fachen, *tr.,* fan to.

Zufall, *m.,* ¨e, chance, accident.

Zufluchtsort, *m.,* –e *or* ¨er, asylum, sanctuary, place of refuge.

Zug, *m.,* ¨e, line; feature; draught (of air), 2081, (of fishes), 2113; troop *or* party, 2137.

zuge'gen, present.

zu'gehen, –ging, –gegangen, *intr.,* s., go up to, move towards; come about, occur.

zu'gesellen, *reflex.,* associate, join.

zu'gestehen, –gestand, –gestanden, *tr.,* concede, grant.

zugleich, at the same time.

zu'kehren, *tr.,* turn towards.

zu'kommen, –kam, –gekommen, *intr.,* s., come to, arrive.

Zukunft, *f.,* future.

Zunder, *m.,* tinder.

Zunge, *f.,* tongue.

Zungendrescher, *m.,* babbler, wrangler, pettifogger.

zürnen, *intr.,* be angry.

zurück, *adv. and sep. pref.,* back, backwards, behind.

zurück'bleiben (ie, ie), *intr.,* s., stay behind, remain back.

zurück'bringen, –brachte, –gebracht, *tr.,* bring back.

zurück'fahren (u, a), *intr.,* s., come back; start *or* shrink back, be startled.

zurück'geben (a, e), *tr.*, give back, return.

zurück'halten (ie, a), *tr.*, hold back, check, restrain.

zurück'kehren, *intr.*, s., return, turn back.

zurück'lassen (ie, a), *tr.*, leave behind.

zurück'nehmen (a, o), *tr.*, take back.

zurück'rufen (ie, u), *tr.*, call back, recall.

zurück'schlagen (u, a), *tr.*, turn back, throw back.

zurück'schrecken, *tr.*, deter, discourage, scare *or* frighten back.

zurück'stoßen (ie, o), *tr.*, thrust back, repel, repulse, spurn.

zurück'treten (a, e), *intr.*, s., step *or* draw back.

zurück'weichen (i, i), *intr.*, s., retreat, retire, fall back.

zurück'weisen (ie, ie), *tr.*, repel, send back *or* away, motion away.

zurück'ziehen, –zog, –gezogen, *tr.*, draw back, withdraw; *intr.*, s., retract, 996; *reflex.*, retreat, retire.

zu'sagen, *tr.*, promise, pledge; *intr.*, assent, agree.

zusammen, *adv. and sep. pref.*, together.

zusam'menbinden (a, u), *tr.*, bind together.

zusam'menbringen, –brachte, –gebracht, *tr.*, bring together, reconcile, assemble, collect.

zusam'menfahren (u, a), *intr.*, s., start (with terror), shudder.

zusam'menfassen, *tr.*, compose, collect; faßt Euren Mut zusammen, summon up your courage, 2175.

Zusammenkunft, *f.*, ⸗e, meeting.

zusam'menlaufen (ie, au), *intr.*, s., run together, assemble.

zusam'menraffen, *reflex.*, collect one's self.

zusam'menschaudern, *intr.*, s., shudder, shiver.

zusam'menschauern, *intr.*, s., shudder.

zusam'menschrecken (a, o), *intr.*, s., start (with terror).

zu'schließen (o, o), *tr.*, close, shut up.

zu'sehen (a, e), *intr.*, take heed, take care.

zu'senden, –sandte, –gesandt (*or reg.*), *tr.*, send to, convey to.

zu'spitzen, *tr.*, point, sharpen.

Zutrauen, *n.*, trust, dependence, faith in (zu).

zutraulich, confiding, trusting.

zuvor, *adv. and sep. pref.*, before.

zuvor'kommen, –kam, –gekommen, *intr.* (*with dat.*), s., forestall, get the start of.

zu'wenden, –wandte, –gewandt (*or reg.*), *tr.*, turn to *or* towards.

zuwider, *prep. and adv.*, against, contrary (to), incompatible (with); wenn es dir —, if you're averse to it, 2064.

Zwang, *m.*, compulsion, coercion, constraint.

Zwangsrecht, *n.*, right of compulsion, right of self-defence.

zwanzig, twenty.

zwar, indeed, in fact, really.

Zweck, *m.*, purpose.

zwei, two; *cf.* 2913, *note.*

zweierlei, *indec.*, of two sorts, two different.

Zweifel, *m.*, doubt.

zweifelhaft, doubtful.

Zweifelmut, *m.*, irresolution, uncertainty.

zweifeln, *intr.*, doubt.

Zweig, *m.*, branch.

zweit, second.

zweiundvierzig, forty-two.

Zwietracht, *f.*, dissension, discord.

Zwietrachtsgöttin, *f.*, –innen, goddess of discord.

zwingen (a, u), *tr.*, compel, force, constrain.

zwischen, between, among.

zwölf, twelve.

ADVERTISEMENTS

Heath's Modern Language Series

GERMAN GRAMMARS AND READERS.

Ball's German Drill Book. Companion to any grammar. 80 cts.
Ball's German Grammar. 90 cts.
Bishop and McKinlay's Deutsche Grammatik. 00 cts.
Boisen's German Prose Reader. 90 cts.
Deutsches Liederbuch. With music. 75 cts.
Foster's Geschichten und Märchen. For young children. 40 cts.
Fraser and Van der Smissen's German Grammar. $1.10.
German Noun Table (Perrin and Hastings). 20 cts.
Gore's German Science Reader. 75 cts.
Greenfield's Grammar Summary and Word List. 30 cts.
Guerber's Märchen und Erzählungen, I. 60 cts. **II.** 65 cts.
Harris's German Composition. 50 cts.
Harris's German Lessons. 60 cts.
Hastings' Studies in German Words. $1.00.
Heath's German Dictionary. Retail price, $1.50.
Hewitt's Practical German Composition. 00 cts.
Holzwarth's Gruss aus Deutschland. 90 cts.
Huss's German Reader. 70 cts.
Joynes-Meissner German Grammar. $1.15.
Joynes's Shorter German Grammar. Part I of the above. 80 cts.
Joynes's Shorter German Reader. 60 cts.
Joynes and Wesselhoeft's German Grammar. $1.15.
Krüger and Smith's Conversation Book. 25 cts.
Manfred's Ein praktischer Anfang. $1.10.
Meissner's German Conversation. 65 cts.
Mosher and Jenney's Lern- und Lesebuch. $1.25.
Nix's Erstes deutsches Schulbuch. For primary classes. Illus. 35 cts.
Pattou's An American in Germany. A conversation book. 70 cts.
Schmidhofer's Erstes Lesebuch. 40 cts. With vocab., 55 cts.
Schmidhofer's Zweites Lesebuch. 50 cts.
Sheldon's Short German Grammar. 60 cts.
Spanhoofd's Elementarbuch der deutschen Sprache. $1.00.
Spanhoofd's Erstes deutsches Lesebuch. 70 cts.
Spanhoofd's Lehrbuch der deutschen Sprache. $1.00.
Wallentin's Grundzüge der Naturlehre (Palmer). $1.00.
Wesselhoeft's Elementary German Grammar. 90 cts.
Wesselhoeft's Exercises. Conversation and composition. 50 cts.
Wesselhoeft's German Composition. 45 cts.
Zinnecker's Deutsch für Anfänger. $0.00.

Heath's Modern Language Series

ELEMENTARY GERMAN TEXTS. (Partial List.)

Andersen's Bilderbuch ohne Bilder (Bernhardt). Vocabulary. 30 cts.

Andersen's Märchen (Super). Vocabulary. 50 cts.

Aus der Jugendzeit (Betz). Vocabulary and exercises. 40 cts.

Baumbach's Nicotiana (Bernhardt). Vocabulary. 30 cts.

Baumbach's Waldnovellen (Bernhardt). Six stories. Vocabulary. 35 cts.

Benedix's Der Prozess (Wells). Vocabulary. 25 cts.

Benedix's Nein (Spanhoofd). Vocabulary and exercises. 25 cts.

Blüthgen's Das Peterle von Nürnberg (Bernhardt). Vocab. and exs. 35 cts.

Bolt's Peterli am Lift (Betz). Vocabulary and exercises. 40 cts.

Campe's Robinson der Jüngere (Ibershoff). Vocabulary. 40 cts.

Carmen Sylva's Aus meinem Königreich (Bernhardt). Vocabulary. 35 cts.

Die Schildbürger (Betz). Vocabulary and exercises. 35 cts.

Der Weg zum Glück (Bernhardt). Vocabulary and exercises. 40 cts.

Deutscher Humor aus vier Jahrhunderten (Betz). Vocab. and exercises. 40 cts.

Elz's Er ist nicht eifersüchtig (Wells). Vocabulary. 25 cts.

Gerstäcker's Germelshausen (Lewis). Vocabulary and exercises. 30 cts.

Goethe's Das Märchen (Eggert). Vocabulary. 30 cts.

Grimm's Märchen and Schiller's Der Taucher (Van der Smissen). 45 cts.

Hauff's Das kalte Herz (Van der Smissen). Vocab. Roman type. 40 cts.

Hauff's Der Zwerg Nase (Patzwald and Robson) Vocab. and exs. 30 cts.

Heyse's L'Arrabbiata (Deering-Bernhardt). Vocab. and exercises. 30 cts.

Heyse's Niels mit der offenen Hand (Joynes). Vocab. and exercises. 30 cts.

Hillern's Höher als die Kirche (Clary). Vocabulary and exercises. 30 cts.

Leander's Träumereien (Van der Smissen). Vocabulary. 40 cts.

Münchhausen: Reisen und Abenteuer (Schmidt). Vocabulary. 30 cts.

Rosegger's Der Lex von Gutenhag (Morgan). Vocab. and exercises. 40 cts.

Salomon's Die Geschichte einer Geige (Tombo). Vocab. and exercises. 30 cts.

Schiller's Der Neffe als Onkel (Beresford-Webb). Vocabulary. 30 cts.

Spyri's Moni der Geissbub (Guerber). Vocabulary. 30 cts.

Spyri's Rosenresli (Boll). Vocabulary. 25 cts.

Spyri's Was der Grossmutter Lehre bewirkt (Barrows). Vocab. and exs. 30 cts.

Storm's Geschichten aus der Tonne (Vogel). Vocab. and exs. 40 cts.

Storm's Immensee (Bernhardt). Vocabulary and exercises. 30 cts.

Storm's In St. Jürgen (Wright). Vocabulary and exercises. 35 cts.

Storm's Pole Poppenspäler (Bernhardt). Vocab. and exercises. 40 cts.

Till Eulenspiegel (Betz). Vocabulary and exercises. 30 cts.

Volkmann's Kleine Geschichten (Bernhardt). Vocabulary. 30 cts.

Zschokke's Der zerbrochene Krug (Joynes). Vocabulary and exercises. 25 cts.

Heath's Modern Language Series

INTERMEDIATE GERMAN TEXTS. (Partial List.)

Arndt, Deutsche Patrioten (Colwell). Vocabulary. 35 cts.
Aus Herz und Welt (Bernhardt). 25 cts.
Benedix's Die Hochzeitsreise (Schiefferdecker). Vocabulary. 30 cts.
Böhlau's Ratsmädelgeschichten (Haevernick). Vocabulary. 40 cts.
Chamisso's Peter Schlemihl (Primer). Vocabulary. 35 cts.
Deutsche Gedichte und Lieder (Roedder and Purin). Vocabulary. 60 cts.
Eichendorff's Aus dem Leben eines Taugenichts (Osthaus). Vocab. 45 cts.
Goethe's Hermann und Dorothea (Adams). Vocabulary. 65 cts.
Goethe's Sesenheim (Huss). From *Dichtung und Wahrheit.* Vocab. 30 cts.
Hauff's Lichtenstein (Vogel). Abridged. 75 cts.
Heine's Die Harzreise (Vos). Vocabulary. 45 cts.
Hoffmann's Historische Erzählungen (Beresford-Webb). 25 cts.
Jensen's Die braune Erica (Joynes). Vocabulary. 35 cts.
Keller's Fähnlein der sieben Aufrechten (Howard). Vocabulary. 40 cts.
Keller's Romeo und Julia auf dem Dorfe (Adams). Vocabulary. 35 cts.
Lambert's Alltägliches. Vocabulary and exercises. 75 cts.
Lohmeyer's Geissbub von Engelberg (Bernhardt). Vocab. and exs. 40 cts.
Lyrics and Ballads (Hatfield). 75 cts.
Meyer's Gustav Adolfs Page (Heller). 25 cts.
Mosher's Willkommen in Deutschland. Vocabulary and exercises. 75 cts.
Novelletten-Bibliothek (Bernhardt). Vol. I, 35 cts. Vol. II, 35 cts.
Raabe's Eulenpfingsten (Lambert). Vocabulary. 45 cts.
Riehl's Burg Neideck (Jonas). Vocabulary and exercises. 35 cts.
Rogge's Der grosse Preussenkönig (Adams). Vocabulary. 45 cts.
Schiller's Der Geisterseher (Joynes). Vocabulary. 35 cts.
Schiller's Dreissigjähriger Krieg (Prettyman). Book III. 35 cts.
Selections for Sight Translation (Mondan). 15 cts.
Shorter German Poems (Hatfield). Vocabulary. 35 cts.
Spielhagen's Das Skelett im Hause (Skinner). Vocabulary. 45 cts.
Stifter's Das Haidedorf (Heller). 20 cts.
Stökl's Alle fünf (Bernhardt). Vocab. and exercises. 30 cts.
Unter dem Christbaum (Bernhardt). 35 cts.
Wildenbruch's Das edle Blut (Schmidt). Vocab. and exercises. 30 cts.
Wildenbruch's Der Letzte (Schmidt). Vocab. and exercises. 35 cts.
Wildenbruch's Neid (Prettyman). Vocabulary. 35 cts.
Zschokke's Das Abenteuer der Neujahrsnacht (Handschin). Vocab. 35 cts.
Zschokke's Das Wirtshaus zu Cransac (Joynes). Vocab. and exs. 30 cts.

Heath's Modern Language Series

INTERMEDIATE GERMAN TEXTS. (Partial List.)

Arnold's Aprilwetter (Fossler). Vocabulary. 40 cts.
Arnold's Fritz auf Ferien (Spanhoofd). Vocab. and exercises. 30 cts.
Arnold's Menne im Seebad (Thomas). Vocab. and exercises. 30 cts.
Auf der Sonnenseite (Bernhardt). Vocabulary. 35 cts.
Baumbach's Das Habichtsfräulein (Bernhardt). Vocab. and exs. 40 cts.
Baumbach's Der Schwiegersohn (Bernhardt). 30 cts. Vocabulary, 40 cts.
Baumbach's Die Nonna (Bernhardt). Vocabulary. 30 cts.
Benedix's Plautus und Terenz; Der Sonntagsjäger (Wells). 30 cts.
Drei kleine Lustspiele (Wells). Vocabulary and exercises. 45 cts.
Ebner-Eschenbach's Die Freiherren von Gemperlein (Hohlfeld). 35 cts.
Freytag's Die Journalisten (Toy). 30 cts. With vocabulary. 40 cts.
Frommel's Eingeschneit (Bernhardt). Vocabulary. 30 cts.
Frommel's Mit Ränzel und Wanderstab (Bernhardt). Vocab. and exs. 35 cts.
Fulda's Der Talisman (Prettyman). 35 cts.
Gerstäcker's Irrfahrten (Sturm). Vocabulary. 45 cts.
Grillparzer's Der arme Spielmann (Howard). Vocabulary. 35 cts.
Heyse's Das Mädchen von Treppi (Joynes). Vocab. and exercises. 35 cts.
Heyse's Hochzeit auf Capri (Bernhardt). Vocab. and exercises. 35 cts.
Hoffmann's Gymnasium zu Stolpenburg (Buehner). Vocabulary. 40 cts.
Keller's Die drei gerechten Kammacher (Collings). Vocabulary. 35 cts.
Keller's Kleider machen Leute (Lambert). Vocabulary. 35 cts.
Liliencron's Anno 1870 (Bernhardt). Vocabulary. 40 cts.
Moser's Der Bibliothekar (Wells). Vocabulary. 40 cts.
Moser's Köpnickerstrasse 120 (Wells). 35 cts.
Riehl's Das Spielmannskind (Eaton). Vocabulary and exercises. 40 cts.
Riehl's Der Fluch der Schönheit (Thomas). Vocabulary. 35 cts.
Schiller's Das Lied von der Glocke (Chamberlin). Vocabulary. 20 cts.
Schiller's Jungfrau von Orleans (Wells). Illus. 60 cts. Vocab., 70 cts.
Schiller's Maria Stuart (Rhoades). Illustrated. 60 cts. Vocab., 70 cts.
Schiller's Wilhelm Tell (Deering). Illustrated. 50 cts. Vocab., 70 cts.
Seidel: Aus Goldenen Tagen (Bernhardt). Vocab. and exercises. 35 cts.
Seidel's Leberecht Hühnchen (Spanhoofd). Vocabulary. 30 cts.
Selections for Sight Translation (Deering). 15 cts.
Stern's Die Wiedertäufer (Sturm). Vocabulary and exercises. 40 cts.
Stille Wasser (Bernhardt). Three tales. Vocabulary. 35 cts.
Wichert's Als Verlobte empfehlen sich (Flom). Vocabulary. 25 cts.
Wilbrandt's Das Urteil des Paris (Wirt). 30 cts.

Heath's Modern Language Series

ADVANCED GERMAN TEXTS. (Partial List.)

Dahn's Ein Kampf um Rom (Wenckebach). Abridged. 55 cts.
Dahn's Sigwalt und Sigridh (Schmidt). 25 cts.
Deutsche Reden (Tombo). 90 cts.
Ein Charakterbild von Deutschland (Evans and Merhaut). $1.00
Frenssen's Jörn Uhl (Florer). 90 cts.
Freytag's Aus dem Jahrhundert des grossen Krieges (Rhoades). 35 cts.
Freytag's Aus dem Staat Friedrichs des Grossen (Hagar). 30 cts.
Freytag's Das Nest der Zaunkönige (Roedder and Handschin). 65 cts.
Freytag's Rittmeister von Alt-Rosen (Hatfield). 50 cts.
Freytag's Soll und Haben (Files). Abridged. 55 cts.
Goethe's Dichtung und Wahrheit (I–IV). Buchheim. 90 cts.
Goethe's Egmont (Hatfield). 60 cts.
Goethe's Faust (Thomas). Part I, $1.15. Part II, $1.50.
Goethe's Hermann und Dorothea (Hewett). 75 cts.
Goethe's Iphigenie (Rhoades). 60 cts.
Goethe's Meisterwerke (Bernhardt). $1.25.
Goethe's Poems (Harris). 90 cts.
Goethe's Torquato Tasso (Thomas). 75 cts.
Grillparzer's Der Traum, ein Leben (Meyer). 40 cts.
Hebbel's Agnes Bernauer (Evans). 50 cts.
Heine's Poems (White). 75 cts.
Helbig's Komödie auf der Hochschule (Wells). 35 cts.
Körner's Zriny (Holzwarth). 35 cts.
Lessing's Emilia Galotti (Winkler). 60 cts.
Lessing's Minna von Barnhelm (Primer). 60 cts. With vocabulary, 65 cts.
Lessing's Nathan der Weise (Primer). 80 cts.
Ludwig's Zwischen Himmel und Erde (Meyer). 55 cts.
Meyer's Jürg Jenatsch (Kenngott). Abridged. 60 cts.
Mörike's Mozart auf der Reise nach Prag (Howard). 35 cts.
Scheffel's Ekkehard (Wenckebach). Abridged. 55 cts.
Scheffel's Trompeter von Säkkingen (Wenckebach). Abridged. 50 cts.
Schiller's Ballads (Johnson). 60 cts.
Schiller's Wallenstein's Tod (Eggert). 60 cts.
Sudermann's Der Katzensteg (Wells). Abridged. Glossary. 60 cts.
Sudermann's Frau Sorge (Leser and Osthaus). Vocabulary. 90 cts.
Sudermann's Heimat (Schmidt). 35 cts.
Sudermann's Johannes (Schmidt). 35 cts.
Sudermann's Teja (Ford). Vocabulary. 30 cts.
Thomas's German Anthology. $2.25.
Wildenbruch's Die Rabensteinerin (Ford). 35 cts.
Wildenbruch's Harold (Eggert). 35 cts.

Heath's Modern Language Series

FRENCH GRAMMARS, READERS, ETC.

Anecdotes Faciles (Super). 25 cts.
Blanchaud's Progressive French Idioms. 60 cts.
Bouvet's Exercises in French Syntax and Composition. 75 cts.
Bowen's First Scientific French Reader. 90 cts.
Bruce's Dictées Françaises. 30 cts.
Bruce's Grammaire Française. $1.15.
Bruce's Lectures Faciles. 60 cts.
Capus's Pour Charmer nos Petits. 50 cts.
Chapuzet and Daniel's Mes Premiers Pas en Français. 60 cts.
Clarke's Subjunctive Mood. An inductive treatise, with exercises. 50 cts.
Comfort's Exercises in French Prose Composition. 30 cts.
Davies's Elementary Scientific French Reader. 40 cts.
Edgren's Compendious French Grammar. $1.15. Part I, 35 cts.
Fontaine's Lectures Courantes. $1.00.
Fontaine's Livre de Lecture et de Conversation. 90 cts.
Fraser and Squair's Abridged French Grammar. $1.10.
Fraser and Squair's Complete French Grammar. $1.15.
Fraser and Squair's Elementary French Grammar. 90 cts.
Fraser and Squair's Shorter French Course. $1.10.
French Anecdotes (Giese and Cool). 40 cts.
French Verb Blank (Fraser and Squair). 30 cts.
Grandgent's Essentials of French Grammar. $1.00.
Grandgent's French Composition. 50 cts.
Grandgent's Materials for French Composition. Each, 12 cts.
Grandgent's Short French Grammar. 75 cts.
Heath's French Dictionary. Retail price, $1.50.
Hénin's Méthode. 50 cts.
Hotchkiss's Le Premier Livre de Français. 35 cts.
Kimball's Materials for French Composition. Each, 12 cts.
Mansion's Exercises in French Composition. 60 cts.
Mansion's First Year French. For young beginners. 50 cts.
Marcou's French Review Exercises. 25 cts.
Pattou's Causeries en France. 70 cts.
Pellissier's Idiomatic French Composition. $1.00
Perfect French Possible (Knowles and Favard). 35 cts.
Prisoners of the Temple (Guerber). For French Composition. 25 cts.
Roux's Lessons in Grammar and Composition, based on *Colomba*. 18 cts.
Snow and Lebon's Easy French. 60 cts.
Storr's Hints on French Syntax. With exercises. 30 cts.
ry of Cupid and Psyche (Guerber). For French Composition. 18 cts.
Preparatory French Reader. 70 cts.

Heath's Modern Language Series

ELEMENTARY FRENCH TEXTS.

Assolant's Aventure du Célèbre Pierrot (Pain). Vocabulary. 25 cts.

Assolant's Récits de la Vieille France. Notes by E. B. Wauton. 25 cts.

Berthet's Le Pacte de Famine (Dickinson). 25 cts.

Bruno's Les Enfants Patriotes (Lyon). Vocabulary. 25 cts.

Bruno's Tour de la France par deux Enfants (Fontaine). Vocabulary. 45 cts.

Claretie's Pierrille (François). Vocab. and exs. 40 cts.

Daudet's Trois Contes Choisis (Sanderson). Vocabulary. 20 cts.

Desnoyers' Jean-Paul Choppart (Fontaine). Vocab. and exs. 40 cts.

Enault's Le Chien du Capitaine (Fontaine). Vocabulary. 35 cts.

Erckmann-Chatrian's Le Conscrit de 1813 (Super). Vocabulary. 45 cts.

Erckmann-Chatrian's L'Histoire d'un Paysan (Lyon). 25 cts.

Erckmann-Chatrian's Le Juif Polonais (Manley). Vocabulary. 30 cts.

Erckmann-Chatrian's Madame Thérèse (Manley). Vocabulary. 40 cts.

Fabliaux et Contes du Moyen Age (Mansion). Vocabulary. 40 cts.

France's Abeille (Lebon). 25 cts.

French Fairy Tales (Joynes). Vocabulary and exercises. 35 cts.

Gervais's Un Cas de Conscience (Horsley). Vocabulary. 25 cts.

La Bedollière's La Mère Michel et son Chat (Lyon). Vocabulary. 30 cts.

Labiche's La Grammaire (Levi). Vocabulary. 25 cts.

Labiche's La Poudre aux Yeux (Wells). Vocabulary. 30 cts.

Labiche's Le Voyage de M. Perrichon (Wells). Vocab. and exs. 30 cts.

Laboulaye's Contes Bleus (Fontaine). Vocabulary. 35 cts.

La Main Malheureuse (Guerber). Vocabulary. 25 cts.

Laurie's Mémoires d'un Collégien (Super). Vocab. and exs. 50 cts.

Legouvé and Labiche's Cigale chez les Fourmis (Witherby). 20 cts.

Lemaître, Contes (Rensch). Vocabulary. 30 cts.

Mairêt's La Tâche du Petit Pierre (Super). Vocab. and exs. 35 cts.

Maistre's La Jeune Sibérienne (Fontaine). Vocab. and exs. 30 cts.

Malot's Sans Famille (Spiers). Vocabulary and exercises. 40 cts.

Meilhac and Halévy's L'Eté de la St. Martin (François). Vocab. 25 cts.

Moinaux's Les deux Sourds (Spiers). Vocabulary. 25 cts.

Müller's Grandes Découvertes Modernes. Vocabulary. 25 cts.

Récits de Guerre et de Révolution (Minssen). Vocabulary. 25 cts.

Récits Historiques (Moffett). Vocabulary and exercises. 45 cts.

Saintine's Picciola (Super). Vocabulary. 45 cts.

Ségur's Les Malheurs de Sophie (White). Vocab. and exs. 45 cts.

Selections for Sight Translation (Bruce). 15 cts.

Verne's L'Expédition de la Jeune Hardie (Lyon). Vocabulary. 30 cts.

Heath's Modern Language Series

ADVANCED FRENCH TEXTS.

Balzac's Le Père Goriot (Sanderson). 80 cts.

Boileau: Selections (Kuhns). 50 cts.

Bornier's La Fille de Roland (Nelson). 30 cts.

Bossuet: Selections (Warren). 50 cts.

Calvin: Pages Choisis (Jordan). 70 cts.

Corneille's Cinna (Matzke). 30 cts.

Corneille's Horace (Matzke). 30 cts.

Corneille's Le Cid (Warren). 30 cts.

Corneille's Polyeucte (Fortier). 30 cts.

Delpit's L'Age d'Or de la Littérature Française. 90 cts.

Diderot: Selections (Giese). 50 cts.

Duval's Histoire de la Littérature Française. $1.00.

French Prose of the XVIIth Century (Warren). $1.00.

Hugo's Hernani (Matzke). 60 cts.

Hugo's Les Misérables (Super). Abridged. 80 cts.

Hugo's Les Travailleurs de la Mer (Langley). Abridged. 80 cts.

Hugo's Poems (Schinz). 80 cts.

Hugo's Ruy Blas (Garner). 65 cts.

La Bruyère: Les Caractères (Warren). 50 cts.

Lamartine's Méditations (Curme). 55 cts.

La Triade Française. Poems of Lamartine, Musset, and Hugo. 75 cts.

Lesage's Turcaret (Kerr). 30 cts.

Maîtres de la Critique lit. au XIXe Siècle (Comfort). 50 cts.

Molière's Le Misanthrope (Eggert). 35 cts.

Molière's Les Femmes Savantes (Fortier). 30 cts.

Molière's Les Fourberies de Scapin (McKenzie). Vocabulary. 35 cts.

Molière's Les Précieuses Ridicules (Toy). 25 cts.

Molière's Le Tartuffe (Wright). 30 cts.

Montaigne: Selections (Wright). 90 cts.

Pascal: Selections (Warren). 50 cts.

Racine's Les Plaideurs (Wright). 30 cts.

Racine's Phèdre (Babbitt). 30 cts.

Rostand's La Princesse Lointaine (Borgerhoff). 40 cts.

Voltaire's Prose (Cohn and Woodward). $1.00.

Voltaire's Zaïre (Cabeen). 30 cts.

ROMANCE PHILOLOGY.

Introduction to Vulgar Latin (Grandgent). $1.50.

Provençal Phonology and Morphology (Grandgent). $1.50.

JUNIATA COLLEGE
2820 9100 038 825 5